***

"*Bioinspired Strategic Design* is not just another business book. Using principles from biology and AI it takes a fresh and innovative look on how these tools can create innovative products and help plan and build more efficient and resilient organizations."

Steve Blank Founding member of the Gordian Knot Center; Adjunct Professor at Stanford University

***

As a CEO in supply chain visibility and resilience, I highly recommend *Bioinspired Strategic Design*. This book offers valuable insights and practical guidance for organizations looking to enhance their strategic decision-making and build resilient operations.

Bindiya Vakil CEO and founder of Resilinc

***

"As life in nature adapts to changing circumstances in order to survive, so too can businesses, organizations, and individuals learn to not only survive but to thrive through the principles of bioinspiration deduced and illuminated by the authors of *Bioinspired Strategic Design*. They show how you can apply the wellsprings of creation to methodically explore and creatively design innovative, robust, and resilient solutions to problems that, in the end, will further human flourishing."

B. Joseph Pine II Coauthor, *The Experience Economy: Competing for Customer Time, Attention, and Money*

***

"How to get creative ideas is the holy grail for companies. In this amazing and innovative book, Drs. Finkenstadt and Eapen argue that nature is an inexhaustible source of inspiration. But how to leverage nature? Packed with practical examples and end-of-chapter exercises, *Bioinspired Strategic Design* shows the way. A must-read for anybody in search of creative inspiration! And who isn't?"

Jan-Benedict Steenkamp Massey Distinguished Professor of Marketing & Leadership, University of North Carolina at Chapel Hill; Author of *Time to Lead: Lessons for Today's Leaders from Bold Decisions That Changed History*

***

"This book is an absolute gem! As natural, analogical thinkers we have much to learn from nature when curious enough to do so. The authors' pioneering explorations involving biomimicry is a must-read for any manager. It is bold, panoramic thinking at its best and a highly enjoyable read as well."

Gerald Zaltman Harvard Business School and Olson Zaltman; Author of *On Not Knowing: The Art of An Open Mind and How Customers Think*

***

"In today's world, where sustainability plays a vital strategic role, nature presents a treasure trove of lessons for the inquisitive learner. This captivating book extends an invitation to explore and implement the simple yet profound principles observed in nature for both survival and success."

Vijay Govindarajan Coxe Distinguished Professor, Tuck School of Business at Dartmouth; Author of *The Three Box Solution*

***

This book provides in-depth insights into how bioinspired design combined with AI can help us address complex challenges faced by businesses, governments, markets, cities, and society. Never more needed and very timely, an extremely valuable read for anyone involved in making strategic design decisions for organisations.

Rachel Cooper, OBE Distinguished Professor of Design Management and Policy at Lancaster University

***

"Mankind has not yet even skimmed the surface of the natural world's multiple capabilities and ability to adapt. So many living things have innate capabilities that technology has yet to even understand, let alone replicate. Dan and Tojin have taken on the task of beginning to harness the principles found in nature and applying them to the design of human systems, in the context of efficiency, resilience, prominence, and design heuristics. This ambitious book seeks to develop critical implications of biomimicry for technological innovation, artificial intelligence, idea generation, scenario planning, and organizational constraints. The result is a delightful book that triggers one's imagination on the possibilities for true nature-driven innovation."

Robert Handfield Bank of America University
Distinguished Professor of Supply Chain
Management, North Carolina State University

***

"Organizations around the world are primarily concerned with efficiency improvement. The authors of this book propose that there are two other critical survivability factors – resilience and prominence – that firms may ignore to their peril. What makes survivability challenging is the complex interplay of these factors based on resources, environmental forces, and different types of observers such as predators, prey, and mates in the natural world, and competitors, rivals, and customers in business environments. A must-read for corporate honchos and emerging leaders alike!"

Geetha Ramamoorthi Managing Director, KBR India

***

"There are books that inspire, and every decade or so, there comes a defining seminal work that offers a new approach to engineering solutions for practically any conceivable problem. *Bioinspired Strategic Design* is one of those pioneering efforts to understand, at a very fundamental level, how we can apply nature-inspired principles to our thought processes governing any meaningful understanding of issues and decision-making. Every design school should have this as mandatory reading; it should be part of Design 101. Frankly, this is a must-read for business school and entrepreneurship students just as much. Any innovator can benefit immensely from the framework Daniel and Tojin have meticulously built."

Vineet C. Nambiar Founder, Mavericks365;
Director, International Business Week

***

"You know those wise people, who seem to answer any question with an insightful story and a powerful example? With this book as your guide, you will be one of those people when it comes to the field of bioinspiration. Filled to the brim with both useful language to use, real-world examples, and inspiring stories, this is one of those books that make you go from outsider to insider in the span of a few hours. Brilliant piece of writing!"

Claus Raasted Director at The College of Extraordinary Experiences; External Advisor at McKinsey & Company

***

"The old mechanic machine type model of organizations and the rigid management practices of the industrial age have run their course. Now, a new model is emerging that we call Management 2.0 animated by an organic perspective of organizations and management. I am proud that a former winner of the Peter Drucker Challenge Essay contest using nature-inspired principles lays the foundation for new innovative and creative management practices for the 21st century."

Richard Straub Founder & President,
Global Peter Drucker Forum

***

"The book provides a novel look at how businesses can learn from living organisms to guide their strategic decision-making. Nature has much to teach us, and this book makes an effort to uncover some of the mysteries that it holds about survival and applies them to human organizations."

Soumitra Dutta Dean, Saïd Business School,
University of Oxford; Former Founding Dean,
Cornell SC Johnson College of Business

***

"Innovation often leads us to seek out the next cutting-edge break-through and search for new sources of knowledge. However, it is worth considering that even today, our most profound source of inventive potential might be found in an ancient fount of inspiration: the natural world. In this fascinating book, Dan and Tojin take the reader on an exploratory expedition to uncover nature's creative principles. At the end of the book, one cannot escape the sense that the journey (and the fun) has just begun."

Jaideep Prabhu Professor of Marketing & Nehru Professor of Indian Business; Judge Business School, University of Cambridge

***

"Nature has always been a great source of inspiration for Product Design. The authors have demonstrated how the ERP framework can help us unleash creative potential in a systematic manner. With generative AI, this opportunity is set to explode and bring about a paradigm shift in divergent thinking. The amalgamation of human creativity with generative AI will take innovations to a new level. A great book to stimulate our thought process in this direction."

Revathi Kant Chief Design Officer, Titan Company

***

"The marvels of nature can teach us so much! Nature optimized its ecosystems and has amazing lessons in areas such as energy efficiency, adaptability, and resilience. Daniel Finkenstadt and Tojin Eapen did an excellent job taking the reader through bioinspired strategic design principles. I recommend anyone involved in innovation and design to read this book, it has many eye-opening learnings."

Jochen Wirtz Professor and Vice Dean, MBA Programmes; National University of Singapore

***

"This book showcases how the profound lessons of nature are interwoven with human organizations and how this unlocks innovative solutions to build a sustainable and adaptable future for our human systems. By exploring the concept of bioinspiration, the book embarks on a journey to unravel the secrets of survival and innovation embedded in the adaptations of living organisms."

Roseline ILORI Founder/CEO, Bridge57 Solutions Limited

***

"The book serves as a fantastic reminder that nature offers the most valuable insights and guidance for navigating our planet. Furthermore, it emphasizes that humans can never surpass nature's power, and we should constantly strive to learn and explore. The book also highlights that trade-offs always exist, and nature chooses the optimal combination based on the changing environment. The presence of comprehensive and perceptive examples of innovative solutions for a sustainable and resilient future help skeptics realize that their knowledge is nearly futile if it contradicts the principles embraced by nature."

Thomas Kuruvilla Managing Partner, Arthur
D. Little Middle East and India; Adjunct Faculty,
Indian Institute of Management, Bangalore

***

"This remarkable book is your go-to manual for innovation and product design in the AI era. The authors transform years of research into practical advice, peppered with numerous examples. In the AI era, don't merely get by – flourish!"

J. Scott Christianson Director, Center for Entrepreneurship and
Innovation; Trulaske College of Business, University of Missouri

***

I have listened to Tojin Eapen on a global webinar, and later read his book. This is not another trivial book on AI. It is a door opener for people who really want to understand how such powerful tool can enhance what the human creativity can achieve. I've been a creative person my entire life, and while I completely believe in the power of the human brain to generate amazing things, AI and Bioinspired Strategic Design provide a completely new angle and perspective on innovation and mind exploration. Amazing stuff.

Ilan Geva President, Ilan Geva & Friends; Sr. Strategy
Director and head of US office, Vmarsh Healthcare

***

"Learning from nature is an interesting activity. The authors Tojin and Daniel have taken this learning several notches up from merely being "interesting." This book gives a structured way of looking at matters most important for business success, like survival, resilience, design, ideation etc. through the eyes of nature. The academic rigor that is evident through the reliable sources referred in the book adds to the credibility of the topics. Businesses will do well to implement the concepts discussed in the book."

Madana Kumar VP and Global Head – Leadership Development, UST; Global Servant Leadership Evangelist and Author of *Not-So-With-YOU*

***

"The idea of drawing parallels from nature and applying those to the business world has always fascinated me. I have known Tojin as a classmate and have recently been following his work. Always impressive! One of the things that stood out for me was the role of reduced prominence in the survivability of a predator – pretty much how we describe startups in "stealth mode." This was not only an insightful read, but also highly enjoyable."

Koreel Lahiri Investment Director - Asia, MDIF

***

"As a keen observer of organizations and how they thrive, survive or fail, I have been keen to understand the underlying causes. This book provides an easily readable explanation and excellent analysis on how external and internal factors affect the future of organizations. CEOs of mature organizations and startups alike could take many lessons from the book to help build prominent organizations by improving efficiency and resilience."

Nirmal N. R. CEO, 3-Wheeler Business, Greaves Electric Mobility

***

"An indispensable guide for leveraging biology's ancient wisdom to foster innovation in organizations."

Brendan O'Toole VP Product, Copeland

***

"It is a very interesting, inspiring, and insightful book for readers looking for fresh ideas and newer directions. *Bioinspired Strategic Design* provides novel insights on adaptability and bio-inspired creativity. It educates us that there is so much to learn from nature around us along with the power of artificial intelligence in strategic decision-making. Kudos to the authors Dan Finkenstadt and Tojin Eapen for penning this masterpiece!"

Neeraj Pandey Professor & Associate Dean - Placement and
Branding; Indian Institute of Management (IIM) Mumbai

***

"Everything in our life is nature's design. In our rapidly changing world, *Bioinspired Strategic Design* offers a fresh perspective on survivability, resilience, creativity, and innovation. Finkenstadt and Eapen skillfully illustrate how individuals, firms, countries, and society at large can leverage the processes found in nature to address challenges presented by our dynamic environment. They explore various efficiency and resilience mechanisms observed in living organisms and organizations, as well as provide bioinspired strategies for product ideation in new product development. Finkenstadt and Eapen present a comprehensive view of how individuals and organizations can draw upon the fundamental principles observed in nature to contribute to making the world a better place."

Kiran Pedada Assistant Professor of Marketing and
F. Ross Johnson Fellow at University of Manitoba;
Visiting Faculty, Indian School of Business

***

"This book is an eye-opener, offering powerful insights for innovation, inspired by principles that govern nature's complex organisms. Packed with thoughtful ideas, compelling examples, provocative AI applications, how-to heuristics, and the robust efficiency-resilience-prominence framework, it is a must-read for those who depend on innovation for growth and longevity of their organizations."

Arun Pereira Global Facilitator, AACSB International
Emeritus Faculty, Richard A. Chaifetz School of
Busines at Saint Louis University, Author of *Papal
Reich* and *The Culturally Customized Website*

***

"*Bioinspired Strategic Design* is indeed an inspiring book that offers a new lens to look at and find solutions from the nature to challenges and opportunities that organisations face. This is a guide to explore and find practical solutions as it is well researched and comprehensive. The authors bring fresh air to the cluttered array of "to do" books."

Kavil Ramachandran Professor of Family Business and Entrepreneurship; Senior Advisor, Thomas Schmidheiny Centre for Family Enterprise; Indian School of Business

***

"At the outset, I would like to congratulate Dan & Tojin for out-of-the-box approach on identifying potential biomimetic solutions as inspiration for solving human/organization problems. Through the concept of studying adaptations and mechanisms found in living systems, how complex challenges faced by all human systems (governments, organizations, communities & so on) can be addressed through bioinspired feasible & viable solutions, is interesting as well as deeply engaging. Several analogues between the way birds & animals are biologically designed may present new nature inspired models for organizations to design their best strategic turnaround plans! I doubt if these deeper insights were ever touched upon by authors in the past & in that sense, it opens an absolutely new sphere to investigate & benefit from. I strongly recommend this book for all business leaders, emerging & mature, to discover an entirely new dimension while exploring innovative solutions to business, society & environment challenges, leaving behind an enjoyable experience."

Avinash Sankhe Director, Shared Services Center at Bureau Veritas

***

"It is no coincidence that organisation and organism share the same root word. The book very effectively analyses natural behaviours through a prism of Efficiency, Resilience and Prominence, whereby we are able to study these behaviours in the natural world and apply them on to various principles relevant for organisations. These having succeeded in the natural world give greater confidence that similar strategies work in the realm of organisations too. Most importantly, it opens up the courage to think in a totally new perspective in every situation by looking for a time-tested bioinspired parallel."

Jacob Chandy Varghese Head of Product Management, EDGE

***

"This book offers a groundbreaking perspective on survival strategies for startups and organizations in challenging settings. Focusing on the ERP model, the book delves into nature's critical balance between efficiency and resilience, drawing parallels with startups, military crafts, and supply chains. The authors skillfully apply nature's adaptability to business survival, presenting a comprehensive framework for navigating hostile environments. This book is an essential read for entrepreneurs, leaders, and strategists seeking innovative approaches to ensure their ventures thrive amidst adversity."

Somnath Datta Director, Customer Excellence; Janssen Pharmaceuticals (Johnson & Johnson)

***

Bioinspired Strategic Design masterfully bridges the gap between the age-old wisdom of nature and the modern challenges faced by organizations. Through a harmonious blend of biological principles and innovative strategies, Finkenstadt and Eapen illuminate a path for businesses to navigate the turbulent waters of the contemporary world. Drawing inspiration from nature's myriad solutions, this book doesn't just advocate for innovation – it embodies it. For those yearning for a fresh perspective that melds the organic with the strategic, this is your compass.

Haresh Raval Board Member, Human Health Project; Global VP of Product, Newegg

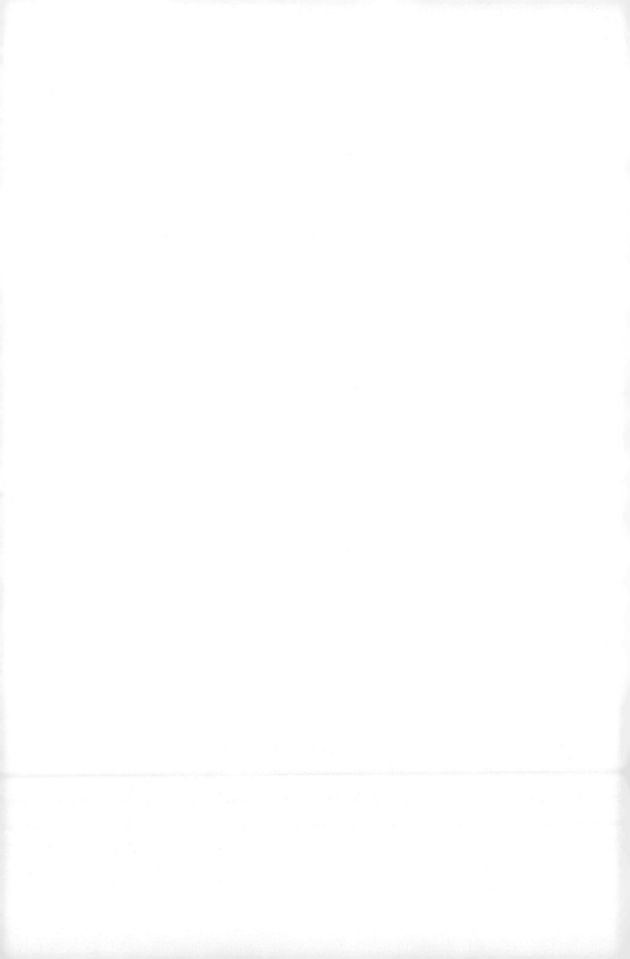

Bioinspired Strategic Design

Organizations are commonly thrust into hostile operating environments where they are required to make strategic decisions that involve significant and costly tradeoffs. Such hostile environments may be endemic such as an economic recession or idiosyncratic such as a predatory action by an adversary. Many features of such hostile environments parallel those of living organisms that also demonstrate fine-tuned strategies to improve their survivability under adverse conditions. How can organizations use these "bioinspired strategies" to survive, and even potentially innovate?

This book shows that the same three capabilities essential for the survival of living organisms in harsh environments – efficiency, resilience, and prominence – are also critical for organizations in their process of navigating through their own hostile environments. Throughout the book, the authors provide organizational executives with a systematic framework for thinking about strategic decision-making in a hostile environment leaning on analysis of real-world cases to draw out ontologies and methods for guiding their teams through disruptions, change management, innovation, and process improvements.

In the first part, organizations are provided with a systematic approach to analyzing three survivability influences – forces, resources, and observers and their interrelationships. While all three influences are active across all organisms (and organizations), the exact nature of their interrelationship and the significance of each influence are unique to every organism (or organization). The framework helps organizations nail down the specific features of their operating environment that can help or hinder survivability by analyzing the three influences. Organizations can respond to external influences by developing three-pronged capabilities – efficiency, resilience, and prominence (ERP) – that respond to the three survivability influences. Organizations often struggle with identifying the appropriate strategies to apply under different conditions. Fortunately, nature provides several mechanisms that can be analogically applied to guide business strategies.

The book contains many illustrations and examples of strategic principles observed among living organisms that can help an organization develop ERP capability. Finally, the book introduces seven strategic design heuristics – Combination, Elimination, Separation, Segmentation, Replication, Dynamics, and Maximization – observed in a living system that can be flexibly utilized to generate ideas to achieve strategic ends.

Bioinspired Strategic Design

Nature-Inspired Principles for Dynamic Business Environments

Daniel J. Finkenstadt
Tojin T. Eapen

A PRODUCTIVITY PRESS BOOK

First published 2025
by Routledge
605 Third Avenue, New York, NY 10158

and by Routledge
4 Park Square, Milton Park, Abingdon, Oxon, OX14 4RN

Routledge is an imprint of the Taylor & Francis Group, an informa business

ISBN: 978-1-032-71530-8 (hbk)
ISBN: 978-1-032-71527-8 (pbk)
ISBN: 978-1-032-71531-5 (ebk)

DOI: 10.4324/9781032715315

Typeset in Garamond
by Deanta Global Publishing Services, Chennai, India

Contents

Acknowledgments

The authors express gratitude to the following individuals, among many others, who have contributed (sometimes unknown to them) in various capacities toward the writing of this book: Rakesh Babu, Bimal Balakrishnan, Barry Bayus, Rich Bettis, Jim Bettman, Rajinder Bhandal, Thomas Chacko, M.K. Chandramohan, Deepu Chandran, J. Scott Christianson, Kiran Das, Jim Flink, Josh Folk, Rick Fernandez, Vijay Govindarajan, Rajdeep Grewal, Stephanos George Eapen, Peter Guinto, Ronald Flores, Rob Handfield, Nowfal Khadar, Frank Lin, Andre Martin, John Metselaar, Christine Moorman, Robert Mowry, Sanjay Nagarajan, Sridev Nair, Vineet C. Nambiar, Mike Nguyen, Kiran Pedada, Jan-Benedict E.M. Steenkamp, Dhinagaran Ramachandran, Bala Ramadurai, Geetha Ramamoorthi, Ed Rogers, Lisa Scheer, Jake Sotiriadis, Richard Straub, Nithin Philip Thomas, Brett Trusko, Lokesh Venkataswamy, Ajay Vinze, Kai Wang, and Valarie Zeithaml.

Dan Finkenstadt would like to thank his wife Amy for providing consistent love and encouragement and recognize the remarkable creativity of his children Amaris, Wilde, and Greyson from which he draws daily inspiration. Also, he dedicates this book to his mother for demonstrating incredible resilience and his uncle Wesley for introducing him to the marvels of nature.

Tojin Eapen thanks his family – Niky, Nesya, Liya, and Ethan Eapen – as well as his parents, brother, niece, and in-laws for their unwavering support throughout this project.

About the Authors

Daniel J. Finkenstadt, PhD, is a professional military officer and previously an assistant professor in the Naval Postgraduate School (NPS) Department of Defense Management offering courses in Enterprise Sourcing. Dr. Finkenstadt is the principal at Wolf Stake Consulting LLC and earned his PhD from the Kenan-Flagler Business School, University of North Carolina, at Chapel Hill (2020). He has over 21 years of defense contracting experience in operational (base level), systems center, headquarters, joint, overseas, and classified environments. He is also a graduate of NPS (MBA, 2011). His research interests are business-to-government markets, professional services (knowledge-based services), generative artificial intelligence, gamification of education, and contingency and scenario planning. He was the founder and Principal Investigator for the new Simulation and Ideation Lab for Applied Science (SILAS) at NPS. He has published multiple articles in the *Harvard Business Review*, including the recent July/August 2023 cover article along with Dr. Eapen. He has published various works in the *National Contract Management Association Contract Management* Magazine, *Defense Acquisition Review Journal*, *Journal of Purchasing and Supply Management*, *International Journal of Operations and Production Management*, the *Milbank Quarterly*, and *California Management Review*. He co-authored the Springer Nature book *Supply Chain Immunity* with Dr. Rob Handfield in 2023. *Supply Chain Immunity* covers supply chain lessons learned during the COVID-19 pandemic.

    *The ideas, positions and opinions in this book are those of the author and do not represent the official position of the United States' government, including the Department of Defense or United States Air Force.

Tojin T. Eapen, PhD, is a passionate advocate, applied researcher, and trusted advisor in the field of sustainable innovation. He is the founder of the Center for Creative Foresight and holds the position of Senior Fellow at The Conference Board. He also serves on the advisory board of Innomantra. His research interests include bioinspired design, augmented creativity, scenario planning, idea management, and sustainable innovation. Previously, he has taught at the Trulaske College of Business at the University of Missouri and UNC Kenan-Flagler Business School. He has also taught as a guest faculty member at the Global Leadership Program of the Tuck School of Business at Dartmouth College. Dr. Eapen has consulted with more than 40 organizations, including Google, Samsung, ABB, KBR, Robert Bosch, NetApp, Qualcomm, Bureau Veritas, SKF, and Newell Brands, providing training and strategic guidance on innovation. He has shared his practical insights through platforms like *Harvard Business Review* and *California Management Review* as well as contributed to conferences like the Global Peter Drucker Forum and various research outlets. Dr. Eapen has also served on the technical advisory group for the ISO 56000 standards on innovation management. His work has been cited by institutions and outlets such as Deloitte, United Nations Development Program, Chamber of Progress, IPSOS, Forbes, Freakonomics Blog, Harvard Business Publishing, ITPro, IE Insights, and Smart Company. He holds a PhD in Business Administration from the University of North Carolina at Chapel Hill, an MBA from the Indian School of Business, and a degree in Electrical Engineering from the National Institute of Technology, Calicut.

Introduction

In all things of nature there is something of the marvellous.

– Aristotle

DOI: 10.4324/9781032715315-1

Bioinspiration, the practice of drawing inspiration from the marvels of nature inherent in living organisms, has always been a wellspring of creative ideas that have catalyzed human innovation. A compelling typification of this phenomenon lies in humanity's enduring yearning to emulate the flight capabilities of birds. The aspiration to soar through the skies can be traced back to ancient times and is enshrined in various age-old legends, notably including the tale of Icarus and Daedalus, which showcases the ancient fascination for bird-inspired flying contraptions. In the 9th century, the Andalusian polymath Abbas Ibn Firnas made a noteworthy attempt to achieve flight by fashioning wings crafted from silk, wood, and feathers. More famously, in the 15th century, Leonardo da Vinci meticulously studied the intricate flight patterns of birds as a means to inform his designs and engender the advancement of flying machines.[1] At the dawn of the 20th century, the Wright Brothers embarked on a remarkable journey inspired by the flight of birds. They ingeniously designed bioinspired warping wings for their aircraft, the Wright Flyer, leading to the most celebrated milestone in aviation history.[2] On December 17, 1903, their relentless pursuit paid off as they achieved the first sustained flight at Kitty Hawk, North Carolina.

In recent times, the principles of bioinspiration have increasingly influenced the development of a large number of innovative products and solutions.[3] The approach of studying and drawing inspiration from the adaptations and mechanisms found in biological organisms to solve technical problems or create new technologies is also known as biomimetics or biomimicry.[4] The term "biomimetics" was coined by American inventor Otto Schmitt, who developed the Schmitt Trigger based on his study of neural impulse propagation in squid nerves.[5] Other notable examples of biomimetic products include Velcro, invented by Swiss electrical engineer George de Mestral, inspired by the way burrs stick to animal fur; the Harare Eastgate Center in Zimbabwe, designed using the principles of termite mounds for temperature regulation and energy efficiency; and the Shinkansen trains in Japan, whose aerodynamic design draws inspiration from the beak of the Kingfisher bird.

Adopting processes found in nature can also improve the performance of human systems. One notable example is the utilization of swarm intelligence techniques, such as ant colony optimization (ACO), in various fields. ACO is an optimization algorithm inspired by the foraging behavior of ants.[6] Ants are able to find food efficiently despite the lack of a centralized control system, and they are able to adapt to changes in their environment, such as the presence of obstacles or the depletion of food sources. ACO has been applied to a wide range of problems, including routing, scheduling, and resource allocation. Over the years, systematic approaches have been developed to assist in identifying potential biomimetic solutions to technological challenges and to determine where to find them. One such approach is Bio-Triz, a method that leverages patterns found in nature to identify and solve problems.[7]

While solutions inspired by nature and living organisms have achieved notable success in various fields, their prevalence still remains almost paltry compared to their vast potential. One area that remains largely untapped is the application of bioinspiration to design and solve challenges faced by human organizational systems, including businesses, governments, militaries, markets, cities, and society as a whole. This is surprising, given that both organisms and organizations share a common overarching goal: survival.[8] Organisms have evolved efficient systems for survival, and human organizations, in turn, have developed complex systems for achieving their goals and addressing the challenges they face. However, despite this shared goal, there has been limited exploration of how the principles and mechanisms found in living organisms can be applied to improve the performance and resilience of human organizational systems. The book aims to address this gap by exploring the potential of bioinspiration in enhancing the design of human organizational systems.

Emphasis and Structure of This Book

At its core, this book is centered around creative idea generation to improve human systems by drawing inspiration from the fundamental principles observed in nature. The astonishing advancement of generative AI technology since 2020 has facilitated novel approaches in studying and harnessing these principles.[9] By studying the adaptations and mechanisms found in living systems, we can gain novel and feasible ideas for addressing the complex challenges faced by businesses, governments, markets, cities, and society. The book aims to provide guidance on how to apply bioinspired principles to systematically generate creative ideas to solve complex problems, drawing on examples from a variety of fields and disciplines.

Chapter 1 explores the concept of survivability in various entities, including organisms, businesses, and countries. It emphasizes the importance of understanding how an entity's actions influence its survival. The chapter introduces three key influences on survivability: resource availability, uncertain environmental forces, and the presence and actions of observers. It discusses the interrelationships between these influences and how they affect an entity's ability to survive. The chapter also introduces the concept of efficiency, resilience, and prominence as factors that contribute to an entity's survivability. Overall, it provides a framework for understanding survival-linked actions and decision-making in different types of entities.

Chapter 2 examines different efficiency and resilience mechanisms observed in living organisms and organizations. It highlights the relationship between these two factors and how they can be applied to achieve similar goals in organizations. The chapter discusses the principles and strategies that organisms use to efficiently manage limited resources and adapt to external environmental forces. It also examines how organizations face resource constraints and need to balance their use of resources while developing strategies to adapt to external forces.

Chapter 3 discusses the concept of prominence mechanisms in living organisms and explores how these strategies can be applied to the organizational domain. It emphasizes the ability of organisms to modify the attention they draw from observers as a critical factor for survivability. The chapter examines different target observers in nature, such as predators, prey, and mates, and how actions and prominence levels differ depending on the observer class. It also explores various prominence-modifying attributes like color, shape, sound, size, location, and motion. Specific strategies observed in nature, including camouflage, apparent death, and distraction, are discussed in the context of predator avoidance and prominence balancing. The chapter also draws analogies between target observers in nature and business environments, considering competitors, customers, business partners, investors, regulators, and the government.

Chapter 4 of the book discusses the concept of natural design heuristics, which are approximate strategies that aid in decision-making. The chapter identifies and describes seven natural design heuristics: combination, removal, separation, segmentation, replication, dynamics, and maximization. These heuristics are illustrated through examples from natural and biological systems. The chapter also explains how these heuristics can be applied to product design, and how they relate to the efficiency, resilience, and prominence factors of a system. The chapter provides detailed explanations and illustrations for each heuristic and explores the training of large language models (LLMs) on different heuristics as a means to facilitate idea generation.

Chapter 5 investigates the concept of mixed design heuristics, which involves the simultaneous application of two or more natural heuristics. The chapter discusses 42 mixed design heuristics that unite two of the natural heuristics. Each mixed heuristic is named by combining the contractions of the natural heuristics. The chapter presents examples and applications of diverse mixed design heuristics in various systems, encompassing living organisms, businesses, products, and military strategy. Additionally, it describes the utilization of LLMs in conjunction with mixed heuristics within the idea generation process.

Chapter 6 focuses on ERP-focused strategic ideation within the context of scenario planning.[10] The ERP (efficiency-resilience-prominence) framework is applied to achieve two objectives: generating suitable scenarios quickly and preparing the organization to respond to multiple scenarios. The chapter describes the limitations of the traditional scenario planning process, related to steps such as scope definition, identifying key stakeholders, identifying trends and uncertainties, scenario research, and strategic ideation. The chapter introduces ERP-focused scenario planning as a solution to these limitations by requiring organizations to assess their efficiency, resilience, and prominence across scenarios and identify gaps in capabilities. The chapter concludes by discussing the use of generative AI tools, such as large language models, to support ERP-focused scenario planning.

Chapter 7 explores the concept of bioinspired product ideation and its application in new product development. It begins by introducing the ERP framework and its role in guiding technological innovation inspired by biological systems. The chapter emphasizes the importance of considering organisms with highly developed capabilities in the ERP factor of interest when seeking ideas for product improvement. It also provides a structured approach, including a series of questions, to systematically identify bioinspired solutions and leverage adaptations from living organisms. The chapter also highlights the application of generative AI tools such as large language models (LLMs) and text-to-image models in bioinspired product ideation.

From Living Organisms to Human Organizations

The fundamental objective of all living entities is to survive and continue their existence. This book's lessons draw heavily from the presumed analogical similarity between living organisms (including plants) and human organizations, which can provide valuable insights into decision-making at a systemic level. This approach consists of two parts: firstly, comparing diverse organisms that are distinct from one another, and secondly, applying common principles found in living organisms analogically to organizational systems.

In nature, it is common to find that organisms instinctively take actions that aim to achieve one of four essential objectives for survival: managing resources, particularly sources of energy; protecting themselves from environmental forces; forming and maintaining relationships with others; and defending themselves against threats from other entities. Furthermore, many living organisms have similar functional components or organs, such as those for sensing, movement, and adhesion, that contribute to these basic objectives. This similarity among organisms allows for the comparison of different organisms, regardless of their habitat or specific methods of achieving these objectives. As most physiological and behavioral adaptations observed in living organisms are related to one or more of the four basic objectives, it is possible to compare solutions across different entities that are otherwise dissimilar. As an example, we can compare the water conservation strategies of the saguaro cactus (*Carnegiea gigantea*) and the dromedary camel, despite the two organisms not being closely related. This comparison may reveal common principles. In fact, the more dissimilar the entities being compared, the more likely it is that common principles will be identified, if they indeed exist. These common principles can then be confidently applied to human systems due to their generalizability. For example, one potential application that could be influenced by the water-conserving strategies of the dromedary and the saguaro is the development of water-efficient systems in vehicle manufacturing, irrigation, or sustainable architecture.[11]

It is not surprising that the objectives of business organizations are analogous to those of living organisms, as both strive for survival. Both also require effective resource management, protection from external forces, the ability to attract customers or partners, and the ability to evade predatorial entities. However, the similarities between specific business organizations and living organisms become more strained when we consider more specific characteristics and behaviors. For example, while business organizations are primarily motivated by profit, governmental organizations may prioritize other goals such as serving the public interest. The predator–prey model is one example of a biological concept that has been applied to business environments, but there are limitations to this analogy. In nature, predator–prey relationships typically occur within a single species, whereas in business environments, these relationships can occur between different types of organizations.

Although the specific ways in which living organisms manifest their survivability-related objectives can be challenging to compare, these differences also offer opportunities for identifying unique and valuable strategies. By considering the reasons behind these adaptations or mechanisms in the context of the common, overarching goals shared by both organizations and organisms, we can gain valuable insights into novel strategies for achieving survival and success in challenging environments. One helpful approach is to examine the unusual adaptations or behaviors observed in certain species in nature, which may not be present in similar species that reside in different environments. To illustrate this approach, let us consider the Arctic fox and the fennec fox, two related species that inhabit contrasting environments and exhibit remarkable adaptations.

The Arctic fox lives in the frigid Arctic regions, while the fennec fox inhabits the hot and arid Sahara Desert. The Arctic fox has a thick, insulating fur coat that helps it withstand the extreme cold temperatures of the Arctic. Its fur changes color with the seasons, transitioning from brown in the summer to a snowy white in winter, providing camouflage against predators. In addition, the Arctic fox has a compact body with short legs and ears to minimize heat loss and reduce exposure to the extreme cold. These adaptations allow it to conserve energy and stay warm, improving its chances of survival in a harsh climate.

On the other hand, the fennec fox has adapted to the scorching heat of the desert in different ways. It has large ears with a high density of blood vessels, which help dissipate heat and regulate its body temperature. These large ears also aid in detecting prey underground by amplifying sound waves. Moreover, the fennec fox has long and bushy fur, which not only provides insulation but also protects it from the intense sun during the day and the cold desert nights. Its kidneys are highly efficient at conserving water, allowing it to survive in an environment where water sources are scarce. Their adaptations highlight the trade-offs involved in their survival. While the Arctic fox prioritizes insulation and energy conservation, the fennec fox focuses on heat regulation and water conservation. Given that these animals are similar to each other apart from their habitat-related characteristics, we can more easily connect the unusual adaptations found in each of the species related to their residing environment.

It is important to recognize that adaptations in living organisms are part of a larger, interconnected system. No adaptation exists in isolation but rather works in conjunction with other adaptations and functions to contribute to the overall well-being of the organism. This means that there are often trade-offs involved; for instance, an animal's size can influence its ability to acquire certain types of resources. Extremely large animals may have an advantage in acquiring certain types of resources with minimal effort, such as the blue whale consumption of plankton, while smaller animals may have to exert more effort to obtain food, such as a squirrel gathering and hoarding nuts. Similarly, an animal's highly developed sensory function may come at the cost of less developed senses in other areas. It is also important to note that animals are highly optimized to their specific habitats, and even slight modifications can disrupt their ability to survive.

The giraffe is a captivating example that demonstrates how adaptations in living organisms are interconnected and involve trade-offs. The giraffe's most distinctive feature is its long neck, which enables it to reach leaves high up in the trees, its primary source of food. However, this adaptation comes with trade-offs as well as other related adaptations.[12] The long neck of a giraffe lets it access a diet source that is unreachable to many other herbivores. By reaching higher leaves, giraffes can obtain a nutrient-rich diet, reducing competition for resources. However, the long neck presents challenges as well. Giraffes require a strong and efficient cardiovascular system to pump blood up to their heads against gravity. To achieve this, giraffes have an enlarged heart and high blood pressure, which are necessary for maintaining blood flow to their brains and to prevent fainting when they lift their heads after feeding at ground level. However, the giraffe's long neck also makes them more vulnerable to predation, as it becomes challenging to defend themselves against predators when their heads are high above the ground. Additionally, their stature requires them to spread their long legs or bend in an awkward fashion to drink from watering holes. This exposes them to attack from large feline predators in their habitat. These trade-offs between the advantages and disadvantages of the giraffe's long neck illustrate the interconnectedness of adaptations and their impact on the overall well-being of the organism.

This book builds on the above insights and introduces a new bioinspired model for designing organizational systems by drawing on natural analogies to improve survivability.[13] The goal of this book is to provide organizations with the tools they need to understand the design of living systems and use the lessons to improve their ability to respond to uncertainty in dynamic and challenging environments. At the core of this book lies the ERP framework, which highlights the vital role of three key capabilities – efficiency (E), resilience (R), and prominence (P) – for the endurance of living organisms in demanding habitats. This framework also underscores the significance of these ERP factors for human organizations grappling with their own challenging environments.

The Squirrel's Trilemma and the ERP Factors

To illustrate the interplay of these ERP factors, we can examine the quandary faced by a squirrel when stockpiling nuts for its winter survival. The trade-offs encountered by the squirrel bear resemblance to those confronted in organizational decision-making within challenging environments. The squirrel faces challenging decisions when it comes to collecting and storing nuts for the winter. On the one hand, it needs to gather as many nuts as possible to ensure its survival through the cold months. It must balance this need with the risks posed by predators and competitors as well as its own physical limitations. In a situation where there is an ample supply of nuts available, the squirrel may be tempted to gather as many as it can as quickly as possible. This strategy, however, is fraught with danger. The squirrel's rapid movements may attract the attention of predators and competitors, putting it at risk of being attacked or having its food stolen. Additionally, the squirrel's focus on gathering nuts may cause it to become distracted and fail to notice potential threats.

A more effective strategy for the squirrel would be to gather nuts at a steady pace, taking regular breaks to rest and scan its surroundings for potential dangers. By moving more deliberately, the squirrel can avoid drawing attention to itself and its food supply. It can also use its breaks to plan the most efficient route for gathering nuts and to assess the amount of food it has already collected. This will allow the squirrel to gather enough nuts to survive the winter without wasting energy or exposing itself to unnecessary risks. In addition to gathering nuts at a steady pace, the squirrel must also take care to hide both the source of its food and its storage location. Early in the gathering process, the squirrel should hide the tree where it is gathering nuts to avoid drawing competitors to the source. Later, it should carefully conceal the location where it has stored its nuts to prevent other animals from finding and stealing them.

Overall, the squirrel's trilemma requires it to balance its need for food and rest, demanding efficiency, while considering the risks posed by environmental forces including immediate and future weather conditions, requiring resilience (Figure 0.1). Additionally, the squirrel must also be mindful of the attention it may attract from predators and competitors, demonstrating the importance of prominence. By gathering nuts at a steady pace and taking care to hide both the source and storage location of its food, the squirrel can maximize its chances of survival through the winter. The squirrel's trilemma underscores the significance of three ERP factors – efficiency,

Figure 0.1   The squirrel's trilemma.

resilience, and prominence – in ensuring survivability against the trifecta threats of limited resources, strong forces, and adverse observers. Similar to the squirrel, firms, governments, and individuals must balance survivability factors of efficiency, resilience, and prominence (ERP) to stay alive during tough times. In this book, we use the ERP model as an analytical framework. Comparing strategies of different living organisms yields general principles of strategic design that potentially extend to other entities that function in dynamic environments. These principles primarily relate to the relative significance of threats, the importance of ERP factors, the nature of interrelationships among the ERP factors, and the tradeoffs involved while taking actions to improve survivability.

This Book in a Nutshell

This book explores the concept of bioinspiration and its potential to enhance the survivability of human organizational systems. By drawing inspiration from the adaptations and mechanisms found in living organisms, we can gain valuable insights and innovative solutions to address the complex challenges faced by businesses, governments, markets, cities, and society as a whole. The book emphasizes the importance of understanding the objectives shared by both organisms and organizations, such as managing resources, protecting against environmental forces, forming relationships, and defending against threats. It highlights the similarities and differences between living organisms and human organizations, providing a framework for comparing and applying bioinspired strategies. Efficiency, resilience, and prominence (ERP) factors emerge as critical for both organisms and organizations in achieving survival and success. The book also offers insights into the use of ERP analogical analysis as a means for interdependent entities to co-create strategies to plan for and overcome dilemmas and trilemmas in hostile environments.

This book seeks to serve as a guide for organizations seeking to harness the power of bioinspiration to enhance their survivability. By studying and learning from the marvels of nature, we can unlock innovative solutions and create a more sustainable and resilient future for human organizational systems. Throughout the chapters, the book explores various aspects of bioinspiration, including efficiency, resilience, and prominence mechanisms, natural design heuristics, mixed design heuristics, ERP-focused strategic planning, and bioinspired product ideation. It introduces concepts and principles from nature that can be applied to improve the performance, adaptability, and resilience of human systems. The book also highlights the role of generative AI tools, such as large language models, in supporting the bioinspired idea generation process. By understanding and applying bioinspired principles, organizations can gain a competitive advantage, improve their decision-making processes, and respond effectively to uncertainty and changing environments.

Notes

1. Richardson, P. L. (2019). Leonardo da Vinci's discovery of the dynamic soaring by birds in wind shear. *Notes and Records: The Royal Society Journal of the History of Science*, 73(3), 285–301.
2. Padfield, G. D., & Lawrence, B. (2003). The birth of flight control: An engineering analysis of the Wright brothers' 1902 glider. *The Aeronautical Journal*, 107, 697–718.
3. Harman, J. (2013). *The Shark's Paintbrush: Biomimicry and How Nature is Inspiring Innovation*. Hachette UK.

4. Benyus, J. M. (1997). *Biomimicry: Innovation Inspired by Nature.* HarperCollins.
5. Harkness, J. M. (2004). An idea man (the life of Otto Herbert Schmitt). *IEEE Engineering in Medicine and Biology Magazine,* 23(6), 20–41.
6. Dorigo, M., & Stützle, T. (2019). *Ant Colony Optimization: Overview and Recent Advances.* Springer International Publishing.
7. Vincent, J. F. V., Bogatyreva, O. A., Bogatyrev, N. R., Bowyer, A., & Pahl, A. K. (2006). Biomimetics: Its practice and theory. *Journal of the Royal Society Interface,* 3(9), 471–482.
8. De Geus, A. (2002). *The Living Company.* Harvard Business Press.
9. Eapen, T. T., Finkenstadt, D. J., Folk, J., & Venkataswamy, L. (2023). How generative AI can augment human creativity. *Harvard Business Review,* 101(4), 56–64. https://hbr.org/2023/07/how-generative-ai-can-augment-human-creativity.
10. Finkenstadt, D. J., Eapen, T. T., Sotiriadis, J., & Guinto, P. (2023, November 30). Use GenAI to improve scenario planning. *Harvard Business Review.* https://hbr.org/2023/11/use-genai-to-improve-scenario-planning.
11. Clements-Croome, D. J. (2013). Lessons from nature for sustainable architecture. In *Intelligent Buildings: Design, Management and Operation* (pp. 25–42). ICE Publishing.
12. Mitchell, G., & Skinner, J. D. (1993). How giraffe adapt to their extraordinary shape. *Transactions of the Royal Society of South Africa,* 48(2), 207–218.
13. Eapen, T., & Finkenstadt, D. J. (2023). Survivability design in hostile environments: Lessons from squids, ships, startups, and supply chains. *Strategic Design Research Journal,* 15(3), 307–317.

References

Benyus, J. M. (1997). *Biomimicry: Innovation Inspired by Nature.* HarperCollins.
Clements-Croome, D. J. (2013). Lessons from nature for sustainable architecture. In Professor Derek Clements-Croome (Ed.), *Intelligent Buildings: Design, Management and Operation* (pp. 25–42). ICE Publishing.
De Geus, A. (2002). *The Living Company.* Harvard Business Press.
Dorigo, M., & Stützle, T. (2019). *Ant Colony Optimization: Overview and Recent Advances.* Springer International Publishing.
Eapen, T., & Finkenstadt, D. J. (2023). Survivability design in hostile environments: Lessons from squids, ships, startups, and supply chains. *Strategic Design Research Journal,* 15(3), 307–317.
Eapen, T. T., Finkenstadt, D. J., Folk, J., & Venkataswamy, L. (2023). How generative AI can augment human creativity. *Harvard Business Review,* 101(4), 56–64.
Finkenstadt, D. J., Eapen, T. T., Sotiriadis, J., & Guinto, P. (2023, November 30). Use GenAI to improve scenario planning. *Harvard Business Review.* https://hbr.org/2023/11/use-genai-to-improve-scenario-planning

Harkness, J. M. (2004). An idea man (the life of Otto Herbert Schmitt). *IEEE Engineering in Medicine and Biology Magazine*, 23(6), 20–41.

Harman, J. (2013). *The Shark's Paintbrush: Biomimicry and How Nature Is Inspiring Innovation*. Hachette UK.

Mitchell, G., & Skinner, J. D. (1993). How giraffe adapt to their extraordinary shape. *Transactions of the Royal Society of South Africa*, 48(2), 207–218.

Padfield, G. D., & Lawrence, B. (2003). The birth of flight control: An engineering analysis of the Wright brothers' 1902 glider. *The Aeronautical Journal*, 107, 697–718.

Richardson, P. L. (2019). Leonardo da Vinci's discovery of the dynamic soaring by birds in wind shear. *Notes and Records: The Royal Society Journal of the History of Science*, 73(3), 285–301.

Vincent, J. F. V., Bogatyreva, O. A., Bogatyrev, N. R., Bowyer, A., & Pahl, A. K. (2006). Biomimetics: Its practice and theory. *Journal of the Royal Society Interface*, 3(9), 471–482.

Chapter 1

Strategic Design for Survivability

It is not the strongest or the most intelligent who will survive but those who can best manage change.

– Leon C. Megginson

DOI: 10.4324/9781032715315-2

Consider different forms of corporeal entities residing in strategic environments that hold survival to be its most important long-term goal.[1] Such a goal would be shared by diverse types of entities located in disparate environments, including biological organisms residing in their natural ecosystems, business organizations active in a competitive industry, agencies operating within a government, or countries maneuvering within a complex geopolitical system. Examples of such entities include:

■ A wolf pack in a harsh wilderness. The pack's long-term goal is survival, and their actions, such as hunting in coordinated groups, establishing territories, and protecting their young, influence their survival.
■ A tech startup in a competitive industry. The startup's actions, such as developing innovative products, marketing strategies, and adapting to market changes, can impact its survival in the industry.
■ A small island nation navigating a complex geopolitical system. The country's actions, such as forming alliances, negotiating trade agreements, and managing internal political stability, can influence its survival and position in the global landscape.

We refer to such entities as *survival-oriented* entities. We propose that there are common lower-level factors that all such entities optimize to survive and stay alive.

For such a survival-oriented entity of interest, say an organism, a business, or a country, commonly, our interest, as an observer, lies in understanding how the entity's actions, past, present, or potential, influence its survival. For example, we might be concerned about how a bison's wandering from its herd led to its demise, how participation in a particular war contributed to the downfall of an empire, or how a business acquisition impacted the success of a company in a foreign market. Furthermore, we may be interested in comparing between actions of diverse entities as well as learning from principles of survival observed in one type of entity (such as a biological organism) and applying it to a different type of entity (such as a business organization).

In this chapter, our goal is to provide a generic framework for thinking about survival-linked actions across different types of entities that can help in organizational decision-making. Such a framework can also help us examine how actions of survival-oriented entities such as the gecko, the angler fish, or the grass snake relate to the actions of individuals, teams, and business units inside human organizations.

Survivability: The Propensity for Survival

The long-term survival of any such corporeal entity residing in a strategic environment often depends on achieving several near-term objectives, which can change continually, based on changing internal or external conditions active around the entity. Each entity senses these changes in conditions and takes action toward achieving its near-term objectives. In general, achieving these objectives can maintain or increase *survivability*, which is the propensity for survival at any point in time of the entity.[2] Similarly, not being able to achieve the objective can lead to a decline in survivability. Repeated failure to achieve its objective can lead to an entity's death, i.e., failure to survive. These near-term objectives include growing sustainably, overcoming competition, avoiding predators, and efficiently managing resources to the degree that it meets their long-term goal of survival. The entity constantly engages in actions toward achieving its near-term objectives, which may or may not be successful. Failure to achieve an objective can result in an entity changing its actions or even modifying its near-term objectives to mitigate a consequent decrease in survivability.

Survivability in strategic environments has emerged as a recurrent theme in daily media coverage, encompassing a broad spectrum of issues, ranging from the extinction of species[3] and public health crises to corporate failures and disruptions in global supply chains. Grasping the concept of survivability is imperative for adeptly navigating the multifarious challenges encountered across diverse domains.

In addition to the above examples, the concept of survivability is relevant in various less publicly conspicuous domains, where the stakes of non-survival may prove even more consequential. National security is inextricably linked to the robustness of critical infrastructure, while cybersecurity is contingent upon the resilience of information systems in the ever-present threat of cyberattacks. The economic stability of nations also relies on the capacity of businesses and financial institutions to weather economic turbulence. In disaster management, the survivability of critical infrastructure assumes paramount importance, and even in the realm of space exploration, a meticulous consideration of survivability is imperative to ensure mission success and the well-being of astronauts.[4]

Comprehending survivability empowers us not only to address the prevailing survivability-relevant challenges across these diverse domains but also to anticipate and prepare for future ones. This chapter draws inspiration from the natural world as a foundational concept for exploring survivability and establishes connections between observations in nature and those in various strategic contexts.

External Influences in Hostile Environments

Hostile environments in nature are characterized by at least three distinct survivability influences: (1) resource availability, (2) certainty of environmental forces, and (3) the presence and actions of active observers. To analyze survival, we begin by considering how each of these three influences threatens or improves survival and modifies the effects of other influences.

Each organism can be viewed as a system that requires external resources for appropriate functioning. For a living organism to survive it needs resources, the most critical of which are energy and energy-convertible resources. Another critical resource is time, which is necessary for finding, converting, storing, or disposing of resources. Energy and time resources are partially exchangeable, i.e., they can sometimes be substituted for each other. For example, the availability of high levels of energy resources can compensate for less time to gather resources. Limitations on energy or time resources can impede the survivability of an organism. Resources such as housing materials and water may be considered energy-relevant resources, even though they strictly do not contribute to energy generation but play a role in energy management. It is therefore clear that resource limitations can impede the survival of an organism.

Damage that adversely impacts system integrity, such as a wound to a physical organ of an animal or emotional stress from isolation, can also result in loss of survivability. Damage is sustained by forces or observers. Forces are non-intelligent entities such as temperature (or cold), wind, currents, etc. that can impact survival by causing physical damage to the organism's body. Acting observers are intelligent decision-making entities that can impact the survivability of other entities. We label them "observers" because the perspective of their interaction with other entities seeking to survive is contingent on their ability to perceive the entity and, in many cases, impacted by the manner in which such entities are perceived. Let us consider the interrelationships involving forces, observers, and resources.

Forces are sometimes harnessed to enhance survivability, such as the use of sunlight to store and convert to energy in plants. However, forces can also directly impact the organism's integrity or damage resource availability. Observer's actions can similarly impact the organism by destroying its physical body or by limiting the availability of critical resources and can be used to enhance survivability (i.e., protecting fellow herd members). Forces in turn can also damage or enable the ability of observers to operate in an environment.

Direct and Indirect Effects of Threats to Survivability

The identified influences (forces, resources, and observers) can directly impact survivability or indirectly through another influence. Moreover, the organism itself can potentially act on the external influence. Thus, we can consider the following direct and indirect effects of the threats on an organism. The directed arrow (→) represents the direction of effect.

1. Force → Organism: The direct impact of environmental forces, such as weather patterns, natural disasters, or climate change, on an organism.
2. Resource → Organism: The influence of available resources on an organism's survival and well-being. Adequate resources, such as food and shelter, are essential for an organism's sustenance.
3. Observer → Organism: The way in which other organisms, often predators or competitors, affect the focal organism through their actions, behaviors, or presence.
4. Force → Resource → Organism: The indirect consequences of environmental forces affecting the availability of resources for the organism. This can include natural disasters impacting resource availability.
5. Observer → Resources → Organism: This relationship relates to how the actions and presence of other organisms can indirectly affect an organism's access to vital resources. Predators and competitors can indirectly impact the resource availability for a focal organism, thereby influencing its survival and well-being.
6. Forces → Observer → Organism: Seasons, as an example, can exert forces that drive procreation cycles, affecting how observers perceive potential mates, thereby indirectly influencing an organism's reproductive success.
7. Organism → Resources → Organism: In some cases, an organism's own actions can deplete or overconsume resources, impacting its own survival and that of other organisms. Overgrazing by herbivores is an instance of this.
8. Organism → Observer → Organism: This category delves into the interactions where an organism's actions influence an observer, which subsequently affects the organism itself. These interactions may include mating displays, territorial behaviors, or defensive actions.

9. Observer → Forces → Organism: Observers, such as humans or predators, can create or manipulate forces that directly affect an organism. This can include hunting, habitat destruction, or climate change.
10. Organism → Forces → Organism: Some organisms possess unique abilities to control external forces, such as certain plants' capacity to modify their environment by altering water flow or wind patterns.
11. Organism → Organism: In some situations, an animal might directly take actions that can increase the risk of its own death. This may be termed as the internal loss of survivability. However, we consider this to be more uncommon and unintentional, given that, in general, the goal of an organism is to survive.

Survivability-Relevant Health Factors

We can assume that all external losses to survivability may be attributed to adverse effects of the three survivability influences we have identified: Forces (Fo), Resources (Ro), or Observers (Ob). Now we can analyze survivability improvements in relation to Fo/Ro/Ob influences by considering three health factors of the organism that promote survivability by appropriately responding to Fo/Ro/Ob threats. These health factors (or survivability capability factors) are efficiency, resilience, and prominence. Each of the ERP factors can be viewed as a generic response function to one of the threat elements as shown in Table 1.1 and depicted in Figure 1.1. We also refer to the three factors collectively as the ERP factors.

Let's delve deeper into how these health factors are connected to the underlying external influences or threats that an organism faces, and how enhancing or adjusting these factors can enhance its survivability.

1. Efficiency: In relation to resources, survivability may be improved by better managing access, conversion, or use of resources. We refer to these components of resource management under the rubric of "efficiency," which is the ratio of output to resources expended. Efficiency

Table 1.1   Threats and Survivability Health Factors Linkage

Influence	Health Factor
Limited resources	Efficiency
Uncertain environmental forces	Resilience
Antagonistic observers	Prominence

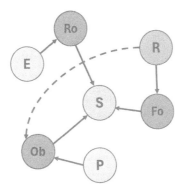

Figure 1.1   Survivability influences and ERP factors.

is thus the measure of the ability of an organism for optimal use of energy and time resources.

2. Resilience: In relation to forces, survivability is damaged by the degrading of an organism's structure. This includes damage to the overall integrity of the organism as well as the destruction of the organism's ability to obtain or utilize resources. We refer to the ability to withstand such force-stresses as resilience. Thus, resilience can protect against non-intelligent forces as well as antagonistic observers.

3. Prominence: Finally, in relation to observers, an organism can improve survival by evading detection or by frightening the observer. Even when the observer's attack is often through the application of a physical force, an entity can improve its survivability by "laying low" and remaining undetected. An entity may also wish to attract an observer such as a mate.

From Organisms to Organizations

Moving from comprehending survivability factors in individual organisms to applying analogous principles in organizational settings is both enlightening and of practical value. While the analogy might initially appear somewhat stretched, it serves as a convenient and valuable framework for grasping how external influences shape the vitality and longevity of organizations, mirroring the impact these influences have on living organisms. The model also captures how the same three health factors are also applicable in the case of organizations. Table 1.2 presents a comprehensive list of influences that are pertinent to both organisms and organizations. These influences are categorized into forces, resources, and observers. This classification enables us to draw more detailed analogical comparisons. For instance, we can draw

Table 1.2 Survival Threats and Health Factors

Survival Influence	Organism-Relevant Influence	Organization-Relevant Influence	Health Factor
Forces	Temperature, climate, weather, current, flood, earthquake	Political stability, market trends, social norms, technology trends, organizational culture	Efficiency
Resources	Food, water, raw materials	Capital availability, skilled workforce, access to raw materials, market demand	Resilience
Observers	Predators, prey, mates, symbiotic partners	Competitors, customers, partnerships, regulators	Prominence

parallels between weather, which affects organisms, and political stability, which influences organizations.

Efficiency is a pivotal health factor for organizations, akin to its significance in individual organisms. Just as an organism needs to efficiently manage its energy and time resources to thrive, an organization must optimize resource allocation, utilization, and output. Efficient resource management allows organizations to navigate the challenges posed by external forces, adapt to changing conditions, and sustain their operations effectively. Resilience is vital for organizations, just as it is for individual organisms when facing various forces. In the business world, resilience means the ability to withstand challenges, adapt to market fluctuations, and ensure the continuity of operations even in the face of adversity. Prominence for organizations involves strategies to either evade competition or stand out in the marketplace. Organizations can enhance their survivability by distinguishing themselves from competitors, delivering distinctive value propositions, and cultivating a robust market presence. In the subsequent sections, we delve deeper into the three health/capability factors and examine their interplay.

Survivability Health Factors: Efficiency, Resilience, and Prominence

We have demonstrated how the dynamic response of an entity to three key influences – limited resources, uncertain forces, and rival attention – determines its survivability. Thus, we can assess the "health" of a focal entity by observing three health/capability factors associated with the entity of interest: efficiency, resilience, and prominence. In the following section, our goal is to examine the interrelationships among these factors and the trade-offs involved in making decisions to enhance overall survivability.

Survivability Factors and Trade-Offs in the Face of External Influences

How can an organism or organization improve its survivability in the face of threatening external influences? First, when the threat consists of limited resources, the entity can improve its survival by improving its efficiency, such as by eliminating different forms of waste. Two of the most critical resources are energy and time, and these are considered exchangeable. Second, to improve its survivability, it can enhance its resilience, which represents the ability to withstand environmental forces and avoid damage. The higher the force the entity is capable of withstanding, the greater the resilience. For a given force, the lower the damage, the greater the resilience. An entity may be resilient to one type of force and non-resilient to another.

What if we need to simultaneously manage both resources and forces? We now confront a common challenge. Typically, we observe a trade-off between efficiency and resilience. The underlying reason for this trade-off is that an entity requires extra resources to be deployed to manage uncertain environmental forces. These extra resources comprise redundancies, reinforcements, or repair systems and can enable an entity to overcome extreme conditions. Thus, a higher level of resilience leads to higher resource demands and consequently lower levels of efficiency. Moreover, high efficiency requires fine-tuning to a specific environmental condition, which can prevent an entity from developing resilience.

Finally, in the presence of antagonistic entities such as predators and rivals, a focal entity can improve its survivability by modifying its prominence. When it comes to efficiency and resilience, the relationship between the health factor and survivability is monotonic. Ceteris paribus, the higher the efficiency or resilience, the better the survivability. In the case of prominence, the relationship with survivability is more complex. Both low- and high-prominence strategies may be applied to avoid or scare a predator. In nature, we see low-prominence strategies employed in biological organisms such as camouflage, hiding, and refuging being used as well as high prominence methods such as deimatic behavior and aposematic coloration[5] against predators. The use of prominence strategies is sometimes complicated by the presence of friendly entities in the environment toward which the focal entity might desire to use a different form of prominence strategy. For instance, an animal may desire to attract a mate at the same time it is trying to avoid a predator. A business firm may attempt to hide its actions from competitors while trying to garner the attention of customers or investors. Moreover, an entity might utilize multiple prominence strategies against an antagonistic entity if one fails or as a means to reinforce the effects. Thus, an entity is well served if it has access to multiple prominence strategies as well as the ability to switch between such strategies.

Influence of ERP Factors on Survivability

It is evident that the focal entity's survivability, as well as success (or lack thereof) in achieving their near-term survival-related objectives, is reflected in changes to one of three generic intermediate survival-relevant health/ capability factors that also influence each other: (1) efficiency (E), (2) resilience (R), and (3) prominence (P). Efficiency characterizes the ability of the entity to conserve resources. Resilience relates to the capability of the entity to withstand and recover from uncertain adversity.[6] Prominence represents the capacity to attract or evade external attention from other decision-making entities in the environment. We refer to these three as the ERP factors, and it is assumed that they mutually influence one another (Figure 1.2).

Each of these factors is assumed to possibly influence as well as be influenced by the other two factors. We depict the interrelationships involving the ERP factors and their relationship to overall survivability using the *Survivability Pyramid* (Figure 1.2). We believe that the degree to which the entity exhibits these factors can determine its survivability at any point in time. The relative importance of each of these factors and their contribution to the entity's survivability can change over time and depend on the extant environmental conditions. Consequently, the changing relative importance

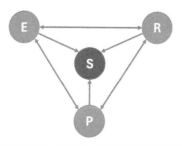

Figure 1.2 Interrelationships among ERP factors.

of the three ERP factors for survivability requires the entity to continually take actions that adjust the degree to which it possesses each ERP factor. We consider these three factors to be generic factors common across all survival-oriented entities. Consequently, looking at how any entity's action effectively makes trades across ERP factors provides us with a shared basis for comparing the actions of different entities. The Survivability Pyramid attempts to provide a universal understanding of actions by distinct entities in heterogeneous environments, enabling a more diverse set of strategic design and decision-making options in the face of uncertainty. If the COVID-19 pandemic taught us anything, it is this – entities had better prepare for strategic decision-making under conditions of extreme uncertainty.[7]

Direct and Indirect Effects of Survivability Factors

To understand the impact of any action on the survivability of an entity and compare the actions of different entities, we find it helpful to consider how these actions impact the ERP factors, both directly and indirectly through other factors, and how the factors, in turn, influence overall survivability. The principle can be summarized as

> the effect of any action on survivability cannot be understood by merely looking at its impact on one of the three ERP factors, efficiency, resilience or prominence that it seeks to modify, but requires looking at indirect effects mediated by the other two factors.[8]

This principle is similar in spirit to the one described in Henry Hazlitt's book, *Economics in One Lesson* (1946), "The art of economics consists in looking not merely at the immediate but at the longer effects of any act or policy; it consists in tracing the consequences of that policy not merely for one group but for all groups."

The key advantage of the above approach is that we can learn from lessons of survival in one context, such as living organisms in nature, and apply it to different settings such as a startup organization in a business market. Commonly, we find an entity (organism or organization) unilaterally directs its actions at modifying only one ERP factor that the entity considers most relevant for survivability at that particular time. What the entity often ignores is the effect of its action on the other two factors. These factors may be less critical for immediate survival but may become considerably more critical shortly after that. For example, a stag's action to abandon its location at a watering hole and run on observing a distant predator increases its resilience (R+) and survivability (S+). However, this action indirectly may also increase its prominence (P+) as it also draws attention from other predators reducing the entity's survivability (S−). We observe an analogical case in business markets, where a company might shift its headquarters overseas to reduce costs or attention from regulators, improving resilience (R+) and survivability (S+). However, the act of moving itself can attract the attention of regulators, who might be inclined to take aggressive actions against the company, reducing its survivability (S−).

In the following sections, we elaborate on how we can utilize the Survivability Pyramid to study the actions of survival-oriented entities. We first consider the direct impact of each of the three factors on survivability. Next, we turn to the indirect effects and consider how each ERP influences the other two factors. Finally, we examine how overall survivability is dependent on changes to ERP factors, both directly and indirectly, via its influence on other factors. Our goal is to demonstrate that evaluating the impact of actions on survivability taken with the unilateral intention of increasing one of the ERP factors requires us to look at the indirect effects of the action on survival via other factors.

Efficiency and Survivability

Efficiency is the ability of an entity to maximize the use of available resources and minimize waste. Efficiency is also defined as "the good use of time and energy in a way that does not waste any."[9] Efficiency is crucial when resources are limited or hard to find. In a resource-scarce environment, organisms that efficiently use resources are more likely to survive for two reasons. First, existing resources can be utilized for more extended periods. Second, high-efficiency levels also allow an entity to redirect its efforts from searching, gathering, and competing for resources that can reduce survivability. A high level of efficiency is achievable in the presence of low variability in internal and external conditions. For example, variation in the amount of food available requires an organism to store excess resources internally for consumption when food is scarce to increase resilience at a loss of immediate efficiency.

Firms have continuously sought lean supply chains to drive down carrying costs and potential waste, freeing up cash and improving near-term financial performance. These lean supply efforts have not always resulted in

survival benefits during extreme demand conditions, such as global pandemics.[10] For business systems, efficiency improvements often involve identifying and eliminating different forms of waste, also referred to as "muda"
in Japanese.[11] The lean manufacturing paradigm identifies seven forms of
waste: transportation, inventory, motion, waiting, overproduction, overprocessing, and defects signified by the acronym TIMWOOD. Efficiency is also
often linked to the "speed" of a system. The higher the efficiency, the faster
the systems can operate. One way entities can achieve higher efficiency is
by implementing multifunctionality, where a component of an entity performs more than one function. Multifunctionality can reduce idle time, as
well as the cost of maintaining a second component. For example, a business department that performs both sales and marketing functions would be
considered more efficient than one involved in only one.

Resilience and Survivability

Resilience relates to the management of uncertain changes in the environment. Resilience is particularly helpful to survival in the light of unexpected
changes and an abundance of resources. Resilience is also linked to the
level of disruption a system can endure without altering its self-organized
processes and structures.[12] An entity can increase its resilience by maintaining slack or redundancy in some form, which comes at the cost of
efficiency. One form of resilience observed commonly in nature involves
animals, such as hibernating bears, storing food internally or externally during winter. The resilience of business and sports teams is represented by
its "bench strength," where substitutes are available for current resources.
The substitutes are available to take over in the case of changes in the form
of demand, increase in demand, or if current sources are incapacitated or
become unavailable.[13] Resilience also involves the ability to recover quickly
from damage. The ability to rapidly repair damage sustained in battle is
a crucial aspect of the survivability design of military aircraft.[14] Such an
ability requires additional resources and maintaining repair-capable systems and repair-dedicated resources to enable the repair process. Repair-
dedicated resources generally do not play a role when the entity is operating
normally.[15]

Resilience also relates to the ability to avoid death or destruction. A
great example of the efficiency–resilience trade-off came to light during the
COVID-19 pandemic. In 2020, many organizations, such as consumer electronics and medical suppliers, faced supply chain difficulties from COVID-19

interruptions. Many had moved to lean inventories to maximize efficiency but found themselves at the brink of extinction when the availability of materials and products on-hand for revenue generation dwindled while global demand surged (a lack of resiliency). There are capabilities, such as agility, that either goal can improve. The trade of efficiency and resilience for maximum agility becomes a condition of uncertainty. For example, removing redundant systems on an aircraft may make it lighter and easier to maneuver at the cost of safety (i.e., reducing resilience for efficiency). However, having a secondary supply source, or even alternate product designs (increasing resilience at the cost of efficiency), may give a product line more agility during massive supply chain disruptions. The former approach of efficiency is agile given high levels of *certainty,* while the latter approach of resilience is agile given high levels of *uncertainty.*

Prominence and Survivability

The third survival-related goal, prominence, relates to an entity's ability to attract or evade the attention of other decision-making ("target") entities in the environment. In order to improve its survivability, an entity might decide to increase its prominence to attract the attention of potential mates, prey, investors, or customers. Conversely, an entity might decrease its prominence to reduce attention from potential predators, competitors, and instigators of hostile takeovers. We refer to these parties as *observers* who have the prerogative and capability to take action toward the focal entity. The desired direction and intensity of the prominence depend on the specific nature of its interaction with surrounding decision-making entities. Occasionally, the same entity can desire both increased and decreased attention from the same target observer. An organism may both desire or attempt to avoid the attention of a potential mate at different times. In a similar vein, a company may try to avoid the attention of certain types of customers, such as bargain hunters, while trying to draw interest from profitable customers.

Prominence's role in survivability is evident in interactions involving a predator and its prey. To improve its survivability (i.e., gain access to critical resources), the predator is often required to reduce its prominence to reduce the attention it garners from the prey, such as seen in the hunting strategy of the tiger. There are several ways in which such a reduction in prominence might be accomplished. The predator might use the advantage of camouflage to blend in with the surrounding foliage. The animal might crouch to appear smaller in size and pace cautiously before it launches its attack. In some instances, to improve survivability, prey may be required to increase prominence. The animal might attempt to appear larger to frighten a prey into submission or scare off a competitor.

From the prey's point of view, the chances of survival are often enhanced if it appears inconspicuous. In other cases, it may appear much more prominent to frighten off a potential predator by startling them. This phenomenon is referred to as deimatic behavior. Appearing unusually large or fast requires excessive resources and can be inefficient if maintained for an extended period of time.[16] Sometimes, a moderate level of prominence on the part of the prey might be linked to the lowest level of survivability. In such a situation, either increasing or decreasing its prominence can improve survivability. The reason for this effect is that a predator's decision to attack a prey may depend on its estimate of the ratio of expected resources gained to the expected effort expended. Perceived size can influence the decision of predator or prey to attack or escape.[17] A prey can influence this evaluation by appearing larger or smaller than its actual self. A larger prey would increase the predator's expectation of resources expended to attack the prey or the potential for damage. This strategy would, in turn, decrease the chances of being attacked by a predator. On the other hand, appearing smaller can minimize the expectation of resources gained and make it unattractive relative to the expected effort expended by the predator. Thus, in certain situations, the prey can both increase and decrease its prominence to improve immediate survivability. Table 1.3 outlines the connection between prominence strategies and outcomes in both the natural world, involving active predators and passive prey, and the business world, involving companies.[18]

In the case of businesses, both the presence or lack of attention may be desirable for survival. For example, a business often desires to attract the attention of business customers to sell more products or investors to gain capital investment. In other situations, a company may decide, "all attention may be bad attention," where the entity may want to attract as little interest as possible from external entities to itself. An example of reducing prominence would be a firm developing a new product and protecting it from competitors before an official market launch, or a public agency or a politician seeking to reduce prominence given negative press. A company with a strategic asset might try to hide to avoid hostile takeovers by reducing its prominence. Several of the world's oldest surviving businesses are relatively small in size. Their relative lack of prominence may have helped them escape potentially harmful attention.[19]

Table 1.3   High- and Low-Prominence Strategies for Predators and Prey

Entity	High-Prominence Strategy	Low-Prominence Strategy
Active predator	Predator appears more prominent to attract the attention of prey or frighten it into submission (white barn owls who scare voles into panic). The firm appears large to attract the interest of investors or dissuade potential competitors.	Predator appears less prominent to avoid the attention of prey before pouncing on it (tiger stripes or chameleon camouflage). The firm appears small during the initial stages of entry into an attractive market to avoid the attention of new players.
Passive prey	Prey appears more prominent (color patterns, physical defenses such as antlers) to dissuade a predator from attacking it. The firm appears large to dissuade interest in a potential takeover.	Prey appears less prominent (chameleon camouflage, remaining still) to escape the attention of a predator. The firm appears small to escape the attention of regulators and larger competitors.

Thus, we can conclude that biological organisms, businesses, and geopolitical entities agencies often employ analogical approaches to modify their prominence to improve survivability. We see that prominence may be both a desirable or undesirable immediate outcome for the entity in the context of its immediate survivability. Depending on the specifics of the situation, the desired outcome may be to increase or attract attention away from a specific entity or group of target entities.

ERP Factor Interrelationships

Next, we consider the interrelationships between the ERP factors. First, let us examine how efficiency and resilience relate to each other. Efficiency and resilience can appear to be contrary factors, even though both can contribute to survival. In general, the benefits of efficiency accrue over shorter periods of time, whereas the benefits of resilience are obtained only over a long-term period.[20] Efficiency relates to the most productive use of time and other resources and minimizing energy consumption. Higher levels of efficiency often imply lower resource consumption on the part of the entity to achieve the desired outcome. Efficiency is particularly desirable when certainty about resource consumption is high, and resources are scarce.

The relative importance of efficiency versus resilience for survival would depend on the degree of unpredictability and variability the entity encounters. For example, compare the role of efficiency and resilience in an entity's fight versus flight response in the presence of a threat. If the entity is efficient, it is likely to be smaller, and faster. In such situations, flight may be a better response. If the entity is relatively resilient, it may be bigger in size, and able to better withstand injury. However, it may be slow-moving. In such cases, fight may be the more appropriate response. Similarly, in encountering a situation that involves surviving a passage through a relatively predictable environment, the emphasis may be on improving efficiency, which is manifested in reducing time and effort and conserving scarce resources. However, in unpredictable conditions, survival often requires resilience and the ability to withstand unexpected losses to critical resources or assets. Achieving these goals involves trade-offs and can come at the cost of other desirable outcomes. ERP factors generally cannot be independently modified. Actions aimed at changing levels of one of the factors typically influence other factors. Actions aimed at increasing efficiency can decrease resilience. Additionally, actions focused on improving efficiency or resilience can modify the prominence of the organism.[21] It's important to acknowledge that short-term resilience or efficiency doesn't necessarily translate to long-term resilience or efficiency. Achieving high levels of both efficiency and resilience simultaneously is challenging. Nevertheless, it's possible for an entity to have low levels of both factors concurrently.

Redundancy and the Efficiency–Resilience Trade-Off

The reason why high levels of efficiency and resilience can be difficult to achieve simultaneously at the same time in the near term can be understood when we look at the role played by redundancy in establishing resilience. The trade-off between efficiency and resilience becomes apparent in various storage media, such as paper, microfilm, magnetic tapes, optical discs, and flash storage, where more efficient media are often more susceptible to failure. Thus, we observe older, less efficient, yet more resilient systems being employed in situations where the cost of failure is substantial.[22] High levels of resilience are often achieved by introducing multiple redundancies such as components, resources, and repair capabilities. These redundancies are maintained at a cost and can impinge on short-run efficiency. An animal may collect and maintain different food reservoirs in summer if it believes that acquiring them would be difficult in the winter.[23] However, these additional reservoirs would require immediate extra effort and the provision of storage and mechanisms that protect the resource from loss or damage. Additionally, they may need to accept increased predation risks in exchange for securing more food. High levels of efficiency, in turn, are often achieved at the cost of reliability by eliminating redundancy, at the cost of resilience and reliability. Improving efficiency in constrained situations often requires an entity to limit resource consumption. Limited resource consumption, in turn, requires eliminating slack in various forms, including stockpiles, excess capacity, and component redundancies. For example, improvements to business efficiency during an economic downturn usually involve laying off "redundant" personnel.

High levels of resilience are required when exploration, such as a search for resources, is an integral part of survival. The significance of redundancy in the efficiency–resilience trade-off is evident when contrasting cave diving with scuba diving. Cave diving necessitates a substantial level of redundancy due to the heightened risk of contingencies in an enclosed environment. In contrast, scuba diving provides a less risky exit route, shifting the emphasis more toward efficiency. Innovative (i.e., exploratory) organizations are often required to maintain higher levels of redundancy, in the form of excess resources, at the cost of efficiency. Efforts to optimize business operations to improve efficiency can be detrimental to resilience and overall survival as expressed in the following quote by Nassim Taleb and his co-authors in a 2009 *Harvard Business Review* article.[24]

> Most executives don't realize that optimization makes companies vulnerable to changes in the environment. Biological systems cope with change … we have two lungs and two kidneys, for instance – that allows us to survive.

The role of redundancy in building resilient entities is evident in many engineered products where safety is paramount. Redundancy can also mitigate the adverse effects of human errors, especially in software products.[25] The level of redundancy necessary is generally proportional to the cost of failure. Safety-critical systems, where malfunction can lead to immediate loss of life, include multiple layers of redundancy. Redundancy also improves resilience as an error-correcting mechanism. An error or defective performance on the part of one component can be corrected by another component of the same type. Aircraft often incorporate redundancy in several critical components to increase resilience. In a multi-engine aircraft, the effects of failure of one engine can be mitigated by other engines. The absence of such redundancies can come at a high cost.[26] However, such redundancy may come at overall decreased efficiency in the short term (i.e., more weight requires more fuel consumption). Entities required to navigate unpredictable conditions where the cost of failure is high often incorporate high levels of redundancy to achieve resilience. For example, the 1962 Citroen 2CV "Sahara" off-road vehicle, designed for oil exploration in desert areas, incorporated several redundant components such as two engines, fuel tanks, gearboxes, and differentials.[27] All of these dual components are exceptionally heavy and create an incredible draw on power resources.

Similarly, we see redundancy as a mechanism for increasing resilience in biological systems both at the level of individual organisms and the overall ecosystem. The desire for resilience may also require entities to add and maintain slack when they can acquire additional resources. The Dromedary camel stores fat for future energy needs in its hump. This is a well-known example of redundancy observed in animals associated with increased survivability in a specific environmental setting – harsh deserts with limited access to food and water. This form of resilience would be wasteful in an environment where food is readily available. In general, for an organism, resilience is a preferred attribute for exploratory tasks, whereas efficiency is prioritized in exploitative endeavors. The overall natural ecosystem also benefits from redundancy among its constituent entities. For example, we observe functional redundancy in nature, where multiple species play similar roles in the ecosystem.[28] In the case of business firms, redundancy might involve holding cash beyond immediate requirements. In the book, *The Living Company*, Arie de Geus identified conservative financing as one characteristic common to long-lived companies.[29] Redundancy also allows for flexibility, given that entities with slack can tolerate exploration and errors.

How Efficiency and Resilience Influence Prominence

So far, we have looked at how actions that increase efficiency can reduce resilience and how an action that increases resilience can harm efficiency. Next, we consider how actions that modify efficiency and resilience influence prominence. Here, we must consider both direct and indirect effects. For instance, in considering how an action aimed at improving efficiency impacts prominence directly, we should also consider how it influences prominence via its influence on resilience. First, let us look at the relationship between efficiency and prominence. We have seen that changes in prominence emerge from (1) the presence of unusual attributes and (2) a relative change in attributes. Take the case of physical attributes such as size. Large size is often associated with prominence. A physically (relatively) large entity naturally commands greater prominence and captures the attention of observers. Thus, an action that leads to increased efficiency can often lead to a decrease in prominence simply because efficient systems are typically smaller than less efficient systems with redundant components. For example, in the process of anhydrobiosis, certain invertebrates tend to shrink in size or contract in size and can withstand extreme dehydration and water loss.[30] A highly efficient business firm employing fewer individuals would be less prominent than a business firm with many employees. However, sometimes there is a secondary mitigating effect. For example, the efficiency gained from leaner operations (smaller size) could also generate higher margins, attracting more investment attention.

Sudden changes in an entity's attributes (such as size, color, or speed) can increase prominence, even if the change is originally aimed at increasing efficiency. Additionally, actions that result in an efficiency gain or loss relative to peer entities can also improve prominence if peers currently obscure the entity. For example, a fish that swims faster compared to its school is apt to be noticed. Similarly, a relative increase or decrease in efficiency compared to a past state can increase immediate prominence. The converse is also true. For example, firms laying off their employees can increase prominence briefly, even though it will lead to lower prominence in the longer term. Even though smallness of size is generally not associated with prominence, a highly efficient (or tiny organism) can appear prominent simply because of its unusualness. For example, a small company with a very high revenue or profit-per-employee would be highly noticeable to potential employees, investors, and competitors. Prominence is also subject to relative attractiveness based on contemporary trends in popularity and policy. More recently, small, commercial startups have become more attractive in public procurement where traditionally, large proven incumbents have reigned supreme. Small business size can also result in positive prominence in government markets where public policy calls for special consideration for such firms. In the United States, small businesses can be designated under a variety of categories such as woman-owned, veteran-owned, minority-owned, 8(a), etc.[31] This designation can lead them to be placed in a place of priority or even the sole source for government contracts. This inverse relationship between firm size and public procurement prominence is driven by public policies that seek to bolster small businesses with federal tax revenue for socioeconomic goals.

In the context of the relationship between resilience, the opposing correlation with efficiency is generally observed, but not always. Resilience typically necessitates the incorporation of some form of redundancy. This implies that a more resilient system is usually "larger" and, consequently, more prominent. An increase in resilience can also increase prominence by inducing a perception of novelty on the part of the observer. In the past, the US federal space launch business was completely cornered by United Launch Alliance (ULA), known for its high levels of mission assurance and reliability. An entity that maintains high levels of redundancies can result in increased size due to the maintenance of redundancies. In certain situations, redundancies can slow down an entity relative to its peers. More recently, SpaceX has begun to overtake ULA in the US space launch business due to its ability to operate faster, cheaper, and with more innovative approaches to rocket reuse. Such a relative decline in speed can make the entity a prominent and attractive target for a predator. In our example, ULA's resilience slowed it to the point that SpaceX was able to pounce and devour ULA's market share.

Resilience also leads to increased prominence if the entity is inordinately involved in resource acquisition. For example, an animal is more likely to be noticed when foraging for food than asleep. Resilient entities can maintain stability in the face of adversity, and this can either enhance or diminish the attention they receive from external entities. Their ability to withstand external forces enables them to become relatively more active when necessary. For instance, during 2020 and 2021, even though 3M and other major PPE suppliers couldn't fully meet the demand in the United States, they still managed to secure business over smaller domestic manufacturers. This was primarily due to their capacity to effectively navigate the challenges associated with COVID-19, even though they depended on potentially risky Asian sources for materials.

Static and Dynamic Survivability: Adaptations in Nature and Business Environments

To overcome threats, entities in a hostile environment commonly utilize adaptations that modify ERP factors. These adaptations may be static, long-term, or dynamic short-term adaptations that modify one or more of the entity's attributes, such as size, form, color, or function. An entity might benefit from static adaptations, such as being larger (or smaller) in size relative to other animals in its environment. An animal might also benefit from dynamic adaptations, such as changing its size quickly, such as observed with the porcupinefish, which can nearly double in size, extending spikes along its body when threatened.

Such adaptation often has a natural bearing on one or more of the three ERP factors. Take the case of static and dynamic adaptations of size in nature. Generally, larger animals are more prominent than smaller ones. Such a difference in prominence can be advantageous or detrimental to the survivability of the animal. An entity that appears much smaller or much larger relative to its reference group can attract increased attention from a predator. In some instances, unusual attributes relative to peers can help animals avoid predation, a phenomenon referred to as apostatic selection. Similarly, quick changes in attributes such as size can exaggerate its prominence and frighten away potential predators. Analogically, a business might benefit from its absolute and relative size, as well as its ability to embellish its size, in the eyes of a potential competitor eyeing its market or during mergers and acquisitions. The most famous case in recent history involved Twitter allegedly underrepresenting the number of fake users on the platform during the majority buyout efforts by billionaire Elon Musk.[32] Most recently, JP Morgan Chase accused the founder of the college financial-planning site, Frank, of misrepresenting the size of its customer base for a $175 million buyout.[33]

Static adaptations such as large or small size can also influence the efficiency and resilience of the animal, based on resource availability, and the significance of external forces. The link between resource availability and an organism's size is described by Foster's rule, also known as the island effect. This rule posits that small mammals on islands tend to grow larger, allowing them to utilize available resources and enhance metabolic efficiency more effectively. Conversely, large mammals on islands develop smaller sizes, reducing their resource requirements and increasing their reproductive output.[34] Depending on the environmental force in question, size may be helpful or detrimental to an animal's resilience. Larger animals may be more resilient to extreme winds, whereas smaller animals may be in general more resilient to extreme temperatures. Dynamic changes to size can also impact the efficiency and resilience of an animal, such as by changing its surface area, which can affect energy dissipation as well as resilience against environmental forces such as deep-sea currents. Similarly, in business operations, a firm may establish robust and trusted sources of supply through strong supplier development, relationship management, and colocation (i.e., the Honda model) that are resilient to uncertainties arising from competition. Others may choose to establish multiple sources of supply that are vetted but easily interchanged in cases of environmental uncertainty. The trade-off for the adaptability and range of multiple sources is that one risks losing in-process efficiencies gained from institutional learning, co-creation, and trust.

Direct and Indirect Effects of ERP Factors on Survivability

It is clear that the relationship between the ERP factors and survivability is not unidirectional and can depend on the specifics of the actions. Indeed, it is possible for a given action to both increase and decrease survivability through its differential effects on the ERP factor. An action might increase survivability through its impact on efficiency but might contribute to a decrease in survivability through its impact on prominence. Consequently, it is essential to consider both the direct and indirect effects of a given action on survivability. The direct effect of a given action may increase survivability, but the indirect effect of the action might decrease survivability through a mediating factor. For example, an increase in resilience may directly lead to increased survivability but may indirectly lead to decreased survivability via an increase in prominence, leading to a net gain, net loss, or net neutral total effect. To illustrate, an entity to maintain resilience is often required to maintain slack or extra resources. In an uncertain environment, the slack can help survivability. However, these extra resources may cause the entity to appear more prominent. An animal that carries extra resources or slack can appear larger relative to animals that do not. This increased prominence can make it a relatively more attractive target. These relationships can be summarized as A → R+ → S+, A → R+ → P+ → S−. Here A→ represents the directed action, and E+/−, R+/−, P+/−, and S+/− represent an increase or decrease in ERP factors and survivability.[35] Additionally, in a resource-deprived environment, an entity with considerable slack may be a target of attention. For example, during a financial crisis, cash-rich companies, which are more resilient, may be more prone to takeover, given that their increased resilience comes to the forefront during a crisis. Thus, actions intended to increase resilience in order to increase survivability should also be evaluated on the basis of its effect on efficiency and prominence.

In the above example, the direct effect of an action on survivability was mitigated by its indirect effects. It is also possible for a factor's direct effect on survivability to be enhanced by an indirect effect through a mediating factor. Consider the impact of an action that reduces the resilience of an entity. The decrease in resilience can have a direct negative impact on survivability, given that the entity has to devote time for resource gathering or repair in the face of adversity. Low resilience can also have an indirect effect on survivability through increased prominence. An entity with low resilience which is incapacitated or is engaged in resource acquisition is often likely to be more prominent. An animal that is wounded or has to constantly search for food (R–) is oftentimes more prominent (P+) as they can less easily hide. This can lead to a decrease in survivability. The relationships can be summarized as A → R– → S– and A → R– → P+ → S–. For example, a company that is engaged in product recall (R–) is likely to be adversely affected both by the direct impact of the recall on survival through reduced profits and through increased prominence manifested in negative publicity. Similarly, a company facing a cash crunch may be required to increase its prominence to raise funds. This increase in prominence can highlight its financial troubles, further decreasing its survivability.

Organizational Application: ERP Factors and Firm Incentives

We propose that entities, especially those making strategic design and decision trades, could benefit by taking a systematic approach to evaluating actions by considering inter-relationships among ERP factors and the indirect effects of the factors on survivability (Table 1.4). ERP factors are interrelated and any evaluation of the actions of an entity that looks at its effect on only one of the ERP factors is incomplete. An action taken with the goal of modifying one of the three ERP factors without considering the other two may be detrimental to its survival.

The above principle, albeit simple, has significant consequences for firm-level strategic decision-making and incentive design. Most decisions in

Table 1.4 Potential Effects on Survivability Involving ERP Factors

ERP Factor	*Potential Effects on Other Factors*	*Potential Effects on Survivability*
Efficiency (E)	E+ → R+; E+ → R–; E– → R+; E– → R– E+ → P+; E+ → P–; E– → P+; E– → P–	E+ → S+; E+ → S–; E– → S+; E– → S–
Resilience (S)	R+ → P+; R+ → P–; R– → P+; R– → P– R+ → E+; R+ → E–; R– → E+; R– → E–	R+ → S+; R+ → S–; R– → S+; R– → S–
Prominence (P)	P+ → R+; P+ → R–; P– → R+; P– → R– P+ → E +; P+ → E–; P– → E+; P– → E–	P+ → S+; P+ → S–; P– → S+; P– → S–

organizations are unilaterally made to enhance a single ERP factor, often without evaluating the potential impact on other factors. Even rarer are the endeavors to identify indirect effects. A reason for this is that individuals tasked with these actions are siloed and provide incentives that align more closely with one of the ERP factors rather than overall survivability. The incentives of the production department may be aligned more closely to efficiency, the incentives of the quality department may be more consistent with unilateral improvements to resilience, and the incentives of the market-ing department may be associated with increased prominence. Thus, busi-ness actions should be incentivized to influence overall survivability rather than its impact on a single ERP factor. Closer alignment of incentives to one of the ERP factors compared to others can lead to sub-optimal decisions for survivability. For example, on the one hand, a company's effort to become lean improves its efficiency. On the other hand, such actions can limit its resilience. It can also potentially reduce its ecological footprint, reducing negative attention from both competitors and customers. Poor resilience (e.g., product recall or delayed product delivery) can also attract negative cus-tomer attention, which in turn can reduce the possibility of survival. These pathways can be summarized as E+ → S+, E+ → R– → P+, E+ → R– → P + → S–, E+ → P+ → S+, and E+ → P– →S–.

The analysis then involves (1) documenting the reasons for the directional relationship, (2) evaluating the degree or strength of the directional rela-tionship, and (3) estimating net effect from bi-directional influences. At the beginning of the analysis, all the potential influences are assumed to exist. The onus is on the investigator to demonstrate that a particular directional relation does not exist for a given relation.

For example, consider the case of an engineering manager in a firm who proposes the action of replacing a product component with a cheap substitute. The manager also claims that such a substitution will result in efficiency savings for the company. Here the proposed relationship is A → E+ → S+. The evaluation of such a claim will subsequently proceed by identifying other pathways from A → S. Some of these pathways include A → R– → S–, A → P+ → S+, and A → P– → S–. The team evaluating the proposal is tasked with explaining how any of the above pathways might result in strengthening or weakening the effects of the originally proposed relationships.

As an additional illustration, imagine a scenario in a retail company. The marketing department is determined to achieve its marketing targets by enhancing prominence (P+) and running a flashy advertising campaign.

However, they do not consider the potential decrease in resilience (R–) or efficiency (E–). Due to inadequate inventory management, the company struggles to meet the sudden spike in demand generated by the campaign, leading to supply chain disruptions, customer dissatisfaction, and a dent in their prominence (P–). In the evaluation process, the team needs to explore how these interconnections might impact the initially proposed relationship (in this case, A → E+ → S+). They must consider alternative pathways like A → R– → S–, A → P+ → S+, or A → P– → S– to comprehensively assess the potential consequences of the proposed action.

Growth, Survival, and the ERP Factors

The ERP model also helps us examine the role of growth in survival. Growth is defined as the "process of increasing size." For a living organism, growth tends to reflect an increase in physical size or stature. Growth can also be indicative of improvements in capabilities such as knowledge and skill. For a business organization, growth is measured in terms of an increase in physical size, as indicated by revenues, profits, market share, number of employees, or geographical footprint. Most commonly, however, growth refers to an increase in sales revenue, and it is common to find CEOs incentivized on revenue growth.

For this reason, it is common to find organizations, in particular publicly listed companies that consider growth as the overarching organizational goal and would consider survival as a goal to be unambitious or even retrogressive. The term "survival" is often associated with poor vision, and companies are encouraged to move from survival to growth mode. Survival is generally associated with desperate actions to improve efficiency during times of crisis. The term "survival mode" in popular use entails a focus on reducing expenses, reducing the workforce, narrowing profit margins, and conserving financial resources.[36] Many argue that prioritizing survivability in business corporations is unnecessary, with growth (associated with increased profits and stock prices) taking precedence. For example, in a 2015 *Financial Times* article discussing corporate longevity, Mor Naaman, an associate professor at Cornell Tech, contended that the sustained existence of established corporations had limited significance, considering the inevitable emergence of new businesses.[37] We regard this limited perspective on survivability as myopic and fundamentally flawed. We believe that it can be demonstrated that survivability, not growth, should be the overarching goal of any business organization.[38] Furthermore, the repercussions of a company's demise (i.e., failure) should be assessed in relation to the role it fulfills within the ecosystem and the initial functional redundancy it offered before its death.[39]

In our view, any short-term corporate objective such as growth should be aligned with a broader, long-term goal of maximizing survivability. It can be shown that (1) the goal of growth can be adequately subsumed within the overall goal of survivability, (2) there exists a limited time where growth is beneficial, beyond which it may be inimical to survival, (3) there is a natural growth rate, outside of which, entities cease to benefit from increased size, and (4) growth is not a sustainable long-term goal for most entities in an ecosystem (balanced co-existence may lead to greater survivability than unfettered growth).

Survivability is deemed a highly desirable objective for a range of organizations, including startups (which also prioritize growth), family-owned businesses, government entities, firms aligned with strategic national objectives, non-profit organizations, and socio-religious institutions. In contrast, survivability may be a less conspicuous goal for profit-oriented publicly traded companies, where shareholders may be primarily focused on profit maximization. Furthermore, aligning executive compensation with enhancements in overall survivability can prove more challenging compared to improvements in any of the three individual ERP (efficiency, resilience, prominence) factors. While many companies have short lifespans, there are some remarkable examples of businesses that have thrived for centuries. In Japan, such companies are referred to as "Shinise," while Les Hénokiens in France and the British Tercentenarians Club recognize businesses that have existed for 200 and 300 years, respectively.[40]

First, to show that growth is subsumed within the goal of survival, we demonstrate that the value of growth to an organism is easily explained in relation to its contribution to survival via the ERP factors. Growth can be viewed as an action that impacts survivability and evaluated on its impact on ERP factors. Growth as an action can bring about an increase in efficiency (e.g., economies of scale), an improvement in resilience (ability to add and maintain slack), and a rise in prominence (increase in physical size). Growth may also be necessary if an increase in size can help a company acquire resources from other entities unwilling to provide similar recourse to smaller entities. Some companies choose to remain small to avoid attention from regulators or tax authorities.[41] Prominent companies are protected by governments or society who sometimes reckon them to be "too big to fail." In a herd, a dominant (and therefore generally more prominent) animal may enjoy protection from others or reduce its predation risk by strategically positioning less-dominant animals in potentially risky positions. This phenomenon is commonly referred to as the selfish herd theory. However, growth can also decrease survivability through its influence on these same three factors beyond an optimal size level. An increase in an entity's size can decrease efficiency and resilience beyond an ideal point. While prominence is helpful for survival in many situations, excessive size can draw adversarial attention from competitors and predators.

Second, growth is temporary and restricted to a limited life stage for most biological organisms, typically when juvenile.[42] A remarkable exception to this principle is the immortal jellyfish (*Turritopsis dohrnii*), which stands as an extraordinary anomaly in nature, challenging the conventional relationship between age and growth. This jellyfish possesses the unique ability to revert to its juvenile stage after reaching maturity, effectively resetting its biological clock. Similarly, growth is critical to survival for most startup business organizations. However, there is an optimal level of size for more mature organisms, beyond which growth ceases to be useful for survivability. Third, even during the juvenile stage, there is assumed to be a natural rate of growth. Deviation from this natural rate can be detrimental to the entity's survival. For example, acromegaly is a hormone condition involving excessive growth in humans that can lead to premature death.[43] Similarly, growth in an adverse environment can be detrimental to an organism's survival. In contrast, dormancy or the absence of growth is a key survival strategy in harsh environments.[44] Likewise, there exists a naturally appropriate stage for large businesses to stop growing. This fact is in stark contrast to an assumption of necessary growth that is the implicit mandate for the CEOs of many large corporations. However, the lack of such a perspective on the appropriate time to stop growing can be detrimental to many successful companies' survivability.

Finally, growth may not be a sustainable goal for most entities in an ecosystem at a given point in time. Excess growth in a resource-scarce environment can increase resource consumption and encourage competition with other entities with whom cooperation may be necessary, or conflict is otherwise needless. Large animals with similar diets in a resource-scarce environment, such as the musk ox and the caribou in the tundra, are often required to fight each other. Excessive growth can increase prominence, resulting in adverse attention from competitors who may view the entity as an emerging threat or from predators. Regulators may target a large corporation for its adverse impact on other business entities in the ecosystem. A business behemoth such as Amazon or Walmart is often the target for calls for a breakup given its perceived detrimental impact on consumers or smaller companies. In short, survival is sustainable; growth is not. The growth of a firm is negatively impacted by both its size and age.[45] Thus it is clear that growth is rarely a meaningful pursuit except as an action that contributes to survival. In fact, if long-term survival is the goal, growth often must be restricted.[46]

Startups and the ERP Model

The survivability triangle and the ERP model provide a framework for analyzing entities that operate in challenging and hostile environments, such as business startups. Given the high failure rate of most startups, survival is a paramount consideration for such firms. Let's consider the case of a startup developing an innovative product that could threaten the dominant position of a well-established firm. On the one hand, the startup benefits from high prominence as it allows them to attract potential customers and investors. However, this increased prominence can also draw the attention of the established firm. The established firm often gains an advantage by employing predatory strategies against the startup, such as temporarily reducing prices to drive the startup out of a lucrative market. In such situations, the startup can employ anti-predatory strategies to either increase or decrease their prominence for survival. Therefore, the concept of prominence-adaptability (P-adaptability), the ability to adjust prominence relative to new conditions, becomes critical for the survival of startups.

Startups face the challenge of finding the right mix between efficiency and resilience. For example, if they focus too much on efficiency by cutting costs, they might struggle when unexpected market changes occur. Conversely, if they overemphasize resilience by allocating too many resources, they can hinder their ability to grow quickly. Striking the right balance enables startups to seize opportunities and handle unexpected setbacks, ensuring their long-term success and competitiveness. Startups frequently need to transition between high-efficiency and high-resilience approaches. For instance, a software startup might prioritize efficiency while developing and launching a new product to meet tight deadlines. But when facing a sudden technical issue, they must swiftly shift to a resilience mode to ensure uninterrupted service for customers. This adaptability, termed "ER-adaptability," is crucial for startup success.

The ER trade-off is also a critical factor in hiring decisions for startups and smaller firms. Consider the case of a startup hiring employees for critical roles in the organization. For high efficiency, it makes sense to hire only a single individual for a task, and in many cases, the same individual performs multiple tasks. It is common to find individual employees wearing multiple hats in a startup organization. However, increased efficiency so gained comes at the cost of reduced resilience. The loss of a vital employee often results in the loss of mission-critical knowledge resources and can lead to the death of the company. Further, efficient human resource models in start-ups (single employees) can negatively impact the efficiency of operations by creating single points of failure and bottlenecks that can slow or even shut down production and delivery once orders start to increase. The ERP model can help startup firms examine existing business structures and actions for possible weaknesses.

Developing Resource Capabilities

Although efficiency is the key capability in resource management, resilience and prominence can also affect it. This is because environmental factors can create limitations and the presence of other observer entities (such as predators) can influence the level of resources, either by supporting the focal entity to collect resources or as potential competitors for scarce resources. Resources in the business world include physical, intellectual, human, and financial assets. Each of these resources goes through different stages of management: foraging (resource acquisition), food consumption (resource use), hoarding (resource storage), and disposal (resource disposition).

In the case of prominence, there are several key principles for resource management. First, the acquisition of new business resources, such as hiring new employees, should be done in a way that competitors are not aware of the sources. This will help prevent the competitors from accessing the same resources, which could harm the focal entity's competitiveness. Second, resource consumption, such as employee training, should not increase the competition for the resource. Third, strategic information about resources, such as data about critical employees, should not be available to competi-tors, as this could lead to the poaching of key employees. Finally, resource disposition, such as information about employee layoffs or terminations, should be kept confidential to prevent competitors from exploiting the situation.

Therefore, there are 3 ERP factors (efficiency, resilience, storage) × 4 resource management stages (acquisition, consumption, storage, disposition) × 4 forms of resource (physical, intellectual, human, financial) = 48 sources of resource-related competencies. By understanding the importance of all three ERP factors – efficiency, resilience, and prominence in resource management, organizations can better prepare for potential limitations and competitors, ultimately leading to a more effective allocation of resources (Table 1.5).

By identifying the areas (of the 48) where the organization's resource management is relatively strong or weak, it can better align itself to cope with the present and potential future business environment. For instance, suppose the organization finds that it lacks efficiency in acquiring resources. In that case, it can modify its current approach to make the acquisition process smoother and more cost-effective. Similarly, if the organization identifies that its resource storage lacks resilience, it can develop strategies to ensure its resources can adapt to changes in the market environment.

Table 1.5   ERP and Resource Management

ERP Factor	Acquisition (Foraging)	Consumption (Feeding)	Storage (Hoarding)	Disposition (Reuse/ Disposal)
Efficiency	Maximum resources identified and acquired in minimum time	Maximum energy in minimum time	Cost-effective in terms of effort and storage capacity	Can be disposed or reused with minimal energy
Resilience	Should be sufficient for immediate and future needs considering current environmental factors	Should be able to provide for unexpected demands and unavailability due to environmental factors	Should be able to withstand changes in conditions that impact storage of resources due to a change in environmental factors	Should be able to withstand forces during disposition
Prominence	Should be such a way that it does not increase the likelihood of predation	Should be such a way that it does not increase the likelihood of predation	The location should not be located by competitors or rivals	Should be able to avoid adverse observers

Survival in Dynamic Hostile Environments

The interactive role of the ERP trifecta factors in maintaining survivability can be illustrated using the challenge of designing survivable military systems.[47] Survivability in the context of military crafts such as fighter aircraft and naval ships is the capability to withstand hostile environments.[48] Lessons from aircraft survivability can contribute to our understanding of business survival in hostile environments. Robert E. Ball defined aircraft survivability as "the capability of an aircraft to avoid or withstand a man-made hostile environment." Ball identified four system-level elements essential for aircraft survivability – detectability, susceptibility, vulnerability, and recoverability (Table 1.6).[49]

Understanding the relationship between these four design elements and ERP factors can help us analyze design-related trade-offs in designing survivable aircraft. Trade-offs in ERP factors are vital for the design of military aircraft but can be easily overlooked. In the book *Zero!* by Masatake Okumiya and Jiro Horikoshi, Mitsusa Kofukuda, Commander of the 6th

Table 1.6   Elements of Aircraft Survivability

Aircraft Survivability Design Element	Definition	Relationship with ERP Factors
Detectability	The likelihood that the aircraft is detected	Low detectability is associated with low prominence and high efficiency. Both high and low detectability can improve survivability based on target observer
Susceptibility	The likelihood that the aircraft gets hit	Lower susceptibility is associated with higher efficiency and lower prominence
Vulnerability	The likelihood that a hit kills the aircraft	Lower vulnerability is associated with higher resilience. Lower prominence is associated with lower vulnerability (i.e., stealth)
Recoverability	The likelihood that the aircraft recovers from a hit	Higher recoverability is associated with higher resilience (i.e., redundant systems). Efficiency could increase recoverability if a system is more energy efficient in times of energy depletion (i.e., loss of fuel due to a strike) and lower weight could allow for easier and longer gliding when power systems are destroyed

Japanese Airforce in World War II, is quoted as saying, "Japanese naval and aeronautical engineers made their greatest technical blunder by concentrating their efforts on increasing aircraft ranges and completely neglecting any attempt to improve an aircraft's ability to survive enemy power."[50] In contrast to Bell's definition, we are also interested in the role of the four elements in contributing to survivability in both hostile and non-hostile environments. We demonstrate the importance of this elaboration by showing the value of both low and high detectability. A lost trekker might benefit from both high detectability (from a search crew) and low detectability (from wild animals). Thus, detectability can be both positively and negatively associated with survival. Similarly, an aircraft with low detectability may escape enemy fire and one with a high level of detectability can avoid being caught in friendly fire when surrounded by enemy aircraft.

Prominence is the ERP factor that is most closely associated with detectability. The more prominent the aircraft, the more likely it is to be detected. We can look at the low- and high-prominence strategies employed by predator and prey (Table 1.3) to better understand how prominence can be modified or controlled in military aircraft to achieve strategic objectives. It is common to see that the use of low-observable technology can improve survivability in combat situations.[51] Military planes can also potentially enhance their survivability by adopting an appearance similar to less threatening aircraft and by being noticeably distinct from enemy aircraft when operating in friendly territory. Consequently, aircraft may gain an advantage from having high visibility in their own territory while maintaining a low profile in enemy airspace. The latter characteristic can help reduce the risk of friendly fire incidents. Military aircraft use stealth technology to reduce detectability, i.e., prominence. However, this may not be the only approach to reducing prominence. An aircraft can potentially escape detection by appearing as an enemy aircraft.

Prominence can also potentially be lowered by appearing like (1) non-threatening aircraft such as passenger planes, (2) objects in the environment, such as birds, and (3) elements surrounding the environment. Prominence can also be decreased by minimizing the rate of attribute change, such as position or speed relative to the environment. For example, a drone might decide to move at the same speed as surrounding aerial objects to escape detection. Survivability is improved if an aircraft expresses low detectability in enemy territory and high detectability in friendly territory. A reconnaissance aircraft would reduce detectability by reducing prominence in enemy territory or navigating in undetectable regions such as the Lockheed U-2

"Dragon Lady."[52] However, a stranded aircraft requiring emergency support would benefit from high prominence toward friendly entities that can potentially rescue it or support it with additional resources. Thus, aircraft can improve their overall survivability if they are able to switch between different levels of prominence based on the target observer.

Detectability is also associated with efficiency. We expect highly efficient aircraft to possess small sizes, faster speeds, and less frequent refueling. Faster aircraft may be less detectable. Efficient aircraft may be less vulnerable to enemy weaponry given their faster speeds. Efficiency also improves survivability via its influence on prominence. Efficient aircraft are generally smaller in size. Also, efficient aircraft would require less time in refueling. Refueling (i.e., resource acquisition) generally results in low survivability because the aircraft can appear more prominent to enemy entities and be temporarily constrained in terms of maneuverability. In contrast, high resilience can increase detectability, given its association with slower speeds and larger sizes. Resilience can reduce detectability, given that less downtime is dedicated to resource acquisition (e.g., refueling) and repair.

Susceptibility is positively associated with efficiency. An efficient aircraft is generally smaller, nimbler, and faster. Thus, it is less likely to be intercepted. However, it may also have inherent weaknesses that come from reduced resilience. An F-16 is efficient but only has one engine, making it more susceptible to power system damage, whereas an A-10 Warthog is bulky, heavy, and slow but can literally sustain full hydraulic system failure and still be flown back to safety.[53] Resilience is associated with low vulnerability.[54] According to Ball, vulnerability can be reduced by using redundant flight-critical equipment, adding equipment to suppress the effects of a hit, and shielding components (as in the case of the A-10). Thus, it is likely that actions designed to decrease vulnerability can improve resilience. Recoverability is the inverse of vulnerability. Thus, actions that improve recoverability should be associated with increased resilience. Analogical to the ERP triangle, we have an SRD triangle that encapsulates survivability design in aircraft. Thus, similar to the ERP model, we expect trade-offs among the SRD parameters.

From Aircraft to Organizations

The lessons from aircraft survivability can help improve organizational design for businesses and agencies required to survive in hostile environments. Hostile environments may be specific to a business or may reflect a broader downturn in economic conditions, such as a recession or an economic depression.[55] An entrepreneurial firm, with an innovative product challenging status quo represented by entrenched players or industry bodies, is a prime example. Like aircraft, such companies are required to demonstrate adaptive prominence. They must appear less prominent toward adversarial entities but more prominent toward customers and investors.

Based on the above analysis, we see the value of adaptability in a hostile environment, which can enable quick switching between ERP factors. Adaptability also requires a well-developed sensing capability to detect changes in external environments and mechanisms to act following the detected changes. This yields the SERPAS (Sense – ERP – Act – Survive) model (Figure 1.3). This model exhibits a superficial resemblance to John Boyd's OODA loop.[56]

We define two forms of adaptability critical to survival – ER-adaptability and P-adaptability. ER-adaptability is the ability to switch between efficiency and resilience regimes. ER-adaptability requires the ability to quickly acquire, maintain, and discard resources. P-adaptability is the capacity to modify levels of prominence. A firm that is highly adept at increasing or decreasing the amount of media attention it receives would be considered P-adaptable. For a living organism, this capacity requires modifying attributes such as size, shape, color, and speed based on changing external conditions. The cephalopod is an exemplar of a P-adaptable organism, whereas the Alaskan bear, with its ability to store and shed large amounts of fat, typifies high levels of ER-adaptability.[57] We refer to the composite of the two types of adaptability as ERP-adaptability.

The SERPAS model can serve as a foundation for introspection for entrepreneurs and intrapreneurs as they progress through the innovation

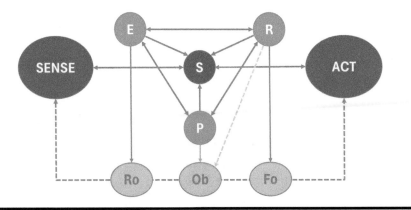

Figure 1.3   The SERPAS model of dynamic survivability.

maturation process. Eric Ries' Build-Measure-Learn model is offered to help startups decide when to pivot or persevere in their value offerings to potential customers.[58] It involves leap-of-faith hypothesis testing and innovation accounting as a means to help new firms or new design teams understand when to keep on their path or move (pivot) toward a new value proposition. The SERPAS model can further assist these teams in making smart value and design trades in their minimum viable products (MVP) as they move through the learn and re-build feedback loops in the Lean Startup methodology.[59] If a startup firm tests a hypothesis that potential customers value higher efficiency in a product and finds that to be false, they can pivot toward hypothesis testing for increased resiliency in their offering. Also, if new firms find that they are trying to break into an emerging market, they may want to strategically plan and time their levels of prominence to maximize investment capital while avoiding outside competition. The model reminds these decision-makers that such strategies cannot be employed in a bubble and such decisions come at a cost to interdependent ERP factors.

Managing Risk Probabilities in System Design for Hostile Environments: MRAP Project

In designing a survival-oriented system, there can also be strategic design trades within each factor that can increase survivability to one risk while reducing it toward another. Total survivability then becomes a matter of risk probabilities, as in the case of the Mine-Resistant Ambush Protected (MRAP) program of the US Military. The MRAP Family of Vehicles (FoV) has been engineered to enhance crew safety and improve vehicle resilience against contemporary battlefield hazards, including IEDs, mines, small arms fire, rocket-propelled grenades, and explosively formed penetrators. Survivability is an explicit goal of this program.[60]

In 2007, the Department of Defense started the development of the Mine-Resistant Ambush Protected (MRAP) Vehicle. It was able to go from concept to the field in less than a year – a rare feat by traditional defense acquisition timeline standards. The process delivered a mine-resistant troop transport vehicle into the area of responsibility in record time. However, the design traded efficiency for resilience. The vehicle was nearly impervious to mines yet was nearly useless for navigating off-camber terrain when compared to its Humvee contemporary. This was a trade-off of terrain navigation and rollover resilience in favor of acquisition efficiency and troop armor resilience. There were other design resilience trades that were made in favor of

near-term troop safety. MRAPs have been found to be at risk for electrocution given their height and producing potential cancer-causing materials
when the safety glass is impacted.[61]

Yes, they may roll over more often (less terrain navigation resilience),
but the chances of rolling over into a lake and drowning are more manageable to mitigate than evading hidden roadside mines (greater explosive
resilience). A comprehensive approach to evaluating the inter-relationship
assumes that each factor has a bilateral influence on each other, and each
factor has a bilateral influence on survivability. Perhaps the developers of the
MRAP used a process to make design trades for survivability across all three
factors. Case studies of the MRAP suggest otherwise and that a single focus
on a particular type of damage survivability decreased maintainability and
system resilience in the area of responsibility.

Survivability Design: Squid, Startup, Ships, and Supply Chains

Hostile environments are often dynamic, with threats evolving rapidly,
necessitating agile adaptations. Therefore, an entity benefits from the capacity to (1) detect changes and (2) make decisions or take actions that enhance
or maintain its ERP health factors. At times, when faced with a threat, an
entity may need to unilaterally modify one of its ERP factors to enhance survivability. However, as previously noted, such alterations can inadvertently
affect the other two factors. Our objective is to investigate the interplay
among the ERP factors, primarily to provide guidance for decision-making
within organizations operating in hostile conditions. This approach informs
the process of survivability design, which pertains to the development of
survivable products and systems.[62]

Next, we will explore four distinct cases: squids, ships, startups, and
supply chains. These focal entities operate in seemingly disparate environments, yet exhibit similar themes, allowing us to assess the generality of the
inter-relationships between ERP factors in hostile environments. The first
case (squids) is a case of individual decision-making in a complex (marine)
environment. In contrast, the other three entities represent complex systems
where decisions and actions are made by coordinated individuals distributed throughout the system. We can categorize these four cases based on
the degree of coordination in decision-making as follows: squid > startups
> ships > supply chains. That is, the squid is the most coordinated in its
actions, as it is a single entity making decisions and taking actions. On the
other hand, the supply chain is the least coordinated, as it involves many

cooperating but independent decision-makers who are somewhat loosely linked to each other. Consequently, our examination of these cases should enable us to identify a broad spectrum of situations involving different types of threats and their diverse responses in hostile environments.

Our primary goal is to identify general principles that can be applied to any organization operating in hostile environments. To achieve this, we conduct a comparative case analysis of the four entities, aiming to reveal similarities, differences, and unique features. While there are several general themes that can be explored within the cases, we will limit our focus to a select few that are relevant to each of the four instances:

- What is the specific nature of threats and their distribution in the hostile environment?
- What are the essential resources that impact survival?
  - How can efficiency improve survivability for the entity?
  - What steps does the entity take to enhance efficiency?
- What are the environmental forces that jeopardize the entity's existence?
  - How can the entity develop resilience against these forces?
- What antagonistic elements does the focal entity encounter?
  - Are there prominent adaptations used to counter rivals and predators?
  - What role does high versus low prominence play in survival?
- What is the relative importance of each type of threat?
- What is the relative importance of the ERP factors?
- What is the nature of the inter-relationship between the three ERP factors?
- What are some of the unique or idiosyncratic features of the entity or its environments that influence its survivability?

Case 1: Squids

Squids are a diverse species that belong to the family of cephalopods, which also includes cuttlefish, octopus, and nautilus.[63] The specific nature of the threat depends on the environment in which the individual species resides. While squids can sometimes face threats such as limited food availability and environmental forces like strong currents, the most significant common threat comes from predators. Different species of squids serve as important food sources for birds, fish, and sharks. Some squids even prey on other squids. Several species have developed numerous adaptations related to prominence in response to predatory threats. The number of prominence adaptation mechanisms in cephalopods has been shown to depend on the complexity of the environment. Certain squid species possess a wide range of prominence adaptations that they can choose to deploy in the presence of predators and rivals.[64] These strategies can be used to attract, avoid, hypnotize, sneak up on, threaten, or alert other entities. Some of these strategies serve a social role. Sentinel squids often alert other squids to the approach of a predator.

The diverse array of prominence adaptations allows for the flexible use of strategies based on situational factors. For example, the choice of prominence mechanisms depends on the size of the predator. When dealing with larger predators like sharks, squids might choose strategies such as hiding or using ink for distraction. For smaller predators, squids may resort to startle behavior. Squids need to balance their use of prominence mechanisms when interacting with antagonistic and friendly organisms. Certain squid species use unilateral prominence displays to communicate different messages to different entities, such as rivals versus potential mates, simultaneously. The size of the squid influences both its prominence and efficiency. Deep-sea gigantism is observed in the giant squid. These creatures inhabit extraordinarily deep waters to reduce their prominence and enhance efficiency. This action helps conserve energy and avoid drawing unwanted attention.

Case 2: Defense Startups

Startups face threats on all three fronts – resources, forces, and rivals. Resource threats for startups are manifested in the non-availability of capital and the absence of qualified personnel. Therefore, efficiency is often crucial for the survival of startups. Ventures that spend their available capital too quickly often face a quick demise. For years, the Department of Defense has grappled with the so-called "valley of death" concerning startups in defense R&D investments. These companies receive initial support and capital to explore their new ideas but have limited funding available to scale and commercialize their inventions. To improve efficiency in terms of human resources, startups often embrace multifunctionality, where departments perform multiple roles, and employees take on multiple responsibilities. Environmental forces related to public policy and the challenges of navigating government markets also impact their survival.[65] External threats include larger competitors that may attempt to steal intellectual property or engage in predatory behavior. There are both benefits and risks associated with stealth for startups. Stealth can help keep a company away from prying eyes. However, the downside of stealth is that it can reduce the likelihood of being noticed by friendly entities such as potential investors and customers.

For instance, over the past five years, the US Air Force has intensified its efforts to mitigate risks to intellectual property (IP) for startups engaged in government contracts. By adopting an innovative approach to Small Business Innovation Research and Small Business Technical Transfer (SBIR/STTR) funding, the Air Force has increased the funds allocated to contracts that do not necessitate compliance with government-specific cost accounting regulations or the forfeiture of IP rights when dealing with dual-use technology startups. Additionally, the Air Force has employed an open-topic strategy within this program to enhance the matching of dual-use technology small businesses with government customers, thereby increasing their prominence. This approach avoids the necessity for these firms to respond to full and open solicitations, which can either diminish their prominence with the government or raise their prominence among competitors.

In a full and open solicitation, the government specifies particular requirements. Firms that do not align well with these requirements may not be evaluated or may opt out of the competition. Historically, even if a company had developed an idea under SBIR/STTR, it might still result in production contracts being solicited to competitors in a full and open manner. With the open-topic model, firms can identify grassroots users for their solutions and compete for direct federal funding to engage in customer discovery across the department. This approach also allows them to potentially secure additional funding to scale their concepts into full-rate production. New organizations such as AFWERX and its AFVentures arm have been instrumental in increasing the prominence of these startups among venture capitalists and significantly boosting private investments in accelerating technology to market. This strategy elevates startup prominence with friendly customers and investors while reducing it with hostile competitors.

Case 3: Military Ships

The type of threat ships face depends on their operational goals and operating environment. Ships themselves must consider potential operational risks and hazards. Long before these challenges occur, most ships must engage in ongoing complex decision-making processes as part of a defense program of record. This necessitates intricate coordination among various public agencies within the executive branch and the legislature. They must also manage decisions related to ERP factors as part of a program involving multiple prime and subcontract developers and vendors. The struggle for financial resources, adherence to schedules, and the allocation of human capital is a constant battle within defense programs. All of these elements are interconnected in a complex network of resource allocation decisions made by the Department of Defense and the broader federal government every year. How programs perform in terms of cost, schedule, and meeting performance goals can create a challenging environment for ships before they ever set sail. If a program consistently falls significantly short of their goals or does so too often, it may face discontinuation. Additionally, if it becomes a prominent political issue, it may be altered or eliminated for reasons that have little to do with programmatic or operational needs.

Beyond political or programmatic risks, most types of ships encounter resource limitations, including energy and time. Such threats are generally minor for most watercraft and rarely result in destructive consequences. A noteworthy example of a watercraft running out of energy resources is the submarine USS R-14 (SS-91), which exhausted its fuel while searching for a tugboat. In this unusual circumstance, the crew had to resort to a makeshift sail created from hammocks and blankets.[66] More significantly, large vessels also confront threats from environmental forces, such as extreme weather, which heighten their instability and expose them to the risk of flooding. These hostile conditions are also experienced by military ships, which must remain vigilant against threats from enemy crafts.

To navigate these challenges, military ships must make trade-offs involving all three ERP factors. For ships, greater efficiency translates to higher speeds (time) and reduced fuel consumption (energy). The outcome of improved efficiency can affect both higher and lower levels of prominence. More efficient ships may achieve greater speed, rendering them more challenging to detect, target, or be intercepted by enemy crafts. However, in certain situations, fast-moving vessels may stand out more against their background, increasing the risk of detection. Higher efficiency often results in lower resilience. Faster ships may need to compromise hull strength in favor of speed, as exemplified by the Littoral combat ship,[67] a class of small combat ships designed for the US Navy, first commissioned in 2008. A similar trade-off is observed in the choice of materials, where aluminum alloys are favored over steel for naval structures. Ships constructed from aluminum alloys are typically lighter and faster. However, vessels made of aluminum alloys may be more susceptible to extreme loads, such as underwater explosions and high-velocity impacts from torpedoes.[68]

Efforts to enhance resilience by reducing vulnerability, such as introducing component redundancy and shielding, can have a detrimental impact on the ship's efficiency.[69] Maintaining low prominence plays a crucial role in the survivability of military vessels, including naval ships, when facing the risk of being targeted by enemy observers. Low prominence aids in avoiding detection and diverting enemy attention. Strategies inspired by nature, such as camouflage, were extensively used in World War II naval ships.[70] Other prominence-reduction strategies employed in military vessels include the use of decoys and signature reduction to decrease susceptibility. However, low-prominence strategies carry a risk in terms of friendly fire. An illustrative example of this is the German passenger ship MV *Spreewald*, which was sunk in 1942 by U-333 because it was in disguise and could not be identified by the German submarine. Therefore, military ships benefit from the ability to adopt differential prominence, allowing them to draw attention from friendly entities while remaining undetected by antagonistic vessels.

Case 4: Strategic Supply Chains

The role of prominence in supply chains is contingent on both internal and external threats as well as the need to attract attention in the case of a defect or failure. An inherent trade-off between efficiency and resilience becomes evident during disruptions.[71] The supply chain challenges that emerged after the COVID-19 pandemic have demonstrated how designing supply chains for high efficiency and minimal waste can result in poor resilience during turbulent times. Before COVID-19, various approaches were taken to address supply chain resiliency. Some entities built up substantial buffer stock, while others developed lean manufacturing processes that enabled just-in-time inventory management. The lessons learned from the post-COVID supply chain experiences show that firms cannot simply stock up for uncertainty, nor can they prioritize cost over the ability to operate during a mass disruption. Firms had adopted a "lean" and "just-in-time" inventory approach that was more about reducing carrying costs than ensuring clear and frictionless access to materials and components necessary for operations and production.

In contrast, government agencies such as the Strategic National Stockpile (SNS) had accumulated stocks of items that had become obsolete and expired, with no immediate sources for replenishment.[72] This resilience-focused approach came at the expense of efficiency and effectiveness. Additionally, for security reasons, the locations of the SNS stockpiles had been kept confidential. This strategy appears reasonable, considering that the SNS was initially established to counter chemical, biological, or nuclear attacks. However, during a widespread pandemic like COVID, the process for accessing its stocks became opaque for the states in need, demonstrating an inefficient trade-off of higher resilience and distribution efficiency for reduced public prominence, all in the name of national security. The unfortunate irony is that more lives were endangered due to the lack of clear SNS access than any risk ever posed by an enemy actor. This underscores the importance of understanding the ERP trade-offs necessary when designing optimal survival strategies in hostile environments. Greater supply chain prominence has been perceived as a threat to national security when malicious actors can trace and exploit critical supply or information networks.

It is also a threat to national security when the government or a firm itself cannot trace the network of suppliers and components. This leaves vulnerabilities in cybersecurity unprotected, provides opportunities for counterfeiting by profiteers, and opens the door to tampering by saboteurs. Additionally, it results in an inability to execute agile, adaptive, and well-coordinated distribution of essential resources efficiently and equitably during major contingencies.[73] Firms do not always desire greater transparency into their supply chains, as this may draw attention to aspects such as cost data affecting negotiated margins, sources of supplies associated with human exploitation, or the firm's inability to responsibly manage a transparent and traceable network of suppliers. It can be a situation where it becomes a problem only if it becomes known. Instances of such issues are widespread in global markets and are coming to light regularly in the aftermath of disruptions caused by events like COVID-19.

Comparative Analysis of Threat Significance and ERP Factors

We find that the importance of different forms of threats may be different across the four cases. This relative difference also highlights the differences in significance between the three ERP factors (Table 1.7).

A comparison of the cases yields general principles that potentially extend to other entities that function in hostile environments. These principles primarily relate to the relative significance of threats, the importance of the ERP factors, the nature of interrelationships among the ERP factors, and

Table 1.7   Comparison of Survivability Cases

Threats/Case	Squids	Ships	Startups	Supply Chains
Significance of limited resources as a threat to survival	Low	Low to moderate	High	High
Significance of uncertain environmental forces as a threat to survival	Low to moderate	Moderate to high	High	High
Significance of antagonistic entities as a threat to survival	High	High	High	Low to moderate
Estimated importance of ERP factors	P > R > E	P > R > E	E ~ R ~ P	E ~ R > P

the trade-offs involved while taking actions aimed at improving survivability in hostile settings:

■ We observe that the importance of the survivability factor is linked to the distribution of the threat. An essential implication is that organizations aiming to enhance their survivability should meticulously assess the relative importance of the three types of threats. If this significance evolves over time, organizations should have the flexibility to adjust their priorities concerning the significance of ERP factors.

■ Business entities operating in hostile environments must take the responsibility of thoughtfully assessing their actions and their potential impact on all three ERP factors. Businesses should remain mindful of the indirect consequences that might arise if they attempt to unilaterally alter one of these ERP factors.

■ In the context of trade-offs between efficiency and resilience, a business stands to gain from the ability to transition between high-efficiency and high-resilience modes, especially in environments characterized by limited resources and high levels of uncertainty.

■ A business gains an advantage by cultivating various adaptive strategies that consider the characteristics and capabilities of adversarial entities in its environment. Nevertheless, trade-offs exist among the different prominence mechanisms available to the entity.

The above principles can be applied to business organizations in additional settings that may be considered hostile such as surviving a recession, when faced with a takeover bid, or overcoming a pandemic.

Implications for Strategic Decision-Making in Organizations

We illustrate how the actions of survival-oriented entities inhabiting diverse environments can be compared by evaluating the impact of these actions on three critical ERP factors: efficiency, resilience, and prominence. The optimal levels of efficiency, resilience, and prominence for maximizing survivability are contingent upon the prevailing environmental conditions. Efficiency is particularly advantageous when environmental conditions, although harsh and resource-constrained, remain relatively stable or reasonably predictable. Conversely, resilience becomes essential when there is a need to withstand unusual or unexpected changes in conditions, such as threats from predatory entities. In general, both efficiency and resilience have a positive direct effect on survivability. However, since they can counteract each other, the net effect on the survivability of an action aimed at enhancing one of these two factors may be minimal or even negative. Prominence, at any given time, can either directly enhance or diminish an entity's survivability. We also demonstrate how a comprehensive understanding of the impact of actions on survivability requires considering both their direct effects on a specific ERP factor and their indirect influence through the other two factors. This perspective is crucial because entities often unilaterally direct their actions toward modifying one of the ERP factors in response to emerging environmental conditions.

Business functions are inherently tied to roles and actions that often create a trade-off between ERP factors. Incentives designed to favor only one of these three factors are likely to have a detrimental impact on survivability. To counter a decline in survivability, organizations can adjust their prominence level. An essential focus within the realm of marketing, a core discipline in the business world, is optimizing prominence strategies for economic success. Instead of merely incentivizing marketers to increase prominence levels, firms should aim for adaptive prominence tailored to the specifics of market conditions. This discussion underscores two key lessons: First, reducing prominence is a potent yet often underutilized approach to enhancing survivability. Second, prominence can frequently be adjusted independently of efficiency and resilience to bolster survivability, potentially mitigating any drop in survivability caused by changes in efficiency or resilience levels. We believe that the model described can aid in the analysis of the impact of complex actions within survival-oriented businesses and organizations. This discussion also emphasizes the critical role of adaptability in ensuring survival. Thriving in hostile environments necessitates the ability to shift between actions that influence different ERP factors. We introduce two capabilities: ER-adaptability, which refers to an organization's capacity to transition between various levels of efficiency and resilience, and P-adaptability, which pertains to the ability to shift between high and low prominence. Organizations capable of adjusting their prominence, efficiency, and resilience levels are the ones most likely to endure.

Innovation versus Ideation in Hostile Environments

When entities consider analogous cases and models to design innovations for survival in hostile environments, such as the current economy, they must be cautious in discerning the nuanced differences between ideation and true innovation. While new ideas hold great promise, their potential can only be harnessed with a well-trained approach, taking into account SERPAS and focusing on ERP factors. All too often, entities become entangled in unfettered ideation, lacking the ability to transition these concepts into tangible innovations.

In 2022, General David W. Allvin, the Vice Chief of Staff of the United States Air Force, underscored the differentiation, stressing the "responsibility of the innovator," while also highlighting the significance of "follow-through" and a profound comprehension of the "business of innovation."[74] Converting an idea into a sustainable innovation necessitates unwavering commitment from the ideator to see their concepts through to widespread adoption by customers in their daily lives or by organizations in their standard workflow. Innovation "customers" encompass all forms of stakeholders, including traditional commercial consumers, citizens, business partners, and internal organizational members. Ideation and innovation are not necessarily separate concepts; rather, they represent different stages within a comprehensive process. For any idea to evolve into a genuine innovation, it must align with Denning and Dunham's definition of a new practice that is adopted by an entity, be it a community, organization, or living organism.[75]

Exercises

1. Conduct a Resources/Forces/Observer (Ro/Fo/Ob) analysis of an organization you are interested in. Examine how Resources are shaped by the effects of Forces and Observers. Critically examine a recent decision made by the organization using the ERP framework.

2. Analyze a recent or impending personal decision using the Resources/Forces/Observer and ERP framework. What are the relevant Resources, Forces, and Observers in your situation? Which of the ERP factors does your decision primarily relate to? How does your decision impact the other two factors?

3. Risk Management in System Design: Discuss the MRAP Project and how it illustrates the trade-offs between efficiency and resilience in system design. Analyze the implications of designing systems for specific risk probabilities in hostile environments.

4. Research and present a case study of an entrepreneurial firm that successfully demonstrated adaptability in a hostile business environment. Analyze how they managed ER-adaptability and P-adaptability.

5. Analyze a real-world business case and apply the SERPAS (Sense – ERP – Act – Survive) model to assess how adaptability can impact the organization's survival. Discuss the implications of ER-adaptability and P-adaptability in the given scenario.

Notes

1. Strategic environments encompass various factors that significantly influence the entities operating within them. These environments are marked by a common set of influences, such as limited resources, unpredictable natural forces, and the presence of observer entities, which can either offer support or pose a threat.

2. For another definition of survivability, see Knight and Sullivan (2000). Knight, J. C., & Sullivan, K. J. (2000). *On the Definition of Survivability* (Technical Report No. CS-TR-33-00). University of Virginia, Department of Computer Science.

3. De Vos, J. M., Joppa, L. N., Gittleman, J. L., Stephens, P. R., & Pimm, S. L. (2015). Estimating the normal background rate of species extinction. *Conservation Biology*, 29(2), 452–462.

4. Castet, J.-F., & Saleh, J. H. (2012). On the concept of survivability, with application to spacecraft and space-based networks. *Reliability Engineering & System Safety*, 99, 123–138.

5. Drinkwater, E., Allen, W. L., Endler, J. A., Hanlon, R. T., Holmes, G., Homziak, N. T., Kang, C., et al. (2022). A synthesis of deimatic behaviour. *Biological Reviews*, 97(6), 2237–2267.

6. Resilience also involves the ability to withstand damage across diverse operating conditions, which may involve varying types and intensities of external forces. For instance, an organism demonstrating strong resilience to high temperatures may exhibit notably lower resilience when exposed to very low

temperatures. Likewise, an entity that is resilient to temperature fluctuations might experience diminished resilience when subjected to high humidity levels.

7. Handfield, R., Finkenstadt, D. J., & Guinto, P. (2021, February 15). How business leaders can prepare for the next health crisis. *Harvard Business Review.*

8. Hazlitt, H. (1946). *Economics in One Lesson.* Harper & Brothers.

9. *Cambridge Dictionary | English Dictionary, Translations & Thesaurus.* (2023). Cambridge.org. http://dictionary.cambridge.org.

10. Handfield, R., Finkenstadt, D. J., Schneller, E. S., Godfrey, A. B., & Guinto, P. A. (2020). Commons for a supply chain in the post-COVID-19 era: The case for a reformed strategic national stockpile. *Milbank Quarterly*, 98(4), 1058–1090.

11. Jones, C., Medlen, N., Merlo, C., Robertson, M., & Shepherdson, J. (1999). The lean enterprise. *BT Technology Journal*, 17(4), 15–22.

12. Gunderson, L. H. (2000). Ecological resilience – in theory and application. *Annual Review of Ecology and Systematics*, 31(1), 425–439.

13. In a soccer game, substitutes are employed when the demands shift (e.g., from defense to attack) or when a starting player becomes injured or fatigued.

14. Ball, R. E., & Atkinson, D. B. (1998). *A History of the Survivability Design of Military Aircraft.* Naval Postgraduate School, Monterey, CA.

15. If resources used to sustain resilience, such as substitute players or repair tools, remain unused for an extended period, their value and quality may deteriorate. Furthermore, maintaining resilient systems under stable conditions is not only inefficient but can also directly reduce survivability.

16. In the realm of military strategy, we often witness periodic displays of strength by countries, like North Korea, which may prove more efficient than engaging in full-scale warfare.

17. Cooper, W. E. Jr., & Stankowich, T. (2010). Prey or predator? Body size of an approaching animal affects decisions to attack or escape. *Behavioral Ecology*, 21(6), 1278–1284.

18. Active prominence involves shorter-term actions targeted at specific entities, whereas passive prominence may not be directed at a specific entity but rather at multiple potential targets.

19. Tamkin, E. (2014, October 20). Keeping it in the family. *Slate.* https://slate.com /business/2014/10/worlds-oldest-companies-why-are-so-many-of-them-in-japan .html.

20. Reeves, M., et al. (2020). *Resilience vs. Efficiency: Calibrating the Tradeoff.* BCG Henderson Institute. https://bcghendersoninstitute.com/resilience-vs-efficiency -calibrating-the-tradeoff/.

21. In specific circumstances, certain actions of an organism can increase prominence to one observer entity while diminishing it for another. For instance, a signal or message might be perceived as noise by a predator but as a mating call by a potential mate.

22. Stack, L. (2019, October 24). Update complete: U.S. nuclear weapons no longer need floppy disks. *The New York Times.* https://www.nytimes.com/2019/10/24/ us/nuclear-weapons-floppy-disks.html.

23. McNamara, J. M. (1990). The policy which maximizes long-term survival of an animal faced with the risks of starvation and predation. *Advances in Applied Probability*, 22(2), 295–308.

24. Taleb, N. N., Goldstein, D. G., & Spitznagel, M. W. (2009). The six mistakes executives make in risk management. *Harvard Business Review*, 87(10), 78–81.

25. Van den Brand, M., & Groote, J. F. (2015). Software engineering: Redundancy is key. *Science of Computer Programming*, 97, 75–81.

26. Baker, M., & Gates, D. (2019). Lack of redundancies on Boeing 737 MAX system baffles some involved in developing the jet. *The Seattle Times*. https://www.seattletimes.com/business/boeing-aerospace/a-lack-of-redundancies-on-737-max-system-has-baffled-even-those-who-worked-on-the-jet/.

27. Mills, J. (2021, September 23). *Are You Brave Enough to Tackle an Adventure with this Citroën 2CV Sahara 4x4?* Hagerty UK. https://www.hagerty.co.uk/articles/auctions/are-you-brave-enough-to-tackle-an-adventure-with-this-citroen-2cv-sahara-4x4/.

28. Scheffer, M., Vergnon, R., van Nes, E. H., Cuppen, J. G. M., Peeters, E. T. H. M., Leijs, R., & Nilsson, A. N. (2015). The evolution of functionally redundant species: Evidence from beetles. *PLoS One*, 10(10), e0137974.

29. De Geus, A. (2002). *The Living Company*. Harvard Business Press.

30. Crowe, J. H., Hoekstra, F. A., & Crowe, L. M. (1992). Anhydrobiosis. *Annual Review of Physiology*, 54(1), 579–599.

31. Clark III, M., & Moutray, C. (2004). The future of small businesses in the US federal government marketplace. *Journal of Public Procurement*, 4(3), 450–470.

32. Patteli, L. (2022). Twitter and musk clash on metrics. *Strategic Finance*, 104(5), 15–16.

33. Feeley, J. (2023, January 11). JPMorgan claims it was defrauded in $175 million acquisition. *Bloomberg.com*. https://www.bloomberg.com/news/articles/2023-01-11/jpmorgan-says-it-was-defrauded-in-175-million-frank-acquisition.

34. Meiri, S., Cooper, N., & Purvis, A. (2008). The island rule: Made to be broken? *Proceedings of the Royal Society B: Biological Sciences*, 275(1631), 141–148.

35. A → R+ → P+ → S– should be interpreted as action A leading to an increase in resilience, subsequently resulting in increased prominence, and ultimately culminating in reduced survivability.

36. Reinink, A. (2010). From survival mode to growth – business growth. *Entrepreneur*. https://www.entrepreneur.com/article/207646.

37. Skapinker, M. (2015). A company is a community of humans. *Financial Times*. https://www.ft.com/content/3770494e-7d7a-11e5-98fb-5a6d4728f74e.

38. The relative value of survivability in comparison to growth can be assessed at both the individual firm level and from an ecosystem perspective. This broader perspective takes into account the potential consequences of a company's failure on factors such as the technical competitiveness of a country.

39. Biggs, C. R., Yeager, L. A., Bolser, D. G., Bonsell, C., Dichiera, A. M., Hou, Z., ... Whiles, M. R. (2020). Does functional redundancy affect ecological stability and resilience? A review and meta-analysis. *Ecosphere*, 11(7), e03184.

40. Napolitano, M. R., Marino, V., & Ojala, J. (2015). In search of an integrated framework of business longevity. *Business History*, 57(7), 955–969.
41. Isenberg, D. J. (2010). How to start an entrepreneurial revolution. *Harvard Business Review*, 88(6), 40–50.
42. Hasegawa, Y., Watanabe, T., Takazawa, M., Ohara, O., & Kubota, S. (2016). De novo assembly of the transcriptome of Turritopsis, a jellyfish that repeatedly rejuvenates. *Zoological Science*, 33(4), 366–371.
43. Nabarro, J. D. N. (1987). Acromegaly. *Clinical Endocrinology*, 26(4), 481–512.
44. Glazer, I. (2002). Survival biology. In R. Gaugler (Ed.), *Entomopathogenic Nematology* (pp. 169–187). CABI.
45. Yasuda, T. (2005). Firm growth, size, age and behavior in Japanese manufacturing. *Small Business Economics*, 24(1), 1–15.
46. Mace, R. (1993). Nomadic pastoralists adopt subsistence strategies that maximize long-term household survival. *Behavioral Ecology and Sociobiology*, 33(5), 329–334.
47. Eapen, T., & Finkenstadt, D. J. (2023). Survivability design in hostile environments: Lessons from squids, ships, startups, and supply chains. *Strategic Design Research Journal*, 15(3), 307–317.
48. Kim, K. S., Hwang, S. Y., & Lee, J. H. (2014). Naval ship's susceptibility assessment by the probabilistic density function. *Journal of Computational Design and Engineering*, 1(4), 266–271.
49. Ball, R. E. (2003). *The Fundamentals of Aircraft Combat Survivability Analysis and Design* (2nd ed.). AIAA.
50. Ball 2003, Preface p. ix.
51. Paterson, J. (1999). Overview of low observable technology and its effects on combat aircraft survivability. *Journal of Aircraft*, 36(2), 380–388.
52. Karas, R. S. (2017). Lockheed preps options as Senate urges new look at unmanned U-2. *Inside the Air Force*, 28(29), 1–7.
53. Shafran, S. N. (2018). Air Force pilot landed damaged A-10 using only "cranks and cables." *Military.com*. https://www.military.com/air-force/air-force-pilot-landed-damaged-10-warthog-using-only-cranks-and-cables.html.
54. Aeronautic engineers are well versed in the concept of various redundancy mechanisms that enhance resilience by mitigating vulnerabilities and bolstering recoverability. This, in turn, enhances the likelihood of survival in combat scenarios.
55. Hall, W. K. (1980). Survival strategies in a hostile environment. *Harvard Business Review* (September–October), 75–85.
56. McIntosh, S. E. (2011). The wingman-philosopher of MiG alley: John Boyd and the OODA loop. *Air Power History*, 58(4), 24–33.
57. The camel also exhibits remarkable ER-adaptability, storing up to 80 pounds of fat in its fatty reservoirs. Additionally, the camel's kidneys and intestines efficiently reabsorb water.
58. Ries, E. (2011). *The Lean Startup*. Crown Business.
59. Blank, S. (2013). Why the lean start-up changes everything. *Harvard Business Review*, 91(5), 63–72.

60. Gansler, J. S., Lucyshyn, W., & Varettoni, W. (2010). *Acquisition of Mine-Resistant, Ambush-Protected (MRAP) Vehicles: A Case Study*. Acquisition Research Program.

61. Hambling, D. (2008). MRAP hazards: Drowning, electrocution, cancer. *Wired*. https://www.wired.com/2008/07/mrap-hazards-dr/.

62. Eapen & Finkenstadt (2023).

63. Hanlon, R. T., & Messenger, J. B. (2018). *Cephalopod Behaviour*. Cambridge University Press.

64. DiMarco, F. P., & Hanlon, R. T. (1997). Agonistic behavior in the squid Loligo plei (Loliginidae, Teuthoidea): Fighting tactics and the effects of size and resource value. *Ethology*, 103(2), 89–108.

65. Josephson, B., Lee, J., Mariadoss, B. J., & Johnson, J. (2019). Uncle Sam rising: Performance implications of business-to-government relationships. *Journal of Marketing*, 83, 51–72.

66. Douglas, R. G. (2004, August). R-14 under way, under sail. *Naval History Magazine*. https://www.usni.org/magazines/naval-history-magazine/2004/august/r-14-under-way-under-sail.

67. O'Rourke, R. (2011). *Navy Littoral Combat Ship (LCS) Program: Background, Issues, and Options for Congress*. DIANE Publishing.

68. Galanis, K. P., & Papazoglou, V. J. (2007). Crack propagation in naval aluminum panels. In *Experimental Analysis of Nano and Engineering Materials and Structures* (pp. 207–208). Springer.

69. Ball, R. E., & Calvano, C. N. (1994). Establishing the fundamentals of a surface ship survivability design discipline. *Naval Engineers Journal*, 106(1), 71–74.

70. Forbes, P. (2011). *Dazzled and Deceived: Mimicry and Camouflage*. Yale University Press.

71. Ivanov, D., Sokolov, B., & Dolgui, A. (2014). The Ripple effect in supply chains: Tradeoff "Efficiency-Flexibility-Resilience" in disruption management. *International Journal of Production Research*, 52(7), 2154–2172.

72. Handfield et al., 2020.

73. Finkenstadt, D. J., & Handfield, R. (2021). Blurry vision: Supply chain visibility for personal protective equipment during COVID-19. *Journal of Purchasing and Supply Management*, 3, 100689.

74. Allvin, D. (2022, May 31). Monthly innovation email.

75. Denning, P., & Dunham, R. (2012). *The Innovator's Way: Essential Practices for Successful Innovation*. MIT Press.

References

Ball, R. E. (2003). *The Fundamentals of Aircraft Combat Survivability Analysis and Design* (2nd ed.). AIAA.

Ball, R. E., & Atkinson, D. B. (1998). *A History of the Survivability Design of Military Aircraft*. Naval Postgraduate School.

Ball, R. E., & Calvano, C. N. (1994). Establishing the fundamentals of a surface ship survivability design discipline. *Naval Engineers Journal*, 106(1), 71–74.

Biggs, C. R., Yeager, L. A., Bolser, D. G., Bonsell, C., Dichiera, A. M., Hou, Z., ... Whiles, M. R. (2020). Does functional redundancy affect ecological stability and resilience? A review and meta-analysis. *Ecosphere*, 11(7), e03184.

Blank, S. (2013). Why the lean start-up changes everything. *Harvard Business Review*, 91(5), 63–72.

Castet, J.-F., & Saleh, J. H. (2012). On the concept of survivability, with application to spacecraft and space-based networks. *Reliability Engineering & System Safety*, 99, 123–138.

Clark III, M., & Moutray, C. (2004). The future of small businesses in the US federal government marketplace. *Journal of Public Procurement*, 4(3), 450–470.

Cooper, W. E. Jr., & Stankowich, T. (2010). Prey or predator? Body size of an approaching animal affects decisions to attack or escape. *Behavioral Ecology*, 21(6), 1278–1284.

Crowe, J. H., Hoekstra, F. A., & Crowe, L. M. (1992). Anhydrobiosis. *Annual Review of Physiology*, 54(1), 579–599.

De Geus, A. (2002). *The Living Company*. Harvard Business Press.

De Vos, J. M., Joppa, L. N., Gittleman, J. L., Stephens, P. R., & Pimm, S. L. (2015). Estimating the normal background rate of species extinction. *Conservation Biology*, 29(2), 452–462.

Denning, P., & Dunham, R. (2012). *The Innovator's Way: Essential Practices for Successful Innovation*. MIT Press.

DiMarco, F. P., & Hanlon, R. T. (1997). Agonistic behavior in the squid *Loligo plei* (Loliginidae, Teuthoidea): Fighting tactics and the effects of size and resource value. *Ethology*, 103(2), 89–108.

Drinkwater, E., Allen, W. L., Endler, J. A., Hanlon, R. T., Holmes, G., Homziak, N. T., Kang, C., et al. (2022). A synthesis of deimatic behaviour. *Biological Reviews*, 97(6), 2237–2267.

Eapen, T., & Finkenstadt, D. J. (2023). Survivability design in hostile environments: Lessons from squids, ships, startups, and supply chains. *Strategic Design Research Journal*, 15(3), 307–317.

Finkenstadt, D. J., & Handfield, R. (2021). Blurry vision: Supply chain visibility for personal protective equipment during COVID-19. *Journal of Purchasing and Supply Management*, 3, 100689.

Forbes, P. (2011). *Dazzled and Deceived: Mimicry and Camouflage*. Yale University Press.

Galanis, K. P., & Papazoglou, V. J. (2007). Crack propagation in naval aluminum panels. In Gdoutos, E.E. (ed.), *Experimental Analysis of Nano and Engineering Materials and Structures* (pp. 207–208). Springer, Dordrecht. https://doi.org/10.1007/978-1-4020-6239-1_102

Gansler, J. S., Lucyshyn, W., & Varettoni, W. (2010). *Acquisition of Mine-Resistant, Ambush-Protected (MRAP) Vehicles: A Case Study*. Acquisition Research Program.

Glazer, I. (2002). Survival biology. In R. Gaugler (Ed.), *Entomopathogenic Nematology* (pp. 169–187). CABI.

Gunderson, L. H. (2000). Ecological resilience – In theory and application. *Annual Review of Ecology and Systematics*, 31(1), 425–439.

Hall, W. K. (1980). Survival strategies in a hostile environment. *Harvard Business Review*, (September–October), 75–85.

Handfield, R., Finkenstadt, D. J., & Guinto, P. (2021, February 15). How business leaders can prepare for the next health crisis. *Harvard Business Review*.

Handfield, R., Finkenstadt, D. J., Schneller, E. S., Godfrey, A. B., & Guinto, P. A. (2020). Commons for a supply chain in the post-COVID-19 era: The case for a reformed strategic national stockpile. *Milbank Quarterly*, 98(4), 1058–1090.

Hanlon, R. T., & Messenger, J. B. (2018). *Cephalopod Behaviour*. Cambridge University Press.

Hasegawa, Y., Watanabe, T., Takazawa, M., Ohara, O., & Kubota, S. (2016). De novo assembly of the transcriptome of Turritopsis, a jellyfish that repeatedly rejuvenates. *Zoological Science*, 33(4), 366–371.

Hazlitt, H. (1946). *Economics in One Lesson*. Harper & Brothers.

Isenberg, D. J. (2010). How to start an entrepreneurial revolution. *Harvard Business Review*, 88(6), 40–50.

Ivanov, D., Sokolov, B., & Dolgui, A. (2014). The ripple effect in supply chains: Tradeoff 'efficiency-flexibility-resilience' in disruption management. *International Journal of Production Research*, 52(7), 2154–2172.

Jones, C., Medlen, N., Merlo, C., Robertson, M., & Shepherdson, J. (1999). The lean enterprise. *BT Technology Journal*, 17(4), 15–22.

Josephson, B., Lee, J., Mariadoss, B. J., & Johnson, J. (2019). Uncle Sam rising: Performance implications of business-to-government relationships. *Journal of Marketing*, 83, 51–72.

Karas, R. S. (2017). Lockheed preps options as Senate urges new look at unmanned U-2. *Inside the Air Force*, 28(29), 1–7.

Kim, K. S., Hwang, S. Y., & Lee, J. H. (2014). Naval ship's susceptibility assessment by the probabilistic density function. *Journal of Computational Design and Engineering*, 1(4), 266–271.

Knight, J. C., & Sullivan, K. J. (2000). *On the Definition of Survivability* (Technical Report No. CS-TR-33-00). University of Virginia, Department of Computer Science.

Mace, R. (1993). Nomadic pastoralists adopt subsistence strategies that maximize long-term household survival. *Behavioral Ecology and Sociobiology*, 33(5), 329–334.

McIntosh, S. E. (2011). The wingman-philosopher of MiG Alley: John Boyd and the OODA loop. *Air Power History*, 58(4), 24–33.

McNamara, J. M. (1990). The policy which maximizes long-term survival of an animal faced with the risks of starvation and predation. *Advances in Applied Probability*, 22(2), 295–308.

Meiri, S., Cooper, N., & Purvis, A. (2008). The island rule: Made to be broken? *Proceedings of the Royal Society B: Biological Sciences*, 275(1631), 141–148.

Nabarro, J. D. N. (1987). Acromegaly. *Clinical Endocrinology*, 26(4), 481–512.

Napolitano, M. R., Marino, V., & Ojala, J. (2015). In search of an integrated framework of business longevity. *Business History*, 57(7), 955–969.

O'Rourke, R. (2011). *Navy Littoral Combat Ship (LCS) Program: Background, Issues, and Options for Congress.* DIANE Publishing.

Patteli, L. (2022). Twitter and Musk clash on metrics. *Strategic Finance*, 104(5), 15–16.

Paterson, J. (1999). Overview of low observable technology and its effects on combat aircraft survivability. *Journal of Aircraft*, 36(2), 380–388.

Ries, E. (2011). *The Lean Startup.* Crown Business.

Scheffer, M., Vergnon, R., van Nes, E. H., Cuppen, J. G. M., Peeters, E. T. H. M., Leijs, R., & Nilsson, A. N. (2015). The evolution of functionally redundant species: Evidence from beetles. *PLoS One*, 10(10), e0137974.

Taleb, N. N., Goldstein, D. G., & Spitznagel, M. W. (2009). The six mistakes executives make in risk management. *Harvard Business Review*, 87(10), 78–81.

Van den Brand, M., & Groote, J. F. (2015). Software engineering: Redundancy is key. *Science of Computer Programming*, 97, 75–81.

Yasuda, T. (2005). Firm growth, size, age and behavior in Japanese manufacturing. *Small Business Economics*, 24(1), 1–15.

Chapter 2

Efficiency and Resilience Strategies

If you want to go fast, go alone, if you want to go far, go together.

–African proverb

DOI: 10.4324/9781032715315-3

In this chapter, we will explore the principles underlying the strategies that living organisms use to maintain efficiency in the face of limited or changing resources, as well as resilience in the face of external environmental forces. By examining these principles, we hope to identify general principles that can be applied to human organizations to achieve similar goals.

Efficiency is the ability of a system, such as an organism or an organization, to effectively manage its resources. On the other hand, resilience is the ability to withstand or quickly recover from external environmental forces. These two factors are closely related, and strategies for improving efficiency and resilience should be considered in tandem. Living organisms must employ their resources efficiently to thrive in environments with limited resources. They often achieve this by making trade-offs involving different resources, such as energy and time. Resilience is a critical component of this process, as it enables organisms to adapt to external forces with a minimal loss of efficiency. Organizations also encounter resource constraints, including limitations on capital, human resources, and technology. To remain viable, organizations must strike a balance in their utilization of these resources and develop strategies to adapt to external forces, such as technological changes, political upheaval, and economic recessions. These strategies should be coordinated to enhance the organization's survival in challenging environments.

It is essential to acknowledge the existence of and understand the reasons behind the association between strategies employed to enhance efficiency and resilience. Trade-offs are inevitable between these two factors, influenced by their specific and often conflicting objectives concerning survivability. These trade-offs emerge from interactions between their respective threats and challenges encountered while attempting to mitigate threats to one factor, all while safeguarding the other. Many resilience strategies involve additional risk mitigation measures, which naturally introduce inefficiencies. Organisms and organizations must grapple with the reality that the future is inherently uncertain, making perfect efficiency unattainable, and resources are finite, limiting the capacity to manage every conceivable risk. Resilience often demands the utilization and maintenance of extra resources, which can impede overall efficiency in ordinary circumstances. For instance, a vehicle that increases its resilience with redundant components, such as the Citroën 2CV Sahara 4×4, may be less efficient in normal operating conditions.[1]

Another reason for the connection between efficiency and resilience pertains to their respective vulnerabilities concerning limited resources and external forces. Environmental factors can trigger fluctuations in resources, affecting both natural ecosystems and business environments. Severe forces can have direct impacts on physical survival while indirectly constraining the availability of valuable resources. For instance, extreme heat can directly affect an organism's ability to regulate its temperature, indirectly diminishing the accessibility of resources like food and water. This analogy extends to organizations as well. Environmental stressors that directly threaten a firm's existence, such as political, economic, or technological factors, can likewise curtail the availability of resources, including capital and labor. A third reason for the connection between efficiency and resilience strategies lies in the frequent encounters with extreme environmental forces during the resource management process of both organisms and organizations. For instance, an animal may confront severe weather conditions while foraging for resources, and an entrepreneurial organization may contend with the effects of economic, political, or social forces during efforts to raise capital from investors.

Both in nature and in business environments, we find entities that are required to manage both low levels of resources and extreme forces. Bristlecone pine trees, among the oldest living organisms, grow in extremely harsh environments with limited resources.[2] They efficiently manage their resources, including water and nutrients, to survive in the arid, high-altitude regions they inhabit. These trees also exhibit resilience by withstanding extreme environmental force and can endure severe cold and high winds. Another organism that exemplifies both efficiency and resilience is the Arctic Tern.[3] These small birds, known for one of the longest migrations in the animal kingdom, demonstrate efficiency in resource management by making trade-offs involving various resources, such as food and time. Additionally, they display remarkable resilience as they endure extreme environmental forces during their migration.

SpaceX's innovation in crafting reusable orbital launch systems exemplifies the delicate balance between efficiency and resilience in the context of innovative technology.[4] The utilization of reusable components significantly enhances cost-effectiveness in space launches. However, this approach introduces usage-related complexities and maintenance obligations that can impact short-term efficiency due to the inherent trade-off between efficiency and resilience. Reusable components require regular inspections, refurbishments, and maintenance to ensure their usability for future launches. Amid external pressures like financial constraints and competition from established firms, SpaceX's strategy of maintaining a delicate balance between efficiency and resilience in rocket design has proven to be remarkably astute.

Levels of Survival Strategies and ER Principles

Survival mechanisms in bio-organisms can be observed at three levels: physiological strategies within individual organisms, behavioral strategies within individuals in response to challenges, and ecological strategies involving several organisms. Efficiency and resilience mechanisms can encompass physiological, ecological, or behavioral strategies.

■ Physiological Strategies: In nature, we observe that individual organisms are equipped with various specialized physiological adaptations to increase their chances of survival. For instance, the presence of keratinous scales in reptiles and certain fish species serves as a protective shield against environmental threats.

■ Behavioral Strategies: Organisms' behavioral adaptations involve actions rather than physiological attributes, although they may necessitate specialized physiological attributes to support these behaviors. For instance, nocturnality, the preference for nighttime activity, is a common behavioral mechanism observed in various species. Nocturnal creatures, such as owls, employ this strategy to take advantage of reduced competition and lower predation risk during the dark hours.

■ Ecological Strategies: Survival extends beyond individual organisms to encompass the interactions between different populations within an ecosystem. A classic example of this is the huddling behavior in penguins. Penguins huddle in tightly knit groups, especially in harsh Antarctic conditions, to conserve energy and maintain warmth. This strategy assists all members in enduring extreme cold and harsh winds, thereby enhancing their chances of survival.

These levels can also be seen in organizational strategies, with physiological strategies relating to an organization's design or setup, behavioral strategies concerning actions, and ecological strategies involving interactions with other organizations.

■ Physiological Strategies: This can be exemplified by the way a company is structured, whether it is publicly listed or privately held, or by a company's long-term investment in robust cybersecurity systems, which serve as protective shields against external threats.

■ Behavioral Strategies: This can be illustrated by company policies, which are potentially modifiable. For example, a company may adopt a flexible work culture, permitting employees to adjust their work hours or locations in response to changing circumstances.

■ Ecological Strategies: Companies often form close-knit partnerships with suppliers, sharing information, and resources. In times of disruption or crisis, this collaborative approach can help all parties conserve resources, reduce costs, and collectively navigate challenges.

To study and classify efficiency and resilience mechanisms, we can consider the stage of resource utilization where these strategies are applicable. In general, the following stages can be identified for any organism in relation to its resource management process: exploration, acquisition, storage, utilization, and disposal. Not all resources involve all five stages. We can observe that acquisition strategies can be physiological, behavioral, or ecological in nature, while utilization is generally physiological.

The ER Principles

We also observe that specific common principles are often used in strategies and mechanisms designed to improve efficiency, resilience, or both. We categorize these fundamental principles as "ER principles," as they can be potentially applied as both efficiency and resilience strategies (Table 2.1). The efficiency principles are reservoir, rest, reduction, reuse, and regularization. The resilience principles include reservoir, replacement, repair, reinforcement, and regularization. Notably, the principles of "reservoir" and "regularization" are included in both the efficiency and resilience categories. It is also essential to recognize that each of these principles has secondary effects that are challenging to disentangle. Take, for instance, the case of "resting." While primarily considered a resource-management strategy aimed at improving efficiency, it can also potentially impact an organism's

Table 2.1   ER Principles

Efficiency	Resilience
Reservoir	Reservoir
Resting	Replacement
Reduction	Repair
Reuse	Reinforcement
Regularization	Regularization

resilience. For example, resting can facilitate the regeneration of protective components that have been damaged, thereby enhancing resilience and ultimately bolstering survivability. Meanwhile, extended or poorly timed periods of inactivity, especially when an organism is subjected to severe external pressures, may jeopardize the organism's overall chances of survival.

In the upcoming sections, we will examine efficiency and resilience principles separately. It's important to note that alterations in resource availability can result from factors unrelated to external forces. For instance, in the natural world, koalas predominantly consume eucalyptus leaves, which possess low nutritional content. These animals possess a specialized digestive system and a slow metabolism that enable them to efficiently extract nutrients and water from the leaves. Similarly, a startup company may encounter constraints in resource access, even when operating in a stable environment devoid of environmental threats. Similarly, the need for resilience may arise independently of the need for efficiency. For example, an organism may live in a resource-rich environment where it is threatened by external forces such as currents. Beavers capture the dynamics of such an environment. Similarly, an organization may have access to adequate resources such as cash but may be threatened by independent forces such as technological disruptions. Finally, it is common to see situations where both efficiency and resilience are necessary. Xeric environments, where resource constraints are driven by harsh environmental forces, are an example of nature. Recessions, where economic forces limit access to financial resources, are an analogous case in the organizational domain.

ER Principles and Efficiency Strategies

We will start by studying strategies utilized by living organisms to improve survivability in environments with limited and fluctuating resources. Such fluctuations in resources can be sudden and unpredictable, or predictable and seasonal. We observe the following four forms of environments where organisms face resource limitations that threaten their survival:

1. Endemic environments where resources are generally scarce, such as deserts.
2. Seasonal environments that experience predictable changes in resource availability, such as monsoon regions.

3. Declining environments where resources are decreasing in a predictable manner, such as deforested areas.
4. Disruptive environments that may experience sudden declines in resources, such as areas of unpredictable forest fires.

While examining how living organisms adapt to such resource-limited environments, we will also examine parallels in the organizational realm. Just like organisms, organizations may face resource constraints such as limited capital, technology, and human resources. These limitations can be endemic, declining, seasonal, or abrupt, just like in nature. Our goal is to identify organizational efficiency and resilience strategies that are analogous to the strategies observed in nature. To do this, we need to consider the flow of resources through exploration, acquisition, conversion, utilization, and storage. In each of these stages, there may be losses due to resource leakage. The factors that impact resources at each stage can also be endemic, declining, seasonal, or abrupt. In doing so, we can identify general business efficiency strategies that parallel those found in nature.[5]

In environments where resource scarcity is an endemic and long-term feature, organisms have developed specific adaptations to reduce their resource needs. These adaptations often take the form of mainly physiological, but also some behavioral, or ecological strategies that allow organisms to survive long term in environments that would otherwise be too harsh for life, given the limited resources. If the resource limitations are endemic, we are likely to observe permanent adaptations. Take, for example, the telecommunications industry. In regions with limited physical infrastructure or high regulatory barriers, companies have developed innovative strategies to reduce their resource needs and remain profitable. Instead of investing heavily in traditional brick-and-mortar infrastructure, some telecom companies have leveraged virtualization technologies and cloud-based services to expand their reach with minimal physical resources.

If the resource limitations are seasonal, we would expect to see a mix of physiological, behavioral, and ecological strategies. For example, consider the food and beverage industry, which experiences fluctuations in consumer demand throughout the year. To cope with this seasonality, companies employ a mix of behavioral and ecological strategies to manage the resource-related limitations. For instance, they may adjust their marketing and product offerings, targeting different customer segments during peak and off-peak seasons. In a resource-declining environment, there may be fewer physiological adaptations and more behavioral or ecological strategies, such as migration to new areas. In such business conditions, companies may diversify their product or service portfolio to mitigate the impact of reduced demand in one sector by expanding into burgeoning markets.

In disruptive environments characterized by sudden shifts in available resources, organisms frequently struggle to adapt. Severe disruptions in resource availability can result in the decimation of entire populations. Nevertheless, even amid these extreme circumstances, certain organisms demonstrate a greater capacity to endure and persist. Consequently, it is imperative to investigate the underlying factors contributing to the variances in survivability under such circumstances. In disruptive business environments, companies with a culture of innovation, a readiness to pivot swiftly, and a sharp ability to identify emerging opportunities may indeed thrive.

Efficiency strategies in both natural systems and organizations frequently employ subtractive approaches to minimize resource utilization by mitigating waste. We refer to these as subtractive strategies because they involve the reduction or elimination of specific activities or substances. We observe several subtractive strategies, such as resting, restricting, refining, and reducing. Yet, in specific scenarios, additive strategies can also enhance efficiency. These approaches entail the addition or augmentation of specific activities or substances. These strategies include reusing, repeating, replacing, and recycling. We can identify some of these efficiency strategies in nature by examining how animals survive in extreme conditions with severe resource deficits in the four types of resource-limited environments we have identified. Next, let us look at some examples of such strategies used to improve efficiency and conserve resources.

Reservoir Strategies

The reservoir principle represents efficiency strategies that involve the storage of a resource for future use and long-term efficiency gains. One strategy involves the ability to stock excess of a resource during periods of high availability to compensate for times when the resource may be less plentiful. In agriculture, farmers use a reservoir strategy through crop rotation. They grow nitrogen-fixing crops like legumes during certain seasons, which store excess nitrogen in the soil. This nitrogen can then be utilized by subsequent crops, reducing the need for synthetic fertilizers. This not only improves crop efficiency but also contributes to sustainable agriculture by conserving resources and reducing environmental impact. In the short term, collecting additional resources and storing them may be inefficient for the organism, but it helps it to withstand changes in resource availability imposed by harsh environmental forces, thereby improving its long-run efficiency. Furthermore, the material in which the resource is stored or converted may also serve other functions, such as offering protection against external forces or enhancing efficiency. For instance, blubber in dolphins serves a crucial role in streamlining, locomotion, and thermoregulation, in addition to its function of storing metabolic energy.[6]

Business organizations also apply reservoir strategies to optimize their operations. For instance, a manufacturing company may stock excess raw materials during times of lower demand or lower prices, allowing it to maintain consistent production even when resource costs fluctuate. This efficient resource management not only enhances the company's cost-effectiveness but also bolsters its resilience by safeguarding against supply chain disruptions or price spikes. Retail businesses, such as clothing stores, often apply reservoir strategies to manage their inventories efficiently. One common approach is to stock excess inventory during periods of low demand or when suppliers offer products at lower prices. This strategy also benefits customers by ensuring product availability and stable pricing.

Resting Strategies

To conserve resources, organisms may rest for a period. Resting can be seen as a strategy of balancing time and energy resources, as seen in the cheetah's strategy of resting for long periods to conserve energy that can be used to achieve high speeds for short periods. Resting strategies may be used in both endemic and seasonal resource-limited environments for organisms. Terms used to describe these strategies include hibernation, dormancy, estivation, cold torpor, overwintering, and brumation.[7] These resting mechanisms may involve physiological or behavioral adaptations. In seasonal environments with predictable changes in resources, resting may be balanced by periods of intense resource acquisition. For example, the well-known strategy used by animals to survive resource deficits in the winter is hibernation. In bears, hibernation is preceded and followed by periods of intense resource acquisition, where the animal tries to build up a large reserve of energy through excessive eating, a phenomenon known as hyperphagia.[8] Similar strategies such as estivation in lungfish and brumation in reptiles involve extended periods of incapacitation. Instead of experiencing long periods of inactivity, reptiles during brumation occasionally stir to drink water, but they may go without food for several months.

Resting strategies, both short term and long term, may be useful for improving organizational efficiency. These strategies can be activated in response to expected or unforeseen changes. Business inactivation strategies, like hibernation, may be applicable to firms that face some form of systematic cyclicality. For example, toy manufacturers who experience peak sales or sporting companies who expect increased business during major tournaments or holidays. The appropriate strategy requires an examination of the cyclical and predictable nature of resource availability. The organization can adopt analogous strategies to enhance its survivability. Can it prepare for periods of inactivity by preparing for excessive consumption during periods of availability, like hyperphagia in bears? Are there secondary resources that can be accessed periodically? For example, a company might enter a state of hibernation with regard to certain categories of employees or infrastructure, such as shutting down part of a plant or utilizing strategic layoffs, but continue business as usual in other areas.

Resting strategies may be less effective in resource-declining or resource-disruptive environments, where changes in resource levels are unpredictable. In these cases, resource acquisition and stockpiling may still be used, but in a much less efficient manner as the utility of these resources is dependent on the state of the environment. In declining environments, resource stockpiling may actually contribute to faster decline. In disruptive environments, it can be even more complex as the resources are only valuable if the unknown or unpredictable should occur and there is a chance that the entity may misappropriate resources for one disruption in favor of another. For example, the strategic national stockpile in the United States had appropriated an inordinate amount of funding toward anthrax vaccines and was ill-prepared for the initial COVID-19 response in 2020.[9]

Reduction Strategies

Efficiency strategies for resource management can include reducing or limiting elements that consume high levels of resources, which in turn can impose limitations on the system. In this case, the trade-off must be acceptable or compensated through another mechanism. For example, kangaroo rats lack sweat glands to conserve water in arid environments.[10] Physiologically they have adapted to prioritize water retention over daytime temperature regulation. Instead, they must use behavioral strategies like nocturnality and the use of burrows to maintain body temperature. Organizations facing resource shortages may eliminate certain functions, such as paid advertising, to conserve resources and use more efficient behavioral approaches like word of mouth to achieve similar goals.

A similar strategy is reducing the size or number of the organs that are a source of leakage of resources. For example, marine fishes have smaller glomeruli, producing less urine, as opposed to freshwater fishes that have large glomeruli, creating large amounts of dilute urine.[11] Decreasing or plugging the leakage of resources by limiting its external interfaces is another common strategy observed in living systems. The small ears of the polar bear prevent loss of heat through leakage, whereas the large ears of the fennec fox allow heat to dissipate. Notice that both increasing and decreasing the size of the interface/exposure can improve efficiency based on the nature of the resource and the environment. In the latter case, the resources saved is an energy-complementary resource, such as water, which is now less required for evaporative cooling. The principle of reduction is also exemplified in the slow metabolism of the wombat and the development of tissues that are tolerant to water loss.

Reduction strategies can also be used to improve efficiency in business and organizational processes. Some common types of efficiency in this context include operational efficiency, labor efficiency, process efficiency, eco-efficiency, product efficiency, material efficiency, and return on investment.[12] To begin, it is important to identify the limited resources of interest. Once these resources have been identified, the next step is to identify sources of resource leakage. For example, raw materials may leak during acquisition, transportation, storage, conversion, or utilization. A resource flow diagram can be used to identify these sources of leakage. In other examples, organizational funds may be leaking due to misuse by purchasing activities. Spend analysis can be utilized to increase what is known as spend-under-management (SUM) to prevent maverick spending or leakage by purchasers who fail to use approved sources that have been established to save money for the organization at an enterprise level and ensure better data sharing and fidelity by the organization for financial decision-making.

The reduction principle can be applied to business or organizational processes to improve efficiency by reducing waste. Organizations can benefit from identifying the interfaces that lead to the exposure and loss of resources. One way to reduce waste in business organizations is to eliminate it, as exemplified by different forms of waste ("muda") represented by the TIMWOOD acronym in the Toyota Production System. These wastes are Transportation, Inventory, Motion, Waiting, Overproduction, Overprocessing, and Defects. Time-consuming processes or sources of wasted resources are common targets for reduction in organizations. Another efficiency strategy is outsourcing, which involves reducing the number of internal resources needed to complete a task or process by hiring external entities to handle it. By outsourcing, organizations can take advantage of specialized expertise and potentially reduce costs associated with employee management. Efficiency may also be improved through the process of automation of repetitive activities. However, automation involves significant trade-offs, costs, and risks including potential job displacement, economic inequality, cybersecurity vulnerabilities, and a need for reskilling and upskilling of the workforce.[13] It is important to carefully consider the trade-offs and the potential secondary and unintended impacts on the organizational components before implementing a reduction strategy.

Reuse Strategies

One set of strategies for improving efficiency involves the principle of reuse, which entails the repeated use of a resource to extract as much value from it as possible. This strategy can be seen in the concentration of urine and dry feces in kangaroo rats and the reabsorption of water in nasal passages through condensation by cactus wrens. Another form of reuse is the collection and return of a resource to an earlier stage of use. This strategy is observed in the California condor, which uses urine to cool its legs through a process known as urohydrosis. Resource sharing or huddling, as observed in animals such as the hyrax, is another form of resource reuse that has ecological implications. This principle can also be seen in the use of metabolic water by animals. Some bird species reuse their nests from one breeding season to the next.[14] Organizations can implement reuse strategies as well. Though not ideal, personal protective equipment such as rubber gloves and surgical gowns were reused during the height of the COVID-19-related supply chain disruptions of 2020. In other cases, reuse can be a more standard practice such as fabrication shops that reuse machine oil as heating fuel. In the case of PPE, the organizations were simply trying to meet demand when supplies were scarce, whereas the fabrication example demonstrates a need to reduce the cost of heating and material disposal for the firm. Additional examples of reuse in a business context include co-working companies that offer shared office spaces, enabling multiple businesses to utilize the same infrastructure, furniture, and utilities. Another instance involves data centers utilizing the heat they generate to provide heating for nearby buildings during the winter months.[15]

Regularization Strategies

Regularization is another principle that can be used to identify efficiency strategies. Regularization is the act of balancing, regulating, streamlining, or changing a system, activity, or situation so that it follows rules and becomes more predictable. One form of regularization is streamlining, which aims to improve both time and energy efficiency. There is often a trade-off between using streamlining versus barriers as a resilience and efficiency strategy. Streamlining and reducing drag can improve efficiency by protecting against external forces, but in some cases, it may be more effective to use barriers. This trade-off is similar to the adoption of hierarchical versus flat structures in different environments. Hierarchical structures may be more effective in stable environments with limited exposure to external forces, while flat structures may be better suited for more turbulent conditions. Another related concern is the choice between single-tasking and multi-tasking, and specialization and generalization in organizations.

One example of the regularization principle in the natural world is the concept of circadian rhythms in animals.[16] Many organisms, including humans, regulate their biological processes based on a 24-hour cycle. This internal clock system helps them maintain predictable and efficient patterns of activity and rest, ultimately conserving energy and minimizing resource wastage. Similarly, in business organizations, the implementation of standardized processes and procedures can be considered a form of regularization. By adhering to established rules and workflows, companies can reduce variability, minimize errors, and enhance predictability, leading to increased operational efficiency. For instance, manufacturing companies often employ Lean and Six Sigma methodologies to streamline their production processes and reduce waste.[17]

ER Principles and Resilience Strategies

Resilience strategies are generally additive in nature, involving an addition of an activity or substance, represented by principles such as reservoir, replacement, repair, reinforcement, and regularization. Nevertheless, there are certain resilience strategies that take a subtractive approach, akin to those previously recognized for enhancing efficiency. The key distinction lies in the fact that subtractive strategies predominantly aim to minimize the impact of a force, rather than mitigating the loss of an external resource. Next, we will explore various resilience strategies observed in living organisms, relating them to the ER principles and examining analogous applications in human organizations.

Reservoir Strategies

Organisms and organizations can significantly enhance their resilience through the implementation of reservoirs, which involves the prudent stockpiling of resources during periods of abundance to mitigate the challenges posed by resource scarcity in the future. A classic example of this principle can be found in desert-dwelling organisms. These creatures have developed the remarkable ability to store excess water when it is available in short bursts, such as morning dew, rare rainfall, or encounters with oases. While this behavior may seem inefficient in the short term, it is essential for their survival in harsh xeric environments. By stockpiling water, they can withstand unpredictable changes in resource availability, thus improving their overall resilience. Desert plants, like the saguaro cactus, are well-known examples of reservoir strategies in nature.[18] During brief periods of rainfall, these plants store water in their swollen trunks or stems. This principle can also be extended to business organizations. For instance, technology companies that build financial reserves during prosperous times can better navigate economic downturns and market fluctuations, demonstrating the dual benefit of efficiency and resilience. Furthermore, the resources stored, such as capital or diversified product lines, may provide protection against external economic forces, enhancing their overall resilience in a dynamic business landscape. In the business world, Apple Inc. is a prime example of a company employing a reservoir strategy.[19] Apple's substantial cash reserves, built up during prosperous times, serve as a financial buffer.

Replacement Strategies

Regeneration is the process through which an organism can regrow or replace a lost organ or body part. This phenomenon occurs in response to a variety of factors, including external forces such as predators or the natural wear and tear experienced by the organism. At the heart of regeneration lies a crucial mechanism where certain cells have the remarkable ability to divide and differentiate into diverse cell types, enabling the formation of new tissue and organs. For instance, specific species of salamanders can fully regenerate limbs through this specialized process.[20] However, the replacement mechanism of regeneration does come with its share of limitations. Firstly, during the regrowth process, there is often a period in which the organ or body part is temporarily unavailable or missing, rendering the organism vulnerable to predators or other threats. Furthermore, the regenerated organ or body part may not function as efficiently as the original, and it may be susceptible to abnormalities or deformities. Lastly, it is important to note that the capacity to regenerate can vary considerably between different species and may be more limited in some organisms than in others.

Just as organisms regrow body parts, businesses commonly attempt to regenerate their business systems after setbacks, such as financial downturns, or major shifts in consumer preferences. This adaptation may involve restructuring, diversifying, or implementing new technologies to replace outdated methods. Family businesses may engage in such restrictive efforts both during transgenerational transfers of control and to ensure their survival across generations.[21] Following the regeneration process, a transitional period may occur during which the company becomes vulnerable to competition and market forces, and the "regenerated" processes or products may not exhibit the same level of effectiveness as the original ones. Military units must have contingency plans in place to replace damaged or destroyed equipment and personnel swiftly. The ability to regenerate forces and assets is essential to maintain combat readiness.

Repair Strategies

Repair is a strategy that involves mending a damaged organ or body part in place, eliminating the need for replacement. This approach can be effective in preserving the function of an organ or body part, especially when it is damaged by external factors like predators or accidents. One notable example is the critical role that DNA repair systems play in upholding the integrity of the genome when it faces replication errors, environmental effects, and the cumulative impact of aging.[22] One advantage of repair is that it can commence before the existing organ or body part becomes entirely dysfunctional, enabling the organism to maintain its function and avoid the risks and costs associated with regenerating a new organ or body part. However, repair systems can be costly to maintain, as they may necessitate specialized cells or tissues, or involve the expenditure of energy and resources to address the damage. Data security breaches are a modern-day threat to organizations. Implementing repair strategies, companies often invest in cybersecurity measures to patch vulnerabilities, regain customer trust, and restore data integrity.

Self-healing is a type of repair commonly observed in living systems and has been the source of inspiration for self-healing composites and polymeric materials.[23] This process entails the activation of specialized cells and tissues in response to injury or damage, involving a range of mechanisms, including inflammation, scarring, and the activation of immune cells to eliminate damaged tissue and facilitate healing. In organizations, repair can take on various forms. It may take the form of a physical restoration following an incident like a factory fire, reputational recovery in response to a public relations crisis such as a product recall, or the reconstruction of a supply chain after a significant disruption affecting key suppliers. In these scenarios, organizations have the flexibility to allocate resources to specific actions, such as funding reconstruction efforts, financing a crisis management team, or securing alternative supply sources.

Reinforcement Strategies

Reinforcement is a mechanism that involves the introduction of a secondary element to provide additional protection against external forces. This can be an effective way to strengthen or protect an existing organ or body part, particularly if it is vulnerable to damage or loss. In some cases, reinforcement may involve simply adding additional units or copies of the existing component, such as adding extra layers of armor or scales to protect against predators. In other cases, reinforcement may involve the use of a more effective material, such as the anti-freeze protein found in Antarctic notothenioids and Arctic cod, which helps to protect the fish's tissues and organs from freezing in extremely cold polar waters.[24] Reinforcement can be a temporary or permanent strategy, depending on the needs and circumstances of the organism. It may be used to provide short-term protection in response to a specific threat or danger, or it may be a more permanent feature of an organism's anatomy or physiology. For organizations, reinforcement can reside at the product/service level or the design of the organization itself. The Mine-Resistant Ambush Protected vehicle is an example of a product designed for reinforcement. Deployed by the forces during Operations Iraqi and Enduring Freedom, the MRAP utilizes a reinforcement design strategy of heavy armoring along with a V-shaped hull design to protect troops from improvised explosive device blasts. Organizations can also arrange their structure using a reinforcement strategy. The military is another notable example. The leadership structure of each US military department includes a civilian secretary responsible for training, equipping, and organizing the service, which is reinforced by a senior military officer who is responsible for military activities, personnel, and operations.[25]

Regularization Strategies

The regularization principle, which involves balancing, smoothing, or reducing unevenness in an organism, activity, or system, plays a crucial role in enhancing efficiency and resilience. This approach minimizes the impact of external forces by more evenly distributing loads or stresses and reducing the vulnerability of individual components. Consider the purple frog, a novel example of regularization in the natural world. With its streamlined body shape and powerful muscles, the purple frog can navigate fast currents in water with remarkable ease.[26] The secret lies in how it distributes the force of the water evenly across its body, resulting in improved efficiency in movement and heightened resilience against the forces of the water current.

This principle can be applied to human organizations as well. For example, in supply chain management, optimizing the allocation of resources and responsibilities can play a critical role in lessening the impact of disruptions, such as supply chain breakdowns or unexpected shifts in demand. Regularizing workflows and processes ensure that the entire supply chain is better equipped to adapt and recover swiftly when faced with external shocks. In businesses, regularization can be seen in organizational structures that distribute decision-making and responsibilities across various departments and teams. By doing so, businesses can reduce their vulnerability to the sudden departure of key personnel or fluctuations in the market, fostering adaptability and long-term success. Similarly, the military employs regularization by diversifying its tactics and training across various terrains, scenarios, and threat types. This ensures that military forces are resilient, capable of adapting to evolving threats and better equipped to respond effectively to a wide range of situations.

Resilience in Action in Nature and Organisms

Beavers are a prime example of an organism that incorporates a range of strategies for resilience in order to thrive in their seasonal and, at times, declining environments. In the case of beavers, resilience is more important than efficiency, as they are adapted to live in a resource-rich environment where they are exposed to a variety of external threats, such as predators, harsh weather, and fluctuating water levels. Moreover, beavers are nature's environmental engineers, and beaver-inspired stream restoration methods can enhance riverscape resilience.[27]

One of the key strategies that beavers use to increase their resilience is the development of specialized anatomy and physiology. For example, beavers have a nictitating membrane on their eyes that allows them to see underwater as well as a thick layer of fat under their skin for insulation and energy storage. They also have nostrils and eyes that can be sealed when submerged, helping to protect them from water-borne threats. In addition, beavers have scent glands that produce castoreum, a waterproofing substance that they use to protect their fur and skin, and their incisors are constantly growing, allowing them to constantly maintain and repair their teeth.

Camels are a prime example of an organism that must demonstrate both efficiency and resilience in order to survive in their endemic environment. They are adapted to live in arid, desert environments where water and other resources are scarce, and they have developed a range of strategies to help them cope with these challenges. These strategies include adaptations for heat management and water conservation, such as thick fur for insulation and a hump of fat for storing energy and regulating body temperature.

Amphibians are capable of surviving in a wide range of conditions due to their ability to live both in water and on land. This flexibility allows them to exploit a variety of habitats and resources and makes them more resilient to changes in their environment. Amphibians, such as frogs and salamanders, are also capable of surviving in a wide range of conditions due to their ability to live both in water and on land. However, as cold-blooded creatures, they rely on the external environment for temperature regulation and may be more vulnerable to changes in temperature and other environmental conditions. One particular type of salamander, the axolotl, is known for its prodigious ability to regenerate, which allows it to survive in a variety of conditions and recover from injuries and damage.

Gila monsters are a type of venomous lizard found in the southwestern United States and northern Mexico. They are known for their ability to store fatty deposits in their bodies, which enables them to be more resilient in certain situations. These fatty deposits can provide a source of energy and insulation during times of food scarcity or cold weather, allowing the Gila monster to survive and recover from challenging conditions. Tardigrades, also known as water bears or moss piglets, are small invertebrates that are often considered to be the most resilient animals on Earth. They are able to survive in a wide range of environments and conditions, including extreme temperatures, high levels of radiation, and extreme dehydration. Tardigrades are able to enter a death-like state called cryptobiosis, in which they shut down their metabolism and become virtually indestructible, in order to survive extreme conditions. Cockroaches are another highly resilient animal, known for their ability to survive on limited resources and go without food and water for extended periods of time. They are also able to withstand a variety of challenges and injuries, including having their heads severed from their bodies and still being able to function.

In a business context, resilience refers to the ability of an organization to adapt and recover from challenges and disruptions. Building resilience in a business can involve a range of strategies, such as maintaining multiple product lines or operating environments to reduce the risk of dependence on any one market or sector. Other approaches might include maintaining cash or raw material reserves or having a surplus of labor available to allow for flexibility in response to changes in demand or production. In business, the concept of resilience through adaptability is prominently demonstrated by Amazon, one of the world's largest e-commerce companies. Amazon's business model incorporates a diverse range of strategies aimed at ensuring efficiency and resilience in challenging economic environments.

An excellent example of adaptability is the United States Marine Corps (USMC).[28] The USMC is renowned for its adaptability in responding to a wide range of challenges and environments. They have a well-established doctrine that emphasizes versatility, allowing them to switch between different mission types rapidly. For instance, they can transition from traditional ground combat operations to humanitarian assistance and disaster relief efforts seamlessly. In nature, we often see organisms exhibit metabolic flexibility in response to changing conditions. For example, when resources are scarce, animals may need to engage in high-energy behaviors in order to acquire them, such as hunting or foraging. However, once they have obtained these resources, they may switch to a lower-energy state in order to conserve energy. The Bedouin goat is one example of an animal that exhibits this kind of metabolic flexibility, as it is able to switch between high-energy and low-energy states in response to changes in its environment.[29] This kind of adaptability can be beneficial for business resilience, as it allows an organization to respond to changes in its operating environment and adjust its strategies and resources accordingly. By maintaining a degree of flexibility and adaptability, businesses can better withstand disruptions and recover more quickly from challenges.

Complementary ERP Mechanisms

Sometimes, adaptations that provide resilience against one force can also be repurposed to improve efficiency in relation to a different resource. For instance, osmoregulatory adaptations in land animals that prevent water loss, such as keratinous scales, provide both physical protection and help to conserve water. Another example is the dual role that blubber plays in streamlining and as an energy reservoir in aquatic mammals, which both increase time and energy efficiency, as well as provide resilience. In many living organisms, fat plays a dual role as a store of energy and as a buffer against external forces. One analogical example is the concept of cross-training employees. Cross-training (also known as multiskilling) involves teaching employees multiple skills or roles within the company, and it serves a dual purpose of efficiency and resilience under appropriate conditions.[30] In the event of a team member's absence or unforeseen challenges arising within the company, employees who have undergone cross-training can step in to address any shortages and ensure the continued smooth operation of business processes, ultimately enhancing the organization's resilience. Cross-training can also improve efficiency by enabling employees to perform multiple tasks. When employees are proficient in different roles, they can switch between tasks more smoothly, reducing downtime and increasing productivity.

Next, let's consider mechanisms that demonstrate a role in both resilience and prominence. One strategy is the use of visible barriers. These can protect against external forces and also reduce interest from an observer by either dissuading them or by making the target less visible. This mechanism can be observed in parrot fish – prior to sleeping, some species produce mucous to form a cocoon that protects them from predators. Much like how parrot fish create a protective cocoon of mucus, businesses can establish a strong digital perimeter that acts as a visible barrier to potential cyber threats. This barrier not only shields the organization from external attacks but also dissuades cybercriminals by making the target appear more challenging to breach.

Efficiency and prominence often work together when resource acquisition is facilitated by increasing or decreasing prominence in relation to other observers. Bats, for example, avoid flying during the day to reduce the likelihood of overheating, which is both an efficiency and prominence strategy. In desert environments, animals are often nocturnal or crepuscular, which also increases their efficiency and reduces their prominence. Another example is the low-energy diet of sloths, which makes them slow-moving and helps them avoid detection. Another prominence-efficiency strategy can be observed in sharks, who use "scare tactics" such as gaping as an intimidation tactic. These displays come at the cost of increased energy consumption and lower efficiency. Businesses operating in niche markets might choose to adopt a low-profile approach, akin to desert-dwelling animals. By doing this, they can streamline their operations, conserving resources while reducing their prominence within the broader market, making them attractive to a specific clientele seeking unique and specialized products or services.

Wood frogs employ strategies that intricately balance efficiency, resilience, and prominence. These frogs have adapted to cold climates by entering a state of suspended animation during winter months.[31] They cease breathing and their heart rates drop significantly (efficiency). To protect themselves, their bodies produce a unique antifreeze compound that safeguards their cells from freezing (resilience). Moreover, their immobility during this period serves the dual purpose of avoiding detection by potential predators (prominence). In a business context, an analogy to the wood frogs' strategy can be seen in software companies that implement automated and disruption-free system updates during off-peak hours, when the software is not being used.[32] These updates maximize operational efficiency by minimizing disruption to users (efficiency) and also ensure system security and performance (resilience). Simultaneously, these updates are scheduled to avoid peak usage times, reducing the risk of inconveniencing or alarming customers (prominence).

Efficiency and Resilience Adaptations in Xeric Environments

In this section, we will explore the use of efficiency and resilience strategies in dry or desert environments, also known as xeric environments[33] where organisms are faced with limited resources and strong environmental forces. A rich description of such an environment can be found in the book *The Empty Quarter* (1933) by British explorer John Philby, which includes an account of his travels across the Rub' al Khali.[34] These forces, such as temperature, humidity, and winds, can have a significant impact on the availability of resources in the environment (Table 2.2). This situation is analogous to an organizational environment in which a strong external

Table 2.2 Ro/Fo/Ob Analysis of Desert Environments

Resources (Ro)	Forces (Fo)	Observers (Ob)
Food, water, time	UV radiation, temperature, humidity, wind, sand	Predators, mates, resource competitors

force, such as an economic recession, threatens a firm by disrupting its daily operations and limiting its available resources. To understand how efficiency can be achieved in this context, we will examine the strategies used by desert organisms to manage critical resources such as water, food, and time.

Animals that inhabit desert environments must adapt to survive the harsh conditions. These environments are characterized by intense ultraviolet radiation, extreme air temperatures, low relative humidity, and minimal rainfall.[35] To maintain their homeostatic state, animals in these environments must carefully manage their water balance and thermoregulation.[36]

To cope with these conditions, animals have developed a range of physiological[37] and behavioral adaptations.[38] For instance, xerocoles, animals adapted to desert life, often adopt a nocturnal or crepuscular lifestyle to avoid daytime heat. They may also employ resilience strategies, such as reinforcing their bodies to prevent moisture seepage and leakage or burying themselves in wet sand to minimize moisture loss. An example of an animal demonstrating these adaptations is the spade-foot toad in the Colorado desert. These toads retain multiple layers of partially shed skin, forming semi-permeable surfaces that reduce moisture loss. Additionally, they bury themselves within wet sand dunes to further minimize moisture loss.[39]

In addition to physiological adaptations, animals in desert environments also display behavioral adaptations. For example, desert-dwelling goats may reduce their metabolism to conserve energy and water. Insects, including beetles and ants, may alter the design of their cuticles in response to xeric conditions, making them more permeable for evaporative cooling.[40] Overall, animals inhabiting desert environments must adapt to survive the extreme conditions. Through a combination of physiological and behavioral adaptations, these animals can maintain their water balance and thermoregulation, enabling them to thrive in these harsh environments.

In addition to the physiological and behavioral adaptations discussed above, animals in desert environments may employ a range of other strategies to cope with the harsh conditions. For instance, some animals may utilize evaporative cooling through panting to regulate their body temperature. This process involves exhaling hot air and inhaling cooler air, leading to moisture evaporation from the respiratory system and resulting in a cooling effect. Another strategy that animals in desert environments may adopt is urinating on their legs, which helps lower their body temperature by increasing the surface area for evaporative cooling. For instance, desert tortoises may salivate on their neck and legs to create a moist surface for evaporative cooling. Additionally, some desert-dwelling animals possess a nictating membrane, a clear protective covering for the eyes, which keeps them moist and shields them from harsh desert conditions, enabling these animals to maintain clear vision and evade predators, even in the dry and dusty desert environment.

These trades also occur in large organizations. For example, the United States Air Force employs category management techniques to enhance its ability to manage resources across a wide range of environmental conditions.[41] Category management is a data-driven business process that requires organizations to analyze and manage common areas of spending in an effort to eliminate unnecessary redundancies, increase efficiency, and enhance mission effectiveness. Most people who hear about this program assume that it simply increases savings by reducing contract prices because it is an arm of the Air Force Installation Contracting Center. However, over the six years since the program has been in full operation, it has achieved $3 billion in savings primarily through changing operational practices, issuing new policies to change employee behavior, and actively managing demand and consumption by its members. Many of these practices relate to the standardization of products, services, and processes, and consideration of the total cost of ownership, which includes more than just unit cost savings; it also considers maintenance costs and resilience to system downtime.

Efficiency and Resilience Macro-Goals

We can contrast generic efficiency strategies found in nature and organizations with resilience strategies by examining three overarching sets of macro-goals. These macro-goals can be likened to the concept of Dominant Logic in organizations.[42] The first set involves optimization versus redundancy, the second set entails specialization versus diversification, and the third set deals with coordination versus interdependence. These macro-goals encompass the implementation of various ER principles.

Optimization/Redundancy

Optimization for Efficiency. Many biological functions in living organisms are highly optimized for the economical performance of essential activities, such as movement, locating food, and reproduction.[43] For instance, numerous animals have streamlined bodies that minimize drag, enabling quick and efficient movement. Similarly, many businesses employ process optimization techniques to eliminate waste and inefficiency in their operations.[44] This may include using tools like Six Sigma or Lean to identify and remove sources of waste or implementing standard operating procedures to ensure consistent, high-quality processes. Some species employ strategies to conserve energy when necessary, such as entering an inactive state or hibernation during periods of low food availability, ensuring they have sufficient energy for survival and reproduction. Similar principles of resource conservation are evident in organizations. Lean management involves principles like value stream mapping and continuous improvement to reduce waste and enhance efficiency within the organization. This often includes engaging employees in problem identification and resolution and using metrics to monitor and enhance performance.

Redundancy for Resilience. Many species have multiple copies of important genes or structures, which allows them to continue functioning even if one copy is damaged or lost. Many organizations have redundant systems and backups in place, which allows them to continue functioning even if one system fails. For example, a company may have backup generators or servers in case of a power outage, or multiple suppliers for critical components.

Specialization/Diversification

Specialization for Efficiency. In nature, it is common to find species that specialize in specific tasks or environments, allowing them to operate more efficiently within those particular domains. For instance, some animals have developed specialized teeth and digestive systems to efficiently process certain types of food. Similarly, many organizations employ specialization through automation and technology to enhance efficiency and reduce costs. This may involve automating routine tasks using software, utilizing robotics for manufacturing processes, or employing data analytics to make more informed decisions.

Diversification for Resilience. Many ecosystems are composed of a wide variety of species, which helps to ensure that the ecosystem can continue to function even if one species is lost. Many species can adapt to diverse environments by altering their behavior or physiology. Many organizations diversify their operations, products, or markets to reduce their risk and increase their resilience. This can involve expanding into new geographic regions, entering new industries, or offering a wider range of products or services. Many species can learn from their experiences and remember important information, which allows them to adapt to new situations and overcome challenges. Similarly, organizations commonly strive to be flexible and adaptable, to quickly respond to changing market conditions or customer needs. This can involve having the ability to quickly change product or service offerings or to shift production or distribution in response to changing demand. Certain markets are more difficult to diversify across. For instance, researchers have found that diversifying across B2B and B2G markets can be both inefficient and contrary to resilience as the transaction costs specific to one market do not easily translate to the other. Due to these asset-specific transaction costs, researchers have recommended specialization over diversification in B2G markets from both an efficiency and resiliency standpoint.[45]

Coordination/Interdependence

Coordination for Efficiency. Many species possess strategies for coordinating and cooperating with each other to enhance their efficiency. For instance, some animals form herds or flocks to facilitate more efficient movement or hunting, or they engage in cooperative breeding, with multiple individuals contributing to raising offspring. Other species coordinate to provide symbiotic support for survival. For example, the remora fish, of the family Echeneidae, attaches itself to sharks, feeding off scraps and parasites on the sharks' skin.[46] This arrangement protects the Remora from predators and offers them energy-efficient transportation while keeping the shark free of parasites that could compromise its health. Similarly, many organizations employ collaboration and coordination strategies to enhance efficiency and productivity. This may involve using tools like project management software to coordinate teams or implementing shared services and cross-functional teams to share resources and expertise throughout the organization.

Interdependence for Resilience. Many species rely on each other for survival, such as through predator–prey relationships or mutualistic relationships. This interdependence helps to ensure the survival of both species. The entire plant and animal food chain is an example of interdependence. Many organizations build collaborations and partnerships with other organizations to share resources, knowledge, and expertise and to gain access to new markets or technologies. This can help to increase resilience by reducing the impact of external shocks and providing access to new opportunities.

Strategies of Mittelstand Companies

Mittelstand refers to small and medium-sized enterprises (SMEs) in Germany, often family-owned and operated, with a strong focus on specialized niche markets. These companies have gained recognition for their capacity to not only survive but thrive in turbulent environments, achieved by effectively balancing the requirements of both efficiency and resilience. The strategies employed by Mittelstand companies can be analyzed in terms of the three sets of macro-goals identified earlier: (1) specialization/diversification, (2) optimization/redundancy, and (3) coordination/interdependence.

Specialization/Diversification: Many Mittelstand companies specialize in a particular product or service and focus on developing innovative solutions for their customers. This allows them to differentiate themselves from larger, more diversified competitors and to build strong relationships with their customers. Specialization can come with certain risks, such as a loss of resilience. However, Mittelstand companies can overcome this by identifying and shifting to new niches as needed. For instance, Körber/Hauni, previously known for producing cigarette-making equipment, successfully transitioned to producing paper-cutting equipment. Their high efficiency is safeguarded using low prominence, as described by Hermann Simon in a 1992 *Harvard Business Review* article.

> These products are therefore invisible to consumers. But more important, Germany's small and midsize companies relish their obscurity. They shy away from publicity, and some have explicit policies of not dealing with the press. As an executive of a leading manufacturer of welding equipment said, "We are not interested in

revealing our success strategies and helping those who have been inert during recent years."

These companies are famously referred to as "hidden champions" and are known for embracing obscurity at both the product and organizational levels.[47] Their products often serve as components within other products or are used in the manufacturing of end products, thus making them rarely visible to end consumers.[48] In this way, Mittelstand companies can maintain their efficiency/resilience balance and continue to thrive despite the challenges posed by specialization.

Optimization/Redundancy: These companies employ a high-efficiency niche strategy, dedicating all their resources toward becoming the leader in a particular niche. This strategy necessitates seeking out new markets far and wide. Despite their small size, Mittelstand companies have a large global network and a strong inclination toward global expansion. Many Mittelstand companies have a global focus and have built a network of international partners and customers. This allows them to access new markets and diversify their revenue streams, which can help to improve their resilience and competitiveness.

Coordination/Interdependence: Mittelstand companies often have long-standing relationships with their customers, suppliers, and employees, which allows them to build trust and loyalty. This can help them to maintain a competitive advantage and to weather economic downturns or other challenges. Many Mittelstand companies invest in the development and training of their employees, in order to build a skilled and committed workforce. This can help to improve productivity and quality and to foster a positive and innovative company culture. Overall, the balance of efficiency and resilience strategies used by Mittelstand companies by focusing on specialization, innovation, long-term relationships, employee development, and internationalization allows them to thrive in niche markets and survive in turbulent environments.

Exercises

1. Examine the efficiency and resilience strategies used by organisms that live in extreme cold conditions. How are the strategies employed by such organisms similar and different from those that live in dry conditions? How can you relate such strategies to an organizational strategy

using an analogical assessment of these strategies to an organization of your choosing?

2. Conduct a Ro/Fo/Ob and ERP analysis of any Mittelstand company. What are some of the strategies commonly employed by this company to overcome challenging environments in the face of current or emerging threats?

3. Study the relationship between resources and forces relevant to an organization of your interest. How much of the resource changes or limitation is driven by forces? What are the challenges that arise from the simultaneous need to manage both resources and forces? How can you apply principles observed in xeric environments to address these challenges?

4. Consider how you can apply any three of the ER principles in your personal decision-making. Examine how a single principle may be applied to improve both efficiency and resilience in your situation.

Notes

1. Kozak, G. (2020, May 18). *The Citroën 2CV Sahara 4x4 Was Just Crazy Enough to Work*. Autoweek. https://www.autoweek.com/car-life/classic-cars/a32475950/the-citroen-2cv-sahara-4x4-was-just-crazy-enough-to-work/.

2. LaMarche Jr, V. C. (1969). Environment in relation to age of bristlecone pines. *Ecology*, 50(1), 53–59.

3. Egevang, C., Stenhouse, I. J., Phillips, R. A., Petersen, A., Fox, J. W., & Silk, J. R. D. (2010). Tracking of Arctic terns *Sterna paradisaea* reveals longest animal migration. *Proceedings of the National Academy of Sciences*, 107(5), 2078–2081.

4. Sippel, M., Stappert, S., & Koch, A. (2019). Assessment of multiple mission reusable launch vehicles. *Journal of Space Safety Engineering*, 6(3), 165–180.

5. *Business Efficiency: What It Is and How To Improve It*. (2022, June). Indeed Career Guide. https://www.indeed.com/career-advice/career-development/business-efficiency.

6. Struntz, D. J., Mclellan, W. A., Dillaman, R. M., Blum, J. E., Kucklick, J. R., & Ann Pabst, D. (2004). Blubber development in bottlenose dolphins (*Tursiops truncatus*). *Journal of Morphology*, 259(1), 7–20.

7. Pinder, A. W., Storey, K. B., & Ultsch, G. R. (1992). Estivation and hibernation. In M. E. Feder & W. W. Burggren (Eds.), *Environmental Biology of the Amphibia*. University of Chicago Press.

8. Fuchs, B., Yamazaki, K., Evans, A. L., Tsubota, T., Koike, S., Naganuma, T., & Arnemo, J. M. (2019). Heart rate during hyperphagia differs between two bear species. *Biology Letters*, 15(1), 20180681.

9. Hamby, C., & Stolberg, S. G. (2021, March 7). How one firm put an "Extraordinary Burden" on the US's troubled stockpile. *New York Times*.

https://www.nytimes.com/2021/03/06/us/emergent-biosolutions-anthrax-coro-navirus.html.

10. Newsom, D. M., & Van Hoosier Jr, G. L. (2012). Kangaroo rat. In *The Laboratory Rabbit, Guinea Pig, Hamster, and Other Rodents* (pp. 1095–1103). Academic Press.

11. Marshall Jr, E. K., & Smith, H. W. (1930). The glomerular development of the vertebrate kidney in relation to habitat. *The Biological Bulletin*, 59(2), 135–153.

12. Vogel, K. (2021, September 2). *Improving Business Efficiency: A Complete Guide*. RingCentral. https://www.ringcentral.com/us/en/blog/business -efficiency/.

13. Borry, E. L., & Getha-Taylor, H. (2019). Automation in the public sector: Efficiency at the expense of equity? *Public Integrity*, 21(1), 6–21.

14. Otterbeck, A., Selås, V., Nielsen, J. T., Roualet, É., & Lindén, A. (2019). The paradox of nest reuse: Early breeding benefits reproduction, but nest reuse increases nest predation risk. *Oecologia*, 190, 559–568.

15. Murphy, A. R., & Fung, A. S. (2019). Techno-economic study of an energy shar-ing network comprised of a data center and multi-unit residential buildings for cold climate. *Energy and Buildings*, 186, 261–275.

16. Vitaterna, M. H., Takahashi, J. S., & Turek, F. W. (2001). Overview of circadian rhythms. *Alcohol Research & Health*, 25(2), 85.

17. Shah, R., Chandrasekaran, A., & Linderman, K. (2008). In pursuit of implemen-tation patterns: The context of Lean and Six Sigma. *International Journal of Production Research*, 46(23), 6679–6699.

18. MacDougal, D. T. (1912). The water-balance of desert plants. *Annals of Botany*, 26(101), 71–93.

19. Sánchez, J. M., & Yurdagul, E. (2013). Why are US firms holding so much cash? An exploration of cross-sectional variation. *Federal Reserve Bank of St. Louis Review*, 95(4), 293–325.

20. Joven, A., Elewa, A., & Simon, A. (2019). Model systems for regeneration: Salamanders. *Development*, 146(14), dev167700.

21. King, D. R., Meglio, O., Gomez-Mejia, L., Bauer, F., & De Massis, A. (2022). Family business restructuring: A review and research agenda. *Journal of Management Studies*, 59(1), 197–235.

22. Yu, Z., Chen, J., Ford, B. N., Brackley, M. E., & Glickman, B. W. (1999). Human DNA repair systems: An overview. *Environmental and Molecular Mutagenesis*, 33(1), 3–20.

23. Harrington, M. J., Speck, O., Speck, T., Wagner, S., & Weinkamer, R. (2016). Biological archetypes for self-healing materials. In *Self-Healing Materials* (pp. 307–344).

24. Harding, M. M., Anderberg, P. I., & Haymet, A. D. J. (2003). 'Antifreeze' glycoproteins from polar fish. *European Journal of Biochemistry*, 270(7), 1381–1392.

25. Defense Primer: The Military Departments. (2023). In *Federation of American Scientists*. Congressional Research Service. https://sgp.fas.org/crs/natsec/ IF10550.pdf.

26. Senevirathne, G., Thomas, A., Kerney, R., Hanken, J., Biju, S. D., & Meegaskumbura, M. (2016). From clinging to digging: The postembryonic skeletal ontogeny of the Indian purple frog, *Nasikabatrachus sahyadrensis* (Anura: Nasikabatrachidae). *Plos One, 11*(3), e0151114.

27. Jordan, C. E., & Fairfax, E. (2022). Beaver: The North American freshwater climate action plan. *Wiley Interdisciplinary Reviews: Water, 9*(4), e1592.

28. Millett, A. R. (1991). *Semper Fidelis: The History of the United States Marine Corps*. Simon and Schuster.

29. Choshniak, I., Ben-Kohav, N., Taylor, C. R., Robertshaw, D., Barnes, R. J., Dobson, A., Belkin, V., & Shkolnik, A. (1995). Metabolic adaptations for desert survival in the Bedouin goat. *American Journal of Physiology, 268*(5 Pt 2), R1101–R1110.

30. Nembhard, A. (2014). Cross training efficiency and flexibility with process change. *International Journal of Operations & Production Management, 34*(11), 1417–1439.

31. Storey, K. B., & Storey, J. M. (1984). Biochemical adaptation for freezing tolerance in the wood frog, Rana sylvatica. *Journal of Comparative Physiology B, 155*, 29–36.

32. Wahler, M., & Oriol, M. (2014). Disruption-free software updates in automation systems. In *Proceedings of the 2014 IEEE Emerging Technology and Factory Automation (ETFA)* (pp. 1–8). IEEE.

33. Fahn, A., & Cutler, D. F. (1992). *Xerophytes*. Gebrüder Borntraeger.

34. Philby, H. St. J. B. (1933). *The Empty Quarter*. Constable.

35. Williams, J. B., & Tieleman, B. I. (2005). Physiological adaptation in desert birds. *Bioscience, 55*(5), 416–425.

36. Austin, G. T. (1976). Behavioral adaptations of the Verdin to the desert. *The Auk, 93*(2), 245–262.

37. Schwimmer, H., & Haim, A. (2009). Physiological adaptations of small mammals to desert ecosystems. *Integrative Zoology, 4*(4), 357–366.

38. Costa, G. (2012). *Behavioral Adaptations of Desert Animals*. Springer Science & Business Media.

39. Mayhew, W. W. (1965). Adaptations of the amphibian, *Scaphiopus couchi*, to desert conditions. *American Midland Naturalist*, 95–109.

40. Beament, J. W. L. (1959). The waterproofing mechanism of arthropods: I. The effect of temperature on cuticle permeability in terrestrial insects and ticks. *Journal of Experimental Biology, 36*(2), 391–422.

41. Landale, K. A., Apte, A., Rendon, R. G., & Salmerón, J. (2018). Using analytics to inform category management and strategic sourcing. *Journal of Defense Analytics and Logistics, 1*(2), 151–171.

42. Bettis, R. A., & Prahalad, C. K. (1995). The dominant logic: Retrospective and extension. *Strategic Management Journal, 16*(1), 5–14.

43. Weibel, E. R., Taylor, C. R., & Bolis, L. (Eds.). (1998). *Principles of Animal Design: The Optimization and Symmorphosis Debate*. Cambridge University Press.

44. Arlbjørn, J. S., & Haug, A. (2010). *Business Process Optimization*. Academica.

45. Josephson, B. W., Lee, J.-Y., Mariadoss, B. J., & Johnson, J. L. (2019). Uncle Sam rising: Performance implications of business-to-government relationships. *Journal of Marketing*, 83(1), 51–72.
46. Xu, Y., Shi, W., Arredondo-Galeana, A., Mei, L., & Demirel, Y. K. (2021). Understanding of remora's "hitchhiking" behavior from a hydrodynamic point of view. *Scientific Reports*, 11(1), 14837.
47. Simon, H. (2009). *Hidden Champions of the Twenty-First Century: Success Strategies of Unknown World Market Leaders*. New York: Springer.
48. Simon, H. (1992). Lessons from Germany's midsize giants. *Harvard Business Review*, 70(2), 115–123.

References

Arlbjørn, J. S., & Haug, A. (2010). *Business Process Optimization*. Academica.
Austin, G. T. (1976). Behavioral adaptations of the Verdin to the desert. *The Auk*, 93(2), 245–262.
Beament, J. W. L. (1959). The waterproofing mechanism of arthropods: I. The effect of temperature on cuticle permeability in terrestrial insects and ticks. *Journal of Experimental Biology*, 36(2), 391–422.
Bettis, R. A., & Prahalad, C. K. (1995). The dominant logic: Retrospective and extension. *Strategic Management Journal*, 16(1), 5–14.
Borry, E. L., & Getha-Taylor, H. (2019). Automation in the public sector: Efficiency at the expense of equity? *Public Integrity*, 21(1), 6–21.
Choshniak, I., Ben-Kohav, N., Taylor, C. R., Robertshaw, D., Barnes, R. J., Dobson, A., Belkin, V., & Shkolnik, A. (1995). Metabolic adaptations for desert survival in the Bedouin goat. *American Journal of Physiology*, 268(5 Pt 2), R1101–R1110.
Costa, G. (2012). *Behavioral Adaptations of Desert Animals*. Springer Science & Business Media.
Egevang, C., Stenhouse, I. J., Phillips, R. A., Petersen, A., Fox, J. W., & Silk, J. R. D. (2010). Tracking of Arctic terns *Sterna paradisaea* reveals longest animal migration. *Proceedings of the National Academy of Sciences*, 107(5), 2078–2081.
Fahn, A., & Cutler, D. F. (1992). *Xerophytes*. Gebrüder Borntraeger.
Fuchs, B., Yamazaki, K., Evans, A. L., Tsubota, T., Koike, S., Naganuma, T., & Arnemo, J. M. (2019). Heart rate during hyperphagia differs between two bear species. *Biology Letters*, 15(1), 20180681.
Harding, M. M., Anderberg, P. I., & Haymet, A. D. J. (2003). 'Antifreeze' glycoproteins from polar fish. *European Journal of Biochemistry*, 270(7), 1381–1392.
Harrington, M. J., Speck, O., Speck, T., Wagner, S., & Weinkamer, R. (2016). Biological archetypes for self-healing materials. In *Self-Healing Materials* (pp. 307–344).
Josephson, B. W., Lee, J.-Y., Mariadoss, B. J., & Johnson, J. L. (2019). Uncle Sam rising: Performance implications of business-to-government relationships. *Journal of Marketing*, 83(1), 51–72.

Jordan, C. E., & Fairfax, E. (2022). Beaver: The North American freshwater climate action plan. *Wiley Interdisciplinary Reviews: Water*, 9(4), e1592.

Joven, A., Elewa, A., & Simon, A. (2019). Model systems for regeneration: Salamanders. *Development*, 146(14), dev167700.

King, D. R., Meglio, O., Gomez-Mejia, L., Bauer, F., & De Massis, A. (2022). Family business restructuring: A review and research agenda. *Journal of Management Studies*, 59(1), 197–235.

LaMarche Jr, V. C. (1969). Environment in relation to age of bristlecone pines. *Ecology*, 50(1), 53–59.

Landale, K. A., Apte, A., Rendon, R. G., & Salmerón, J. (2018). Using analytics to inform category management and strategic sourcing. *Journal of Defense Analytics and Logistics*, 1(2), 151–171.

MacDougal, D. T. (1912). The water-balance of desert plants. *Annals of Botany*, 26(101), 71–93.

Marshall Jr, E. K., & Smith, H. W. (1930). The glomerular development of the vertebrate kidney in relation to habitat. *The Biological Bulletin*, 59(2), 135–153.

Mayhew, W. W. (1965). Adaptations of the amphibian, *Scaphiopus couchi*, to desert conditions. *American Midland Naturalist*, 74 ,95–109.

Millett, A. R. (1991). *Semper Fidelis: The History of the United States Marine Corps*. Simon and Schuster.

Murphy, A. R., & Fung, A. S. (2019). Techno-economic study of an energy sharing network comprised of a data center and multi-unit residential buildings for cold climate. *Energy and Buildings*, 186, 261–275.

Nembhard, A. (2014). Cross training efficiency and flexibility with process change. *International Journal of Operations & Production Management*, 34(11), 1417–1439.

Newsom, D. M., & Van Hoosier Jr, G. L. (2012). Kangaroo rat. In M. A. Suckow, K. A. Stevens, & R. P. Wilson (Eds.), *The Laboratory Rabbit, Guinea Pig, Hamster, and Other Rodents* (pp. 1095–1103). Academic Press.

Otterbeck, A., Selås, V., Nielsen, J. T., Roualet, É., & Lindén, A. (2019). The paradox of nest reuse: Early breeding benefits reproduction, but nest reuse increases nest predation risk. *Oecologia*, 190, 559–568.

Philby, H. St. J. B. (1933). *The Empty Quarter*. Constable.

Pinder, A. W., Storey, K. B., & Ultsch, G. R. (1992). Estivation and hibernation. In M. E. Feder & W. W. Burggren (Eds.), *Environmental Biology of the Amphibia*. University of Chicago Press.

Sánchez, J. M., & Yurdagul, E. (2013). Why are US firms holding so much cash? An exploration of cross-sectional variation. *Federal Reserve Bank of St. Louis Review*, 95(4), 293–325.

Schwimmer, H., & Haim, A. (2009). Physiological adaptations of small mammals to desert ecosystems. *Integrative Zoology*, 4(4), 357–366.

Senevirathne, G., Thomas, A., Kerney, R., Hanken, J., Biju, S. D., & Meegaskumbura, M. (2016). From clinging to digging: The postembryonic skeletal ontogeny of the Indian purple frog, *Nasikabatrachus sahyadrensis* (Anura: Nasikabatrachidae). *Plos One*, 11(3), e0151114.

Shah, R., Chandrasekaran, A., & Linderman, K. (2008). In pursuit of implementation patterns: The context of Lean and Six Sigma. *International Journal of Production Research*, 46(23), 6679–6699.

Simon, H. (1992). Lessons from Germany's midsize giants. *Harvard Business Review*, 70(2), 115–123.

Simon, H. (2009). *Hidden Champions of the Twenty-First Century: Success Strategies of Unknown World Market Leaders*. Springer.

Sippel, M., Stappert, S., & Koch, A. (2019). Assessment of multiple mission reusable launch vehicles. *Journal of Space Safety Engineering*, 6(3), 165–180.

Storey, K. B., & Storey, J. M. (1984). Biochemical adaptation for freezing tolerance in the wood frog, Rana sylvatica. *Journal of Comparative Physiology B*, 155, 29–36.

Struntz, D. J., Mclellan, W. A., Dillaman, R. M., Blum, J. E., Kucklick, J. R., & Pabst, D. A. (2004). Blubber development in bottlenose dolphins (*Tursiops truncatus*). *Journal of Morphology*, 259(1), 7–20.

Vitaterna, M. H., Takahashi, J. S., & Turek, F. W. (2001). Overview of circadian rhythms. *Alcohol Research & Health*, 25(2), 85.

Wahler, M., & Oriol, M. (2014). Disruption-free software updates in automation systems. In *Proceedings of the 2014 IEEE Emerging Technology and Factory Automation (ETFA)* (pp. 1–8). IEEE.

Williams, J. B., & Tieleman, B. I. (2005). Physiological adaptation in desert birds. *Bioscience*, 55(5), 416–425.

Xu, Y., Shi, W., Arredondo-Galeana, A., Mei, L., & Demirel, Y. K. (2021). Understanding of remora's "hitchhiking" behavior from a hydrodynamic point of view. *Scientific Reports*, 11(1), 14837.

Chapter 3

Prominence Strategies

Camouflage is a game we all like to play, but our secrets are as surely revealed by what we want to seem to be as by what we want to conceal.

–Russell Lynes

DOI: 10.4324/9781032715315-4

Living systems rely on the critical ability to modify (i.e., increase or decrease) the attention they receive from other observers to ensure their survivability.[1] We refer to this capability as "prominence." In this chapter, we will explore how living organisms employ well-developed strategies to manage their prominence and extend these strategies to the organizational domain. An organism's size or appearance inherently provides certain prominence-related advantages and limitations. For instance, larger animals or those with vibrant colors are often more easily detected than smaller ones. Furthermore, many organisms exhibit complex and fine-tuned strategies to regulate their prominence among diverse observers, including mates, predators, prey, competitors, and herd members. We are also interested in understanding how prominence interacts with the other two health factors: efficiency and resilience.

In this chapter, we also explore how the prominence mechanisms observed in nature can be analogously examined in the context of organizational actions. Our objective is to introduce various prominence mechanisms observed in nature and assess their applicability in a natural setting before adapting them to business contexts. To analyze these mechanisms effectively, we must identify distinct strategy dimensions, including the classes of target observers, the direction of entity changes, and the types of entity attributes. In this chapter, we will:

■ Examine how actions differ based on the class of target observers in nature, including predators, prey, mates, resource competitors, collective members, parent–child relationships, parasitic and symbiotic partners. It is worth noting that any entity can also be a target observer for its own target. We will also consider how the choice of increasing or decreasing prominence can depend on the class of the target observer. We will identify natural analogies between target observers in nature and business environments based on the relative symmetry of expected gains.

■ Consider how prominence can be adapted using various attributes, such as color, shape, sound, size, location, and motion. We find that both static extreme states and dynamic variations in attributes can be used to maintain or modify prominence levels. We will illustrate this principle using common attributes such as size and colors.

■ Describe specific strategies observed in multiple species, examining the strategies observed in nature and what we can learn from them about survival. We will explore apparent death, camouflage, protean behavior, deimatic behavior, nocturnality, distraction, and line-of-sight modification. These are typically referred to as predator-avoidance strategies, but we will describe how these can be applied to other classes of observers. We will also examine prominence balancing strategies, which may be used when an organism needs to attract and evade attention simultaneously.

■ Evaluate special cases of prominence strategies, wherein a target observer may learn from observers of another class who share a desire for similar outcomes. One example is the adoption of predator strategies by prey when facing their attackers or the utilization of a prey's mating prominence mechanisms by predators to deceive and attract their prey.

Classes of Target Observers in Nature

Prominence as a survival strategy is primarily relevant in the presence of other decision-making entities. We refer to such entities as target observers. Prominence-related actions by an entity are always directed at a target observer. The term "target observer" indicates that the entity's prominence strategy is built around the expected perspective of a specific observer of interest. These considerations can be either positive or negative but are always focused on increasing the entity's survivability. Thus, we can only fully specify the level of prominence of an entity by referring to the target observer of interest. Prominence represents the amount of attention (both degree and duration) that the entity obtains from the target observer of interest. In a natural environment, the most important target observers for decision-making entities include predators, prey, and mates. This group also includes competitors from different species, group members in a herd, and symbiotic partners. Notice that the entity itself is a target observer from the perspective of its own target. Thus, the actions of the entity and the target often counteract (predator/prey) or mirror (mating) each other.

For each entity, there is generally a primary direction of change (increase or decrease) in prominence, typically observed toward a specific target observer, as commonly seen in biological organisms. These are listed in Table 3.1. When facing a target observer that is a predator or prey, the primary (i.e., most typical) directional change in an organism involves reducing prominence. When facing a predator, a prey organism seeks to hide to evade detection and make an escape. Similarly, in the context of facing a potential prey, low prominence helps predators sneak up on the target and minimize the overall effort for acquiring resources.

Table 3.1 Directional Relationships for Prominence

Target Observer	Primary	Secondary
Predator	Decrease	Increase
Prey	Decrease	Increase
Mate	Increase	Decrease

However, remarkably, the organism is sometimes able to use the opposite ("secondary") directional change to achieve similar ends as the primary direction. Thus, for each class of target observers – predators, prey, and mates – we can identify plausible situations where both increasing and reducing prominence may be valuable, as highlighted in Table 3.2. In a predator–prey interaction, the outcome typically results in asymmetric changes in survivability. If the predator is successful in its strategy, the prey is not, and vice versa. Thus, the prominence strategies compete with each other. In contrast, in mating relationships where high prominence is used, we expect symmetric changes in survivability. That is, both the target and the observer improve their survivability.

We have discussed how decreasing prominence is the primary approach when dealing with both predators and prey, aiming to avoid detection. However, in many instances, we encounter situations where increasing prominence is also employed with these observers (Table 3.2). Both predators and prey can enhance their survivability by increasing their prominence in specific ways, especially by utilizing high levels of prominence to warn or frighten off the predator or to induce fear and submission in the prey. For example, butterflies flash bright colors when evading predators to startle them (exhibiting deimatic behavior), while predators, such as many large birds, utilize a flush-pursue strategy to startle their prey and then chase them down and capture or kill them.[2] In the context of mating relationships, the primary directional change involves increased prominence. However, there may be situations where decreasing prominence is also necessary, such as when avoiding undesirable mates or during periods outside of mating seasons or stages of life.

Natural Analogies in Organizational Environments

Next, we can explore how strategies that modify prominence, observed in biological organisms, may be applied to business organizations. To make

Table 3.2   Prominence Directions for Target Observers

Target Observer	Decrease Prominence	Increase Prominence
Predator	Decreasing prominence to hide or avoid detection from the predator. Decreasing prominence to diminish attractiveness in the eyes of the predator.	Increasing prominence to appear threatening to the predator. Increasing prominence to distract or deceive through heightened attractiveness.
Prey	Decrease prominence to appear non-threatening before pouncing on the prey. Decrease prominence to prevent fear-induced aggressive responses before the attack.	Increase prominence to frighten into submission, shock, startle, or compel movement and reduce the effort in conflict by the prey. Increasing prominence to attract prey before an attack.
Mate	Decrease prominence to avoid undesirable mates during the mating season. Decrease prominence to appear non-threatening and attract potential mates.	Increase prominence to attract a desirable mate during the mating season. Increase prominence to appear threatening or induce fear in non-desirable mates.

this comparison, we must first identify analogous observers in nature and connect them to those in organizations. These analogous observers represent distinct categories of external decision-making entities that a business, such as a firm, might adjust its prominence levels toward to enhance its chances of survival. In the case of business firms, these target observers typically encompass customers, competitors, business partners, suppliers, investors, regulatory bodies, media, and government entities. We will investigate natural analogies between the target observers for a biological organism and those for a business organization. These analogies are delineated in Table 3.3, which provides a comprehensive overview of both common and relatively uncommon relationships.

For the sake of simplicity, we categorize each observer entity in business environments into one of three classes: predator, prey, or mate. If the interaction between the target observer and the entity is likely to result in symmetric outcomes, with both parties benefiting from the interaction, we categorize the target observer as a mate. In cases where the outcome is asymmetric, with one party benefiting more than the other, we categorize it as a predator/prey relationship.

Table 3.3 Analogical Relationships in Natural and Business Environments

Target Observer	*Common Analogical Class*	*Uncommon Class*
Competitor	Predator, prey	(Mate)
Customer	Mate	(Predator), (Prey)
Business partners	Mate	(Predator), (Prey)
Investor	Mate	(Predator), (Prey)
Regulator	Mate	(Predator), (Prey)
Government	Mate	(Predator), (Prey)

To comprehend the necessity of examining both common and uncommon analogical categories, let's consider the case of competitors and their corresponding analogies in the natural environment. Competitive actions typically lead to asymmetric outcomes, such as one company gaining market share at the expense of another or securing a business deal from a competitor's existing customer. Therefore, the natural analogy resembles a predator–prey relationship. Consequently, we anticipate that predator/prey strategies are analogically relevant for a business's interactions with its competitors. Nevertheless, in certain situations, competitors may engage in actions that result in symmetric outcomes. These actions might involve partnerships to establish joint ventures, the formation of buyer cartels, participation in standards committees, coordinated activities that are disadvantageous to shared resources (suppliers and employees) but advantageous to both companies, and mutually supported merger and acquisition (M&A) activities. In these cases, the appropriate analogy is that of a mate, and prominence strategies associated with mating would offer more insightful guidance for firm decision-making.

In the case of customers, as well as other target observers such as partners, investors, and suppliers, where more symmetric outcomes are anticipated, the natural analogy is that of a mate. Nevertheless, it is worth considering secondary associations where customers, business partners, investors, or regulatory agencies could assume roles resembling predators or prey. Actions in which an organization itself behaves as a predator toward any of these entities are sometimes unethical or illegal, and, in such cases, they should be primarily scrutinized to identify actions that should be avoided or appropriately responded to. However, it is conceivable that certain predatory strategies may be viewed as legitimate, such as a company increasing its prominence levels to deter new entrants in a market.

Regulatory bodies exhibit significant variation in a global economy, and while they should be treated with respect, companies may choose to steer clear of corrupt markets or regions as part of a strategy to avoid becoming prey. An illustrative case in point would be the substantial business prospects that emerged during Operations Enduring Freedom and Iraqi Freedom. Some companies that opted to enter these markets could have reaped substantial profits by assuming greater risks. Nevertheless, many of them opted to abstain from or withdraw from these markets due to the pervasive regulatory corruption orchestrated by bodies that facilitated operations within those operational zones.[3]

Predatory actions can also be examined in the context of how these strategies may be prevented or avoided from the perspective of the target observer. Instances where the target observer, such as an investor, assumes a predatory role can be scrutinized to consider appropriate responses that enhance survivability. For example, a customer might take actions aimed at deceiving or disadvantaging the company, acting in a manner akin to a predator. If the company is aware of or familiar with such actions, it can draw lessons from prominence strategies employed by prey against predators. Similarly, unexpected predatory actions by target observers, such as partners or investors, can be studied to identify appropriate predator-avoidance strategies that are observed in nature.

Target Observers for Business Organizations

Much like natural entities, a business organization may achieve favorable outcomes by adjusting the prominence of the same target observer, by either increasing or decreasing it. Table 3.4 outlines situations where bidirectional changes in prominence can be relevant, specifically focusing on competitors and customers as target observers.

Prominence Adaptability

In dynamic environments where an entity encounters various types of target observers, such as a moving animal encountering potential predators, prey, and mates, the ability to swiftly adjust prominence levels is crucial for survival. We refer to this capability as "prominence adaptability" or "P-adaptability." P-adaptability is particularly vital for organisms facing fluctuating environmental conditions, including changes in the physical landscape and exposure to diverse target observer entities. In contrast, animals with

Table 3.4 Prominence Direction and Target Observers for Business Entities

Target Observer(s)	Decrease Prominence	Increase Prominence
Competitors (Predator)	Diminish attention for a strategic new product by downplaying its significance.	Enhance the visibility of a strategic investment to deter similar actions. Showcase significant partnerships with key partners/customers to discourage predatory moves by market competitors.
Competitor (Prey)	Minimize competitors' awareness during efforts to acquire a competitor's customers, products, or market share.	Amplify visibility to provoke a competitor into unwise actions, induce the disclosure of business secrets, or deter resistance to competitive actions.
Customers (Mate)	Diminish prominence during product development. Reduce attention from less attractive customers. Lower visibility to pique curiosity about the product. Mitigate negative attention related to corporate social responsibility issues, product recalls, etc.	Boost customer engagement before a new product launch. Employ standard marketing strategies and engage in business development activities to expand market share.

relatively stable day-to-day environmental conditions may find P-adaptability less significant. For example, less mobile creatures benefit from static camouflage, while constantly moving animals gain from dynamic camouflage. Many bio-organisms exhibit high P-adaptability, and businesses can glean valuable insights by studying the prominence-modifying behaviors of these creatures.

P-adaptability is essential for companies operating in highly dynamic environments, where they must respond to the actions of various target observers, including customers, competitors, and business partners. For businesses, similar to bio-organisms, P-adaptability signifies the capacity to swiftly adjust prominence by either increasing or decreasing it. The ability to adapt one's prominence has never been more crucial or prevalent than in this era of nearly continuous news cycles and global interconnectedness, where even small news stories can reach potential mates or predators.

Moreover, most developed countries are saturated with cameras and video capabilities. Firms must possess the awareness, strategic planning, and capability to adapt prominence in a wide range of scenarios to enhance their survivability, particularly as they operate in global environments where corporate social responsibility, sustainability, and activism are at the forefront of concern for most relevant target observers including customers and regulators.[4]

Prominence Reduction: An Underutilized Organizational Strategy

We observe a notable contrast in the emphasis placed on prominence-reducing actions in businesses and organizations compared to bio-organisms. While the significance of increasing prominence is well recognized, as evident in the necessity to widely promote a new product, the ability to swiftly reduce prominence is much less acknowledged and developed in human organizations. Conversely, in biological systems, prominence-reduction mechanisms are generally a more common and advanced aspect of many organisms' survivability, when compared to prominence-increasing mechanisms. Prominence-reduction strategies, such as camouflage, are widespread across many species, whereas prominence-increasing mechanisms, like deimatic behavior, are relatively less common. Given this observation, it appears that prominence-reduction mechanisms hold greater importance for survivability. Therefore, it would be reasonable to extensively explore the incorporation of prominence-reduction strategies into the toolkit for businesses aiming to enhance their survivability, in addition to traditional strategies.

Prominence Strategies as a Response to Predatorial Actions by Competitors

To identify potential areas of application for camouflage and other anti-predator strategies in the business world, we must first examine instances of predatory behavior within business practices. Competitors' predatory actions can significantly undermine a company's stability, and such actions may also be viewed as unjust by the targeted company or impartial observers. Moreover, these predatory actions can restrict the targeted company's ability to respond, exacerbating the harm incurred. In response to such predatory behaviors, companies may employ camouflage or other anti-predator strategies to safeguard themselves. For instance, a company might reduce its marketing or advertising efforts to render itself less conspicuous to potential predators. Alternatively, it may employ more discreet, targeted marketing campaigns that are less likely to be noticed by non-affiliated parties. Another approach is to operate in a manner that makes it challenging for competitors to detect or target the company, such as offering services during unconventional hours or in atypical locations. This approach can make it more difficult for competitors to mount effective actions against the company, ultimately enhancing its survival prospects. Examples of predatory actions include:

■ Hostile takeover of a company to eliminate it. In this scenario, a company acquires a competitor with the intention of eradicating competition. This predatory action is perceived as benefiting only one of the two parties involved. Such an action should be differentiated from a merger, which is perceived to be mutually beneficial to both companies.

■ Another form of predatory action that can be observed in the business world involves lawsuits aimed at undermining the target company's ability to concentrate on its core business. These lawsuits may be initiated by competitors or other parties with the intention of generating legal obstacles and diverting the target company from its primary business objectives. Smaller companies, often the targets of such predatory actions, may lack the resources or capacity to effectively counter these adversarial actions. Governments have also witnessed behaviors such as frivolous protests of public procurements designed to obstruct new entrants from capturing the market share held by incumbents.[5]

■ Poaching or the depletion of critical resources, including employees, suppliers, sources of resources, or partners, can have severe consequences, especially for smaller firms that rely more heavily on these resources. Losing such resources can potentially lead to the demise of the company, making the act of preying on these resources a predatory action. For instance, a larger company may entice the technology executive of a smaller firm with a higher salary, intending to undermine the company's technical expertise. Comparable practices have been observed in firms poaching talent or establishing advocates through the revolving door in government leadership.[6]

■ Predatory actions may encompass harming the ecosystem in which a competitor operates, potentially involving the destruction of resources crucial for a smaller company's survival. For instance, a larger company might illegally dispose of hazardous waste into a river that a smaller company relies on as a water source. Such an action would significantly impair the smaller company's ability to conduct its operations and could be categorized as a predatory action.

■ A predatory company may employ short-term tactics that a larger company can weather but could prove fatal for a smaller counterpart. Such actions often involve predatory pricing strategies or promotional campaigns devised to intimidate and undercut the smaller rival's business. Predatory pricing is when a company intentionally reduces its prices to levels below its cost or profit margins, with the goal of driving its competitors out of the market. The predatory company can afford to engage in this practice due to having superior resources, economies of scale, or access to more affordable capital than its competitors. This strategy aims to establish an unfair advantage by compelling smaller companies to either lower their prices or cease their operations.

■ Predatory companies can also use promotions and marketing tactics to undermine their smaller competitors. For example, a larger company could offer substantial discounts or loyalty rewards programs to their customers, making it difficult for smaller businesses to compete. In some cases, predatory companies might even engage in false advertising or other unethical practices that damage the reputation of their smaller competitors. Firms can also establish offensive marketing campaigns against competitors such as the active rivalry between popular fast food chains Burger King and McDonald's.[7]

Attributes and Prominence Strategies

Biological organisms modulate their prominence levels through the adjustment of attributes like color, shape, sound, smell, taste, size, and motion. Among these attributes, color is one of the most well-known mechanisms for achieving prominence. The use of color for prominence can be both static and dynamic. In static coloration, the organism's color mimics the colors in its immediate surroundings, but it remains unchanged when the organism moves to a different environment. This type of coloration represents a longer-term adaptation and is particularly beneficial for organisms that are relatively immobile. However, it's important to note that static coloration can still affect prominence levels if there is an underlying change in conditions. For example, an organism with static skin color that matches the surrounding foliage may be inconspicuous, but if there is an alteration in the foliage, such as when trees are cut down, the organism could suddenly become highly visible.

Dynamic or adaptive coloration entails alterations in coloration, where the color itself or patterns can rapidly or gradually adapt to shifting external conditions, encompassing changes in weather and the colors of the surrounding environment.[8] Dynamic coloration is exhibited through strategies that can either reduce prominence, such as camouflage, or enhance it, as seen in deimatic behavior. Deimatic behavior aims to increase prominence by creating a noticeable color contrast between the entity and its environment.[9] Utilizing dynamic coloration, whether to enhance or diminish prominence, can serve as both a predator-avoidance strategy and a prey attraction strategy.[10]

Form attributes, such as shape and size, are frequently adjusted to attain varying levels of prominence. Organisms can enhance their prominence by both increasing their apparent size and dynamically adapting their structure. For instance, the puffing-up strategy, characterized by a rapid expansion in size, is observed in various animal species. Examples include the porcupine fish and pufferfish, which inflate when confronted by a predator, and bears, which puff up to appear larger.[11] Some animals employ shape-shifting strategies, exemplified by the mutable rain-frog (*Pristimantis mutabilis*). Such strategies are more commonly observed in defense against predators. Conversely, an increase in prominence can also be utilized by predators.

Attributes related to movement and sound can also be subject to modification. Predators employ alterations in size along with variations in sound and motion to heighten their prominence with the intent of intimidating, frightening, or startling their prey. At times, this strategy is most effective when transitioning from an inconspicuous position to an extremely prominent one, as seen in cases of complete stillness followed by rapid motion to startle prey. For instance, predatory birds use swift movements to startle their prey.[12] The objective is to compel the prey to take actions that favor the predator. Enhancing prominence through rapid movements can be a strategy to instill fear, as exemplified by the behavior of owls that swiftly fly to terrify prey into disclosing their hiding place.[13] Frightening can also serve as a strategy to temporarily immobilize the prey, hindering its ability to respond with a fight-or-flight reaction.[14] This can result in resource savings, as the predator would need comparatively less effort to capture the prey. Attributes like smell and taste can also be employed to heighten or conceal prominence.

Prominence Mechanisms in Nature for Predators and Prey

One of the primary functions of prominence in the animal kingdom is to evade predator detection. We observe that certain types of anti-predator

Table 3.5 Anti-predator Strategies Utilizing Prominence

Strategy	Definition
Camouflage	Entity resembles the surrounding environment or objects to avoid being detected.
Nocturnality	Entity hunts or acquires resources at night when the target observer is inactive.
Line-of-sight modification	Entity operates in locations where the target observer is not actively observing.
Thanatosis or apparent death	Entity simulates death to reduce attention or interest from the target observer.
Deimatic or startle display	Entity modifies attributes to startle or frighten the target observer.
Aposematism	Entity employs bright coloration to signal potential predators about potential negative consequences.
Protean behavior	Entity exhibits unexpected patterns of movement to confuse the predator.
Distraction	Entity diverts attention by drawing focus toward one entity to reduce attention toward another.
Schooling	Entity appears as part of a group to evade detection.
Refuging	Entity positions itself behind another object or entity to obscure visibility from the target entity.

prominence mechanisms are recurrent across unrelated organisms. Among the most well-known anti-predator strategies are alarm signals, aposematism, apparent death, deimatic behavior, distraction displays, crypsis, camouflage, nocturnality, mimicry, and the unkenreflex. Many of these strategies also encompass prominence-adaptive mechanisms. Table 3.5 provides a brief description of common anti-predator strategies that involve the use of prominence.

At times, it proves beneficial to switch or alternate between high and low prominence. For instance, one method to attain heightened prominence involves pulsation. An organism that typically maintains a low prominence can increase the attention it receives through pulsation, accomplished by swiftly altering its attributes. Such pulsations can involve buzzing sounds and flickering visual displays, as observed in fireflies. Furthermore, a low-prominence strategy in one environment can translate into a high-prominence strategy in another. For example, an entity displaying generally dull and inconspicuous colors may appear prominent in an environment surrounded by vibrant hues. Similarly, a business feature that is considered a standard part of service in one market can transform into a competitive advantage or an unexpectedly prominent feature in another.

Organisms are occasionally required to exhibit bilateral prominence, simultaneously displaying high prominence to certain observers while maintaining low prominence to others. There are various strategies that can be employed to achieve this. One approach is through prominence segmentation, where one part of the organism demonstrates one form of prominence, while another part displays a different form. For example, the Superb Bird-of-Paradise in New Guinea appears as an ordinary-looking bird until it needs to attract a mate, at which point it extends a bright electric blue feather band under its neck to create a stunning display. Similarly, businesses can address the prominence dilemma by becoming inconspicuous to competitors while being exceptionally appealing to potential partners, customers, and investors. Another strategy involves utilizing multiple communication channels, such as high-frequency sounds, or different attributes, like sight versus smell.

Many of the prominence strategies observed in nature are devised to diminish prominence, as both prey and predators share the primary goal of evading detection. Nevertheless, some circumstances necessitate increased prominence, as exemplified by startle displays. Distraction is typically employed as a defense mechanism by prey, but it can also serve as a predatory strategy, as demonstrated by wolves, pygmy squids, and rattlesnakes. Prominence can be heightened through contrast or changes relative to a previous state. For instance, a business that is known for extensive advertising may garner increased attention if it suspends its advertising, creating dynamic-contrast prominence. Attributes including color, shape, size, smell, and motion can all be modified to alter levels of prominence. A large object can reduce its prominence by moving relatively slowly; however, in a group of fast-moving organisms, a slower one tends to draw attention to itself. Prominence can be decreased (or even increased) by altering the observer's ability to perceive the overall form of the organism.

Countershading, a strategy observed in nature where an organism's coloration is darker on one side, can be employed to both heighten and diminish prominence. This principle also finds application in the realm of business organizations. A countershading strategy, wherein a segment of the organization appears distinct from the rest, may be utilized by firms to either stand out or appear less conspicuous, depending on its implementation. If certain parts of the business blend with the surrounding environment or other businesses, it may create the perception of a smaller presence than it actually has. However, the disparity in appearance can also draw attention through contrast effects. For instance, some companies offer prominent services such as manufacturing and logistics while maintaining the capability to conduct R&D for others on a need-to-know basis.

Additional strategies that hinder an observer's ability to detect an organism by obscuring its appearance include disruptive coloration and differential blending. These strategies disrupt the observer's capability to perceive the entity as a cohesive organism. In the context of business, disruptive contrast can also be analogically applied. For instance, a company might employ different names in various countries to create the impression of being a smaller entity. Several anti-predator strategies can also be used by predators against prey and are listed in Table 3.6. The analogical strategies for businesses and organizations can be found in Table 3.7.

In the upcoming section, we will explore prominent strategies observed in nature, commencing with camouflage, the most renowned of such strategies. Generally, in the context of camouflage, the subject of interest is the prey and the observer in question is the predator. Camouflage serves the

Table 3.6 Related Prominence Strategies for Predator and Prey

Strategies	Predator	Prey	Prominence
Camouflage	Hides from prey before an attack	Hides from predators before or during an attack	Decrease
Nocturnality	Hunts at night when prey is sleeping	Active at night to avoid predators	Decrease
Line-of-sight modification	Predator avoids prey's line of sight	Prey avoids predators' line of vision	Decrease
Apparent death	Appears to die to attract prey	Appears to die to dissuade attack from predator	Decrease
Deimatic or startle display	Frightens prey into submission or startles prey to change location	Frightens away predator	Increase
Protean behavior	Utilizes an unpredictable movement pattern to confuse prey	Employs an unpredictable pattern of movement to confuse predator	Decrease
Distraction	Distracts prey before attacking	Distracts predators before escaping	Increase or decrease

Table 3.7 Predator-Avoidance Prominence Strategies for Business Firms

Strategies	Firm Actions
Camouflage	The firm adopts the appearance of other companies or its surroundings to avoid detection of its actions. In high-risk areas, entities like government agencies and NGOs may also try to blend in as local commercial organizations.
Nocturnality	The firm operates during times or seasons when it is less likely to be observed or threatened by competition.
Line-of-sight evasion	The firm conducts its activities in locations or markets where its competitors are unable to observe its actions.
Apparent death	The firm intentionally appears inactive or dormant to divert the interest of competitors (or regulators).
Deimatic or startle display	The firm employs displays of strength or aggressive marketing to intimidate or deter competitors.
Protean behavior	The firm adopts unexpected patterns of behavior to confuse or mislead competitors.
Distraction	The firm presents a false display of prominence to divert the attention of competitors from its true activities.

purpose of reducing visibility, with the primary altered attribute being color. Camouflage can be either static or dynamic. Subsequently, we will apply the principles gleaned from camouflage strategies to the corporate realm, where the observer of concern is a competitor.

Camouflage

In nature, camouflage is a widely recognized strategy for deception, often discussed in conjunction with crypsis and mimicry.[15] Early investigations into adaptive coloration for camouflage were carried out by Abbot Thayer[16] and Hugh Cott.[17] While color is the most frequently adapted characteristic for camouflage, sound and texture can also contribute to this strategy. The adaptation of animal coloration can be rooted in an entity's long-term habitat environment, and certain animals even exhibit season-dependent camouflage. For instance, species such as the Arctic fox, collared lemming, and long-tailed weasel change their coat color seasonally.[18] The rate at which camouflage changes varies among species, with faster adaptation rates indicating more versatile organisms capable of concealing themselves in a broader array of environments.[19] For animals unable to adjust their camouflage but compelled to relocate, the ability to return to a secure environment when threatened is essential. The effectiveness of a camouflage strategy can also hinge on whether the organism is stationary or in motion.[20] In the presence of a predator, such animals might opt to quickly move to a location where they can blend in with their surroundings.

The effectiveness of camouflage relies on the observer's capacity to discern disparities between the subject and its surroundings. For instance, certain forms of camouflage that rely on similarity in visible light might prove ineffective under UV light. Furthermore, plant coloration can undermine camouflage.[21] Motion camouflage represents a distinct concealment strategy where an organism moves at the same rate as its surrounding environment to evade detection.[22] In situations where organisms must conceal themselves within highly variable environments but lack the ability to dynamically adapt their appearance, they may resort to compromise camouflage. This entails selecting a coloration that offers a moderate level of protection in both environments, a strategy employed by species such as wall lizards, shore crabs, and moths. Alternatively, they may utilize disruptive markings to confound the visual processes of potential observers.[23]

Animals can employ camouflage techniques to safeguard their assets, such as nests, eggs, or offspring. For instance, lapwing eggs provide an excellent illustration of this protective camouflage. Camouflage and the strategy of dormancy are frequently combined, as dormant animals may utilize camouflage techniques to shield themselves by concealing in locations where they can seamlessly blend into their surroundings. Beyond color-based camouflage, patterns and textures are also employed. Camouflage serves as an effective predation strategy, enabling predators to seamlessly merge with their environment and approach prey without raising alarm. Moreover, camouflage also finds application in mating and various other organism–observer relationships.

In the modern world, camouflage techniques inspired by nature have found applications beyond the natural realm, where survival is of paramount importance. The military sector stands out as a primary beneficiary of this approach, incorporating camouflage into clothing and equipment to seamlessly blend with the environment. The concept of camouflage was initially closely examined during World War I, significantly influencing military strategies, and it continues to evolve. For example, the development of "invisibility cloaks" has the potential to revolutionize military approaches to camouflage, as these materials can bend light to conceal subjects from view.[24] However, camouflage's relevance extends beyond the military domain; it plays a critical role in the design of infrastructure systems to enhance survivability. In cybersecurity applications, camouflage is employed to safeguard critical infrastructure systems against potential cyberattacks.[25] By drawing inspiration from the camouflage techniques observed in nature, various artifacts, including military clothing and vehicles, have been developed or adapted to improve survival in hostile environments.

Forms of Camouflage

The term "camouflage" encompasses a diverse array of strategies employed to elude detection and recognition. Animals employ various techniques to achieve this, including obliterative shading, disruptive coloration, background matching, and shadow concealment. An essential form of camouflage is masquerade, wherein the entity evades recognition by altering its appearance to resemble an inconspicuous object, such as a leaf, stick, or bird dropping. Table 3.8 provides an overview of camouflage methods.[26]

While camouflage is typically employed as a means to reduce visibility, there are situations in which it can inadvertently lead to increased prominence for the camouflaged entity. In some of these scenarios, such increased visibility can be detrimental to the organism's survival. Objects that appear camouflaged in visible light may become remarkably conspicuous in infrared or ultraviolet light, as observed in certain scorpions. Instances where an entity is exceptionally attuned to its environment that can make sudden environmental changes over time result in heightened prominence, rendering the entity an easier target. However, in certain cases, camouflage can bring about increased prominence in a manner that benefits the entity. For instance, an organism might employ camouflage to blend with a secondary entity, or multiple organisms may amalgamate to create a single blended entity, giving the illusion of a single, large, and prominent presence.

Organizational Camouflage

Next, let's delve into how the insights gained from studying camouflage strategies can influence the adjustment of visibility within business environments, particularly in situations where companies confront potentially predatory actions. While our main focus is on the lessons derived from camouflage tactics in business settings, these fundamental principles also extend to other domains like geopolitical strategies. Many of these principles offer direct parallels that businesses can utilize to evade detection or recognition.

Table 3.8 Forms of Camouflage

Form	Description
Masquerade	The entity's body features resemble those of other objects in its local environment, causing predators to mistake it for unattractive entities.
Background matching	The entity's body exhibits colors or patterns that match its surroundings, allowing it to blend seamlessly with the background and evade easy detection by predators.
Disruptive coloration	The entity's body displays markings at its margins that disrupt the body's outline, making it challenging for predators to identify the prey.
Surface disruption	The entity's body features false edges that are more noticeable than its actual body outline, creating visual confusion for potential predators.
Countershading	The part of the entity's body surface nearest to a light source is darker in shade than the part farther away, providing a visual illusion that aids in concealment.
Distractive coloration	The entity's body carries small markings that divert a predator's attention away from the body's outline, helping to avoid detection.

The potential applications of camouflage encompass safeguarding business operations from predatory actions, where specific aspects of the company or its activities are concealed to evade the attention of potential threats. Moreover, some of these strategies can be adapted for various tactics aimed at avoiding predators and reducing prominence.

■ Firstly, camouflage can be employed in the context of protecting business ideas and projects. A fledgling idea is often vulnerable to being replicated or co-opted by competitors. Similarly, a new product may be at risk of being copied or imitated, leading to a loss of market share or competitive advantage. In such cases, camouflage can be utilized to conceal the true nature of the idea or product until it is ready to be released to the market. This may involve concealing information about the product or idea, using nondescript language in communications, or creating a false trail of information to deter potential competitors. In some cases, it may be beneficial and ethical to deliberately mislead competitors with false or misleading information to confuse them and prevent them from gaining an accurate understanding of the business idea or product. In many cases, new development products are held in sensitive compartmented information facilities (SCIFs). By employing camouflage techniques in this manner, businesses can safeguard their intellectual property and maintain their competitive edge in the market.

■ Secondly, camouflage can be beneficial to companies seeking to enter new geographical markets or market segments while avoiding detection or arousing suspicion from competitors or other stakeholders. For instance, if a company is planning to enter a new market or segment that is already dominated by established players, it may use camouflage to obscure its intentions and activities until it has established a foothold. This may involve creating a shell company, using a different brand name, or adopting a low-profile approach to marketing and advertising. By using camouflage in this manner, a company can effectively "fly under the radar" of its competitors, giving it time to build relationships with customers and stakeholders and establish a strong foothold in the market. Moreover, camouflage can also be useful for companies that are seeking to disrupt existing markets or segments, as it can help them avoid drawing unwanted attention or scrutiny from regulators, competitors, or other stakeholders. However, it is important to note that the use of camouflage in this manner should be carried out ethically and transparently, with due consideration for the impact on customers, employees, and other stakeholders.

■ Thirdly, camouflage can be a valuable tool for companies seeking to protect strategically important components of their business from competitors or even other stakeholders. For example, a company may use camouflage to hide a critical part of its operations, such as a key supplier or distribution network, from the prying eyes of its competitors. By using camouflage in this manner, a company can protect its competitive advantage and prevent its competitors from gaining access to important information or resources. Similarly, a company may also use camouflage to conceal unattractive or threatened components of its business, such as underperforming subsidiaries or products, from the scrutiny of customers or investors. This can help to avoid negative perceptions of the company and allow it to focus on its more profitable or strategic areas of operation. However, some of these actions may be perceived as unethical or illegal.

■ Fourthly, camouflage can be utilized by companies to protect vulnerable or inexperienced business units or employees from external threats. For instance, a company may use camouflage to shield new or weak business units from being targeted by competitors, allowing them to establish themselves and grow without undue interference. Similarly, a company may use camouflage to protect its employees from being targeted by malicious actors, such as hackers or corporate spies. In addition to using camouflage to protect business units and employees, companies may also use it to safeguard critical resources, sources, and supply routes. By hiding these assets, a company can reduce its vulnerability to attacks or disruptions, such as theft, sabotage, or natural disasters.

▪ Fifthly, camouflage can be used by companies to conceal the identity or actions of their leadership or critical employees from competitors or other external parties. For instance, a company may use camouflage to hide the movements or actions of its top executives during sensitive negotiations or strategic planning sessions. Similarly, a company may use camouflage to conceal the identity of critical employees who are involved in key projects or initiatives that are critical to the company's success. By using camouflage to hide the identity or actions of its leadership and key personnel, a company can protect itself from unwanted attention and interference and maintain a strategic advantage over its competitors.

▪ Sixthly, a company, especially a young startup, may find it helpful to use camouflage to conceal the identity of its investors or funding sources. This can be particularly important in cases where the company's investors or funders may not want to be publicly associated with the company, or where the company's competitors may try to leverage this information to their advantage. For example, a startup may use camouflage to hide the identity of its investors during fundraising rounds, to prevent competitors from poaching investors or launching preemptive attacks. Similarly, a company may use camouflage to conceal its funding sources to protect itself from unwanted attention or scrutiny from regulators or other external parties.

▪ Seventhly, camouflage can be employed by a company to carry out stealth marketing tactics aimed at customers without being detected. However, such actions may raise legitimate concerns about privacy and ethics. In response, customers may also employ camouflage techniques to protect themselves from predatory actions by companies. This can include the use of ad-blockers, VPNs, and other privacy-preserving technologies. As companies become more sophisticated in their marketing tactics, customers may also become savvier in their use of camouflage techniques to avoid unwanted marketing and preserve their privacy.

■ In some cases, a company may also choose to camouflage its operations during a business failure to avoid detection by creditors or investors, or to limit liability (such as an LLC). This could also involve restructuring or reorganizing the company in ways that make it difficult to track its assets or liabilities. Camouflage can also be used in the context of mergers and acquisitions to avoid drawing attention to sensitive negotiations or deals. In such cases, companies may choose to operate under a different name or use a shell company to maintain confidentiality and prevent leaks.[27]

Use of Specific Camouflage Strategies

In a business environment, strategies akin to camouflage techniques, including background matching, disruptive coloration, masquerades, and surface disruption, can effectively counter predatory actions by competitors. Here are some potential approaches that businesses can employ.

Background matching is a camouflage strategy that organizations can use to evade detection by seamlessly blending in with their surrounding environment. This approach creates the illusion that the entity is an integral part of the surroundings, potentially causing observers to mistake it for something else. In a business context, this can prove to be an effective method for companies to steer clear of attracting undesirable attention from competitors or other stakeholders. Businesses can employ the background matching strategy in several ways. For instance, a startup aiming to lower its visibility could opt to work from a shared workspace instead of leasing a high-profile office. Alternatively, some firms may opt to function as subcontractors for larger companies involved in public procurement, thereby limiting the government's access to comprehensive insights into their operations and preventing unwanted oversight. This way, the company can seamlessly integrate with other businesses in the same domain and avoid drawing undue attention.

Another method for businesses to utilize background matching is by adjusting to the local culture and business norms in foreign countries. In simpler scenarios, businesses may alter the standard branding, colors, and design of their signage or facilities to seamlessly integrate into a new environment. For example, think of chain restaurants like McDonald's seeking acceptance in highly scrutinized development zones. In more comprehensive cases, when a company is launching a new unit in a foreign country, it might opt for a brand name that resonates with the local culture, hire local employees, or adopt business practices prevalent in the local market. This approach can assist the company in blending seamlessly into the local business environment, avoiding standing out as a foreign entity. Furthermore, businesses can establish partnerships with government agencies or other companies as a means of assimilating into the environment. By presenting these projects as independent ventures, the company can steer clear of attracting unwanted attention and remain inconspicuous.

Ironically, diminishing the level of differentiation of a company or product can serve as a potential camouflage technique. Differentiation is traditionally regarded as a pivotal marketing element, frequently utilized by companies to set their products or services apart from those of their competitors. Nevertheless, this very differentiation can also make them conspicuous and subject to unwanted attention. By curbing differentiation, a company can seamlessly merge into its environment and avoid drawing undue notice. This strategy can be especially appropriate in highly competitive industries where standardization and conformity are the norm, and differentiation can result in increased scrutiny from competitors. On the other hand, some firms, such as private label manufacturers, maintain a steady revenue stream by forgoing differentiation at the product-brand level and competing primarily on cost and production quality.[28]

Masquerade

Masquerading is a camouflage strategy that organizations can effectively employ to appear as something other than their true identity. This tactic involves portraying themselves as a company in a different business, one less likely to draw unwanted attention from competitors or other stakeholders. For instance, a company operating in a fiercely competitive growth industry might opt to masquerade as a business in a different sector that is less prone to hostile scrutiny. This approach allows the company to avoid attracting unwarranted attention from rivals and remain discreet. Moreover, aside from assuming a different industry facade, businesses can also use masquerading to present themselves as a different type of company within their own sector. For example, a B2B company may choose to present itself as a consumer-oriented enterprise to deter competition from other B2B firms. Another method, at times employed unethically or illegally, involves companies creating false identities or personas. This can be particularly effective in online settings, where companies can establish counterfeit profiles or accounts to collect information or manipulate public opinion.

Disruption

Disruption is another effective camouflage strategy that companies can employ to reduce recognition and avoid unwanted attention from competitors or other stakeholders. This strategy involves disassembling the overall structure of the company or its actions so that different parts of the entity do not appear related to each other. In nature, disruptive coloration, surface disruption, and countershading serve as examples of this strategy. In a business context, companies can achieve disruption through a variety of methods. For instance, a large firm might break itself into smaller units to decrease its overall visibility and avoid attracting unwanted attention. Similarly, a large retail chain might launch a new company under a different name in a new country to prevent associations with the parent company. Some firms may blend masquerading with a disruption strategy to operate as both a consulting firm and a product development firm. This can provide them with strong influence over customer requirement development and decision-making for products sold by their other segments. In public procurement, this has been recognized as a conflict of interest, leading to the requirement for many firms to formally separate the two business units to prevent these conflicts from occurring. Another way that businesses can employ disruption is by intentionally mixing up, muddling, or breaking up their actions to avoid detection. For instance, a company may implement price increases, but then combine them with price decreases or actions such as shrinkflation to prevent customers from noticing the changes.

Distraction

Distraction is a powerful camouflage strategy that businesses can employ to decrease attention toward a focal target by increasing the prominence of another target. This strategy is particularly useful when a company wants to divert attention away from a critical action or aspect of the business. One way to achieve distraction is through the use of decoy actions. These actions are designed to shift the attention of the observer away from a problematic or offensive business action toward something more attractive and innocuous. For example, a company might launch a marketing campaign or public relations event that captures the public's attention, thereby diverting attention from any negative news or focus on the company. Another example of distractive camouflage is outsourcing services to a different provider, especially those that involve direct engagement with a predatory entity. By doing so, the company can divert attention away from its main operations and avoid attracting unwanted attention from competitors or other stakeholders. It is important to note that the above strategies can also have negative consequences if they are not executed properly. If the strategies are too obvious or poorly executed, they can actually draw more attention to the business and make it more vulnerable to predatory strategies.

Nocturnality and Line-of-Sight Evasion

Nocturnality is a strategic approach in which a predator or prey increases its activity during the night when the observer is less attentive or incapable of retaliating. This approach allows the predator to expend less energy and face less resistance from the prey, making it a desirable strategy in many situations. In the organizational context, nocturnality can be utilized as a competitive strategy by companies. They can choose to provide services at times, seasons, or dates when their competitors are relatively inactive, such as during holidays or outside regular business hours. By doing so, the company can potentially avoid detection and gain an advantage over its competitors.

Similarly, nocturnality can also serve as an effective strategy used by prey to acquire resources without fear of being attacked. For instance, a startup that is concerned about attracting hostile attention from its competitors can opt to work during times, days, or even seasons when its competitors are less active, providing them with an opportunity to acquire resources without facing any threats. Another related strategy is line-of-sight evasion, where the entity operates in locations outside the predator's line of sight. This approach can be valuable for both predators and prey, allowing them to avoid detection and surprise their targets. Examples of this can be found in organizations such as law enforcement and the military. However, firms can also employ this method, for instance, by choosing to use off-peak logistics to avoid detection when delivering products to the market and reduce costs, leading to a competitive edge.

Apparent Death

Apparent death, also known as thanatosis, is a survival strategy employed by some organisms to avoid predation. This strategy entails the organism feigning death, rendering itself unattractive to potential predators.

Additionally, the organism becomes immobile, reducing the likelihood of detection by predators. Companies facing hostile competitors seeking to eliminate them can also employ this strategy. By feigning death, a company can curtail activities, such as marketing communications, that would typically be noticed by external observers. This can create the perception of decline, making the company less appealing to potential competitors who might assume it is on the brink of failure. Feigning death proves effective as a survival strategy for organisms or entities that are close to death or injured. By appearing lifeless or inactive, the organism or entity can minimize the predator's interest, affording it the time and space needed for recovery from its injuries, ultimately aiding in recuperation and strength restoration.

In the business context, a company facing poor performance due to competitive actions, such as a major player reducing prices to eliminate competitors, might benefit from adopting a "pretend to be dead" strategy. By scaling down its marketing activities and presenting an image of decline, the competitor may ease its aggressive actions, allowing the company to seize the opportunity to recover and regain its competitive position. Recently, many online direct-to-consumer firms have shifted to a "Click and Mortar" model. Some companies, which seemed to face challenges in the highly competitive online market, have reemerged with brick-and-mortar options that have gained popularity in the post-COVID-19 pandemic world. In this context, physical shopping represents a return to normalcy for consumers.

Deimatic Behavior

Deimatic behavior is a defensive strategy used by prey to startle or frighten a predator. It involves enhancing the prominence of the prey to create a sudden and surprising change that can intimidate the predator. This behavior is often achieved through sudden changes in attributes such as color, size, or sound. The effectiveness of deimatic behavior depends on the ability to surprise the predator and provoke a sudden response. While deimatic behavior is typically employed as a predator-avoidance strategy, it can also be utilized by predators against their prey. Businesses can employ sudden actions, such as reducing prices or expanding their marketing reach, to intimidate their competitors and gain a competitive advantage. For businesses, employing deimatic behavior can be an effective way to respond to predatory advances by competitors. By implementing abrupt changes in their business strategy, such as price reductions or increased marketing reach, they can make themselves less attractive targets for predatory companies. This can prompt the predatory company to reevaluate the resources or efforts required to over-come the prey, leading to their withdrawal from further attacks.

Aposematism

Aposematism or aposematic coloration is a defensive strategy used by prey to warn potential predators of their toxicity or danger. It involves the use of bright colors or patterns to signal that the animal is not a suitable prey item. Unlike deimatic behavior, aposematism does not entail dynamic changes in behavior. It remains unclear why aposematic coloration is effective as an anti-predator strategy, but one explanation is that unusual characteristics such as bright colors are associated with unknown risk-reward trade-offs. An animal with unusual characteristics may be linked to a unique ability to pro-tect itself. In a business setting, aposematism can be applied by employing highly differentiated attributes that introduce uncertainty about the entity's capacity to retaliate against potential predators.

Aposematism in a business context can be seen as warning signs aimed at informing competitors about the risks associated with adversarial engage-ment. By introducing uncertainty regarding the risk-reward trade-off of interacting with a specific business, it can discourage predatory behavior and prevent detrimental outcomes for both parties. The success of such a strategy hinges on the credibility of the warning signs. Unusual character-istics exhibited by the target may be linked to atypical risks to be faced, leading to the perception that engaging with such a business could result in unexpected and undesirable consequences. The effectiveness of apo-sematism stems from the uniqueness of the attributes the entity presents, making it challenging for competitors to estimate the potential risks and rewards of engagement. Aposematic features might be connected to a potent ability to retaliate against attacks, further discouraging predatory behavior. Organizations may opt to employ strategies like aligning with key customers or strong complementary partners to signal greater risk to potential competi-tors. If competitors perceive that the strategic partnerships of a focal firm or organization create unreasonable costs or barriers to entry in a market, they may refrain from challenging the focal entity.

Protean Behavior and Distraction

Protean behavior is a survival strategy adopted by organisms to escape predators. It entails erratic and unpredictable movements that confuse the predator, making it difficult for them to track the prey's path. Prey may utilize a variety of motions, such as zig-zags, spins, loops, or bounces, which the predator finds challenging to follow.[29] In a business context, protean behavior can be employed as a strategy by a firm to outmaneuver its competitors.

Competitors often make assumptions based on a firm's past actions and anticipate its future moves accordingly. However, a protean firm behaves unpredictably, making it difficult for competitors to predict its next move. A firm may even take unexpected actions that appear contrary to its perceived self-interest to mislead its competitors. Protean behavior is effective when the prey or firm is much more agile and nimble than the predator or competitor. A predator can also employ protean behavior to catch its prey. Instead of a direct attack, the predator may use an indirect route to surprise the prey, and these behaviors may also be observed in pack hunting. This strategy can lull the prey into complacency, making it easier for the predator to catch it. Another related strategy is distraction, where the prey tries to divert the predator's attention to increase its chances of survival. Distraction can also be utilized by entities, such as birds, to protect themselves. For instance, a bird may pretend to be an easy target to divert the predator's focus away from its nest or eggs.

Schooling, Hiding, and Refuging

Schooling is a behavior that organisms adopt as an anti-predator strategy, improving their chances of survival by joining a group such as a school or a herd. The collective nature of these groups can offer several advantages that enhance the efficiency and resilience of the individual organism. The act of schooling can have a dual effect on the prominence of an organism. On the one hand, it can reduce the prominence of smaller individuals, making them harder to locate within the group, which can deter potential predators. A predator chasing prey would find it challenging to track down a specific individual within a school. On the other hand, schooling can increase the visibility and prominence of the group as a whole, making it appear as a single large entity, which can dissuade predators from attacking the collective.

Joining a collective, such as a school, requires an organism to be of a similar size and appearance to others within the group. A larger entity may not find it advantageous to join a school since it would be required to share a larger part of its resources and may stand out even more within the collective, making it an easy target. Similarly, a much smaller entity may struggle to survive, as it may be relatively ignored in collective actions. Conversely, a much smaller entity may also be considered an easy target for a predator due to its contrast with other members. In addition to offering protection against predators, joining a school can provide other benefits. Schools can enhance the efficiency of an organism's movements, as well as provide opportunities for social learning and information sharing. Moreover, being part of a collective can offer a sense of safety and security, reducing stress levels and improving an organism's overall well-being.

A small business entity can often protect itself and access resources by joining a larger collective, just as animals do in the wild by forming schools or herds. By uniting with others, businesses can benefit from economies of scale, shared resources, and increased bargaining power with suppliers and customers. This can help level the playing field against larger competitors and provide a greater chance of survival. Similarly, predators such as sharks and wolves benefit from hunting in groups, where they can coordinate their actions and take down prey more efficiently. This strategy is also used by businesses that form strategic partnerships or alliances, where they can share resources, knowledge, and expertise to achieve common goals. An example is that of oil cartels and buyer collectives.[30]

Hiding is another strategy that both prey and businesses can use to protect themselves. A small prey may hide behind a larger animal that its predator may be unwilling to threaten. This can deter the predator from attacking the smaller prey, as any attack may be perceived as an attack against the larger animal, which may retaliate to the predator's disadvantage. Similarly, businesses may choose to position themselves near larger companies to gain access to resources and support. This can help smaller businesses thrive and survive by leveraging the reputation and resources of the larger entity. Businesses may also employ covert operations to protect themselves from competition or gain an advantage, and they may themselves be used as part of such operations organized by intelligence agencies.[31]

A shell business may serve as a cover for a larger operation, or it may maintain a low profile by operating in a niche market or disguising itself as a different type of business altogether. In nature, we can observe how smaller male European tree frogs, *Hyla arborea*, will hide close to attractive males to gain access to females.[32] This strategy allows them to capitalize on the larger male's attractiveness and protect themselves from predators while still achieving their reproductive goals. Similarly, businesses may form strategic partnerships with larger, more established companies to gain access to new customers, markets, or technologies. Firms may also choose to employ hiding for nefarious purposes, such as industrial espionage.

Predator–Prey Prominence Strategies Applied to Mates and Customers

Interestingly, the strategies used by predators and prey to protect themselves can also be applied in the context of mates, and analogically, competitors and customers of organizations (Table 3.9). For instance, predators or prey may choose to act during times when their targets are less likely to be effective, such as at night or when visibility is low. Similarly, businesses may choose to move their undesirable activities to locations or times when customers are less likely to observe them to avoid negative attention. This could involve outsourcing manufacturing to cheaper locations overseas or conducting sensitive operations during off-peak hours.

Conversely, some of these strategies can also be used to attract attention. For example, the strategy of apparent death can be used to increase attention from predators, prey, or mates. A predator may let its guard down if it believes its prey is already dead, while an animal may provide attention or

Table 3.9 Prominence Strategies for Customers and Competitors

Target Observer(s)	Customers	Competitors
Camouflage	Decrease prominence during beta testing. Decrease attention from unattractive customers.	Decrease attention to strategic new products.
Nocturnality and line-of-sight evasion	Decrease attention to some activities that will be deemed unattractive by moving them to a time or location where the customer is inactive.	Decrease attention to some activities that will be deemed threatening to competitors by moving them to a time when the customer is inactive.
Apparent death	Decrease attention to unattractive actions or attractions from an unattractive customer by appearing to be inoperative.	Decrease attention to competitive actions by pretending to be inactive or dead.
Startle display	Increase attention from customers before a new product launch.	Increase attention to strategic investment to dissuade similar moves from the competition.

resources if it believes its mate is in danger. Similarly, businesses may sometimes feign weakness or the threat of closure to elicit sympathy and support from customers. In such cases, apparent death is followed by the entity's return to life, which can surprise, delight, or anger the observer. Moreover, businesses may also modify their line of sight to increase their visibility to potential customers. This can involve using targeted advertising or marketing strategies that align with the interests and preferences of specific customer groups or even newsjacking (where a firm attaches itself to a trending topic). For instance, a company may use social media platforms to promote its products or services to a younger demographic, while using more traditional advertising channels to reach older consumers.

Observations on Courtship Rituals and Implications for Marketing Actions

The actions of an entity toward a target observer, who is a mate, often involve actions intended to increase prominence. Courtship rituals are a prime example of actions that increase prominence, and they include displays of rich colors, patterned movements, and vocalizations. These displays are competitive in nature, with multiple potential partners displaying similar actions to draw the attention of a desired mate. Another strategy observed in courtship is the generation of a new artifact, such as a nest designed to attract attention. In animals, courtships are typically one-sided displays, with males engaging in such rituals to attract the attention of a female. Some animals engage in multi-modal signaling, where both visual and auditory signaling are employed. Certain organisms, such as crested auklets, engage in mutual courtship displays.

However, there are certain risks associated with prominent courtship displays. They can be resource-intensive, consuming energy and time, which can lead to reduced efficiency and resilience. Increased prominence is also intended to dissuade or frighten other potential mates of the target observer, as seen in the peacock's display.[33] Additionally, increased prominence can draw the attention of predators or frighten away potential prey. In some cases, it may be advantageous to decrease one's prominence to a potential mate. For example, if a mate is uninterested or already in a relationship, an individual may not want to draw unnecessary attention to themselves. In such cases, the individual may modify their behavior or actions to be less noticeable.

Similar prominence strategies can also be observed in the business world, where companies may not want to draw attention to certain actions or behaviors that may be unattractive to customers. They may also want to draw attention away from certain market segments to enable them to collaborate with other firms and encourage better co-creation/collaboration. Teaming arrangements with complementary firms tend to be much more open than teaming arrangements with firms that could be future competitors. We often observe this in the defense industry, where some large entities are forced to team with similarly sized firms that specialize in specific technologies to be integrated into the focal firm's solution. They are compelled to team but tend to do so at only the minimum level needed to complete the integration. Meanwhile, the same focal firm may be much more collaborative and create much more value with a teaming firm that has no business in the focal firm's primary market.

The observations made about mate-seeking behaviors in the natural world have interesting parallels with the strategies employed by business firms in attracting customers. In the case of business firms, the actions taken toward potential customers are usually one-sided displays, similar to the courtship rituals observed in nature. These displays typically involve changes or enhancements to the attributes of the firm that are intended to be attractive to the target observer (customer). Examples of such changes may include marketing promotions, price adjustments, new product introductions, and changes in physical locations. To maximize the effectiveness of their mate-seeking actions, business firms often employ multi-modal prominence displays. For example, a firm may combine advertising with price promotions to increase its attractiveness to potential customers. Such displays are intended to increase the likelihood that the target observer will take notice of the firm and its offerings.

Prominence Attributes, Emotions, and Business Actions

We can observe that both attraction and repulsion can be induced in low and high-prominence states. In Table 3.10, we have listed how distinctive static attributes or changes to attributes can elicit emotions like curiosity,

Table 3.10 Prominence Linked Emotions

Emotion	Low Prominence	High Prominence
Attraction	Curiosity	Dazzle
Repulsion	Dread	Fear

Table 3.11   Attributes and Prominence Mechanisms

Attribute	Static	Dynamic
Color	Distinctive color as a source of attraction or repulsion	Distinctive color variations as a source of attraction or repulsion
Size/shape	Unusual shape as a source of attraction or repulsion	Unusual changes in shape as a source of attraction or repulsion
Sound	Distinctive sound as a source of attraction or repulsion	Distinctive changes in sound as a source of attraction or repulsion
Motion	Distinctive location as a source of attraction or repulsion	Distinctive motion as a source of attraction or repulsion

dread, dazzle, or fear. Typically, in the context of animals, these attributes include color, shape/size, sound or motion (Table 3.11).

In the case of dread-inducing actions, animals often employ a strategy of remaining still and blending into their environment to avoid detection. For example, an alligator lying quietly in a pond can induce a feeling of dread in potential prey or predators due to the fear of the unknown. This moderate emotion of repulsion is derived from the uncertainty of what the hidden entity might do.

On the other hand, fear-inducing actions involve high-prominence mechanisms that frighten the target observer. This can be achieved through sudden and startling behaviors, such as a snake striking at its prey suddenly or a tiger leaping from a bush to chase down its prey. In attraction strategies, entities use low-prominence mechanisms to generate curiosity and interest from the observer. This can be achieved using subtle and understated displays that pique the interest of the observer by withholding information. For example, an animal may hide itself in the foliage, revealing itself partially, enticing observers to search for it. Alternatively, entities can use high-prominence mechanisms to induce attraction through dazzle displays, commonly seen in mating displays. These displays can include vibrant colors, intricate patterns, and elaborate dances or movements that capture the attention of potential mates. These emotions are linked to prominence-inducing mechanisms employed by animals, and similar strategies can be observed in organizational contexts. For instance, a business may utilize subtle marketing tactics to spark curiosity and interest in a new product, or it may employ elaborate and attention-grabbing promotional displays to dazzle potential customers.

In the animal kingdom, color is an important visual element that signifies differentiation and can induce both attraction and repulsion. Similarly, in the business world, color plays a crucial role in visual brand identity, representing the organization's personality, values, and messaging. A vibrant and distinctive color scheme can attract customers and set the brand apart from competitors. However, excessive differentiation in color could draw unwanted attention from competitors and make the company more vulnerable.

Sound is another critical element of animal communication, representing their voice and unique form of expression. It can serve to communicate with potential mates or even potential predators. The Tiger Moth uses acoustic mimicry to warn bats of their noxiousness. In the same way, the form of communication for businesses, such as marketing messages, customer service, and investor relations, represents their voice and unique way of expressing themselves. The tone, language, and style of communication can attract or repulse customers and investors. Size and location are also important factors that influence the prominence of animals in their environment. In the same way, size and location play a critical role in the physical presence of businesses. Large and visible headquarters, factories, and stores can attract customers and investors, while also signaling the company's dominance in the industry. However, too much visibility can also attract unwanted attention from competitors or regulators, and strategic location changes can induce fear and uncertainty.

Motion is another attribute that animals use to signal their presence and dominance in their environment. Businesses also use motion to signal their actions and changes in strategy, such as opening new stores, expanding into new markets, or rebranding. These actions can attract or repulse customers and investors, depending on the perceived impact and risk. Thus, the analogies between animal behavior and business strategy suggest that distinctiveness can induce both attraction and repulsion, and that changes in distinctiveness can also generate similar emotions.

Prominence Balancing and Market Strategies

In animal behavior, there are often important trade-offs related to prominence, where the animal must balance its energies between actions aimed at predator avoidance, resource consumption, and resource acquisition. These trade-offs highlight the importance of adapting to changing environmental conditions and the need to redirect energy to different activities as circumstances dictate. For example, let's consider the case of a squirrel gathering and storing nuts. In the absence of a predator, the squirrel can focus on balancing immediate consumption with the storage of resources for future use. However, in the presence of a predator, the energy requirements for the squirrel increase and less time is available for resource acquisition. As a result, the squirrel may need to focus more on predator avoidance, which may mean that it has to sacrifice some of its resource-gathering activities. The squirrel may also expend high levels of energy in its effort to evade detection by a predator.

This trade-off between predator avoidance and resource acquisition is also observed in other animals. For example, some animals may engage in less conspicuous foraging behavior when predators are present, while others may increase their vigilance and decrease their feeding time. These behaviors illustrate how animals can balance the competing demands of predator avoidance and resource acquisition.

In the business world, similar trade-offs are also observed. Firms must balance their energies between actions aimed at attracting customers and actions aimed at avoiding competitors. In a competitive market, a firm may need to redirect its resources to focus more on competitor analysis and strategy development. Conversely, in a less competitive market, a firm may be able to focus more on attracting customers through advertising and promotional activities. Thus, understanding trade-offs related to prominence can help firms develop effective strategies to adapt to changing market conditions.

When animals are balancing the need to mate and the need to avoid predators, they often also face difficult prominence-related trade-offs. These trade-offs can also be observed in the business world. For example, a company that wants to attract customers may inadvertently attract competitors as well. Conversely, a company that is too focused on avoiding competitors may miss out on opportunities to attract new customers. However, in the absence of predatory competitors or mating pressures, a company can focus on achieving a balance between efficiency and resilience, without being overly concerned about prominence. This can be achieved by investing in resource exploration and consumption. A company can explore new markets and invest in research and development without worrying too much about competitors.

In fact, in the absence of predators, a company can increase its prominence without worrying about competitive threats. This can be achieved by increasing its presence in the marketplace and becoming a more recognizable brand. The increase in prominence that comes with feeding and foraging is not inimical to mating success, which generally benefits from increased prominence. Companies that do not have to deal with predatory competitors find it much easier to balance other objectives. They can focus on their core business and invest in long-term growth strategies without worrying about short-term competitive threats. This allows them to make more strategic decisions and invest in the future, rather than being forced to constantly react to competitive pressures.

The ultimate success of an entity's efforts to modify its prominence depends on both the capabilities of the task observer and the environmental characteristics of its surroundings. For instance, in the case of fish, strategies like hiding or seeking refuge are more effective in certain types of complex marine environments, such as kelp forests and coral reefs, as opposed to the deep ocean. Within a specific class of task observers, an entity may employ prominence strategies that vary depending on situational factors like the size of a predator. When faced with predators of different sizes, an organism may exhibit startle behavior to increase its prominence or seek refuge to reduce it. Similarly, when approaching prey, an entity may utilize loud sounds to intimidate (high prominence) or employ camouflage to stealthily approach (low prominence).

The above patterns can also be observed in the context of business markets. Each business functions as a survival-oriented entity, and its survival hinges on the level of prominence it presents to various observers, such as competitors, customers, investors, partners, and regulators. The desired direction of prominence may also differ based on the specific observer. For example, in the case of a technology startup, survival can depend on the startup's ability to effectively manipulate its prominence. Just as a fish's survival depends on its prominence strategies in different marine settings, a startup's success is also affected by its ability to adjust its visibility based on its operating landscape, investor whims, customer demands, competitor actions, and regulatory oversight. Depending on the situation, the startup may need to switch between high-profile tactics to startle competitors and attract customer attention or low-key strategies to evade competitive threats.

Prominence Adaptability Lessons from the Cephalopods

The ability to adapt an entity's prominence is beneficial in both natural and business environments. Prominence adaptability, or P-adaptability, refers to an entity's capacity to modify the degree and direction of its prominence to enhance its survivability when confronted with multiple target observers and changing conditions in complex environments. In a natural setting, an organism derives advantages from P-adaptability concerning both interspecific entities, such as mates or resource rivals, and intraspecific entities, like predators, prey, parasites, and hosts. Similarly, a P-adaptable business organization would be capable of swiftly and flexibly adjusting its prominence in relation to other interspecific observers, such as competitors and business partners, as well as intraspecific entities, such as customers and investors. It's worth noting that P-adaptability is not equally valuable for every organism. For instance, a creature like the blue whale does not derive significant benefits from P-adaptability due to its extreme size, easy access to food (krill), and lack of natural predators. An example of a business firm that might derive limited benefits from P-adaptability is a government-protected monopoly or a regional utility company. In the following sections, our goal is to comprehensively explore P-adaptability and derive valuable insights by studying cephalopods, such as octopuses, cuttlefish, and squids, renowned for their mastery of prominence adaptation in the natural world.[34]

P-Adaptability and Environmental Complexity

The optimal level of P-adaptability is dependent on the complexity of the environment, which is determined by both observer and environmental characteristics. For instance, in a marine environment, the appropriate level of P-adaptability for a sea creature depends on factors such as the type and number of observer species and the physical characteristics of the sea environment, such as the texture and color of the landscape, variability in water temperature, and velocity of currents. In a typical business setting, the ideal level of P-adaptability for a business firm is determined by the number and type of customers, competitors, and partners, as well as the variability in PESTLE (Political, Economic, Social, Technological, Legal, and Environmental) factors.

P-adaptability can be expressed both concurrently and dynamically. An organism living in a complex and dynamic environment can enhance its survivability by (1) concurrently adapting multiple prominence strategies and (2) dynamically changing between different high- and low-prominence strategies based on emerging situational factors in the environment.

Concurrent P-adaptability is significant when observers of different types are present at the same time and can be realized in different ways: (1) multi-interpretation, (2) multi-channel, and (3) multi-location. In multi-interpretation concurrency, a prominence-related action is interpreted differently by different observers. For example, a bright color (aposematic) display may be attractive to a mate and startle a predator. In multi-channel concurrency, one form of communication may be used to attract, while another may be used to avoid. For instance, an animal might use a visual display to threaten a predator while using auditory signals to call a parent for help. In multi-location concurrency, one part of a signal or display may be designed to generate one form of prominence (attract), while the rest is used to create a different one (signal avoidance). In dynamic P-adaptability, the entity modifies its prominence over time based on changes in observers, surrounding conditions, or feedback on a previous strategy. For instance, an animal may switch to a new prominence strategy if a previous approach fails.

Even though P-adaptability is valuable to organisms, modifying their prominence can be costly, requiring the ability to detect changes and make appropriate modifications to attributes such as color and structure. Businesses operating in complex and dynamic environments face similar challenges to those in natural environments, as they must develop systems to sense changing conditions and modify prominence strategies for individual observers like customers over time, as well as demonstrate different levels of prominence among various observers such as customers, competitors, and investors. Thus, businesses can look to nature for guidance on when and how P-adaptability can be suitably employed.

In nature, we find several examples of highly P-adaptable organisms, such as chameleons, the gray tree frog, the puffer fish, and the golden tortoise beetle. However, one group of marine animals stands apart for their sheer range of prominence modification techniques and P-adaptability – the cephalopods. Some of the abilities related to prominence are so remarkable and unique among living organisms that cephalopods, sometimes controversially, have been referred to as "alien" or "other-worldly" life forms.[35]

Cephalopods: Chameleons of the Seas

Cephalopods are the largest and most intelligent of marine invertebrates, deriving their name from the Greek words for "head" and "foot." They belong to the mollusk family and consist of four types: squids, cuttlefish, octopus, and nautilus. With over 750 identified species, they exhibit a high degree of diversity in size, ranging from tiny squids like Idiosepius to colossal squids that can exceed 10 meters in length. Cephalopods are categorized into two clades, Nautiloidea and Coleoidea, with the latter further subdivided into Decapodiformes and Octopodiformes. These remarkable creatures have a long history, with depictions on Minoan Crete pottery dating back to 1650 BC. Aristotle also described their behavior in his work, *History of Animals*, around 350 BC. They have left their mark on popular culture, with the mythical Kraken from Norse myths being one of the most famous examples. Cephalopods have served as inspiration for innovative products, including adaptive clothing and soft robotic arms modeled after the flexible appendages of the octopus.

In this section, our goal is to summarize prominence-related adaptations observed in cephalopods and identify principles that could potentially assist organizations in managing prominence. A comprehensive discussion of the behavior of cephalopods and their prominence strategies can be found in Hanlon and Messenger's work on "Cephalopod Behavior."[36] The Cephalopod Page, maintained by Dr. James B. Wood, provides numerous research and learning resources related to cephalopod species.[37]

Cephalopods are an incredibly adaptable species and possess a wide range of biological features that allow them to modify their prominence. While they are often referred to as the "chameleons of the sea," their camouflage abilities go beyond those of the famed color-changing reptile species.[38] An examination of these abilities can provide valuable insight into P-adaptability in other environments, including business markets. It is important to note, however, that not all species of cephalopods possess the same prominence-adaptation mechanisms. These mechanisms are limited to a smaller subset of the diverse species of cephalopods. While no single cephalopod species possesses a comprehensive set of the prominence mechanisms observed across various species, their overall P-adaptability offers valuable lessons for businesses.

One important lesson for businesses drawn from observing cephalopods is that perfect P-adaptability is rarely desirable. Instead, businesses should focus on understanding the competency required to adapt prominence based on the expected variations in internal and surrounding conditions and the nature of task observers. By understanding these factors, businesses can better adapt to changing circumstances and remain successful in their respective markets. Many firms and governments have discovered, post-COVID-19 pandemic, that making predictions to inform strategy is costly and likely impossibly complex due to the uncertainty of the future. Many have shifted toward strategic foresight and planning for a range of low-probability, high-cost scenarios. Strategic networks and mutual aid planning have become central P-adaptability concerns for these organizations to prevent failure during catastrophic events.

Prominence Adaptations in Cephalopods

Cephalopods are well known for their remarkable, almost mythical, ability to adapt their color and texture. They have a range of adaptation mechanisms, including camouflage, mimicry, and bioluminescence, which set them apart from other organisms. For example, the mimic octopus is a master of mimicry, with the ability to mimic a large number of creatures, such as flounders, while on the move. As formidable predators themselves, cephalopods also employ various prominence techniques, such as squirting ink for distraction, which can be a life-saving strategy. The firefly squid is another fascinating example, using bioluminescence for mating, predation, and evading predators. By controlling the chromatophores, color-changing cells under the surface of the skin, they can adapt their light based on internal and external conditions and evade predators by employing counter-illumination. The male Caribbean reef squid, *Sepioteuthis sepioidea*, uses color patterns generated by controlling the chromatophores, which are color-changing cells under the surface of the skin, to communicate as part of courtship rituals. Cuttlefish also use color to hypnotize their prey, increasing their prominence, and employ tactical deception by displaying different prominence mechanisms to different classes of observers. Deep-sea gigantism is another feature observed in cephalopods, serving as both an efficiency improvement mechanism and a prominence modification strategy. These intelligent predators also employ multiple strategies found in vertebrates, including ambushing, luring, stalking, pursuit, speculative hunting, and hunting in disguise.

It is evident that cephalopods are highly adaptable in their natural environments, utilizing various mechanisms to achieve prominence. While these mechanisms differ across species, they provide a comprehensive set of lessons on adaptability. The goal is to summarize these lessons and apply them to the business domain. Specifically, there are three themes of interest in studying cephalopod adaptations and applying them to business entities. Firstly, what are the structural aspects of cephalopod biology that allow them to be adaptable, and can this knowledge inform the design of business organizations? Secondly, what are the different prominence modifications employed by cephalopods, and are there equivalents in the business domain? And thirdly, how do cephalopods react to different task observers, and how can this be analogically useful in understanding a business's reaction to relevant observer entities? By exploring these themes and drawing parallels between the natural world and the business world, we can gain insights into effective strategies for business organizations to adapt and thrive in dynamic and ever-changing environments.

Business Lessons from Cephalopods

As part of our study, we looked at various cephalopod species to identify the different prominence adaptations they employ and how they utilize them. Through our analysis, we were able to identify several key dimensions on which these adaptations differ, providing valuable insights into the diversity of P-adaptability mechanisms employed by cephalopods. Drawing on these observations, we have compiled Table 3.12 summarizing some of the most important lessons we have learned about P-adaptability in cephalopods and how they may be applied to help businesses achieve greater prominence adaptability. These insights highlight the importance of understanding the specific competencies required to adapt to different internal and external conditions and the need for businesses to adopt a flexible approach tailored to the specific nature of their environment and the tasks they perform.

Sensing System

Sensory mechanisms are vital for achieving P-adaptability, and both centralized and distributed sensing mechanisms offer unique advantages. Cephalopods are renowned for their well-developed sensory systems, featuring both centralized and distributed components. For instance, cephalopods possess highly developed camera-like eyes akin to humans, as well as the ability to detect light using their multiple arms. They can also reflexively modify their skin color and pattern with light-activated, eye-independent chromatophores. Businesses can benefit from both global, centralized monitoring and local, distributed sensing. Global monitoring assists in anticipating impending changes and adapting accordingly, while local monitoring is valuable for tracking subtle shifts and exploring various locations. This may encompass the examination of diverse local environments and monitoring various target observers, such as customers, partners, and competitors.

Units within a business engaged in local scanning may be granted local autonomy to take actions that influence local prominence. Scanning within business environments can inform current and future strategies, including the use of scenario planning within organizations. Prominent companies like

Table 3.12 Prominence Adaptability in Cephalopods and Business Implications

Cephalopod Feature	*Implication for Business P-Adaptability*
Sensing system	Businesses benefit from both centralized and distributed information-gathering systems. Centralized systems allow for longer-term global scanning, while distributed systems support short-term local planning. Firms must be able to sense what is happening within a business with robust business intelligence as well as what is happening in the external environment with robust market intelligence.
Attribute adaptation	Businesses can benefit by having attributes that are both modular and adaptive, including form, structure, and communication.
Flexible form	Businesses can improve survivability by being able to modify their physical structures, such as breaking up larger units into smaller interconnected units or moving units closer together.
Life-cycle changes	Businesses often need to modify prominence strategies over their lifetime, adapting them to different task observers, including competitors, customers, and investors.
Differential prominence	Businesses need to be able to demonstrate different levels of prominence toward various observers simultaneously. This allows businesses to tailor their approach to individual customers, such as through individualized marketing.
Distraction	In highly competitive environments, businesses can employ distraction as a potent method to gain prominence. This involves strategic capture management techniques, where companies deliberately seek opportunities in unexpected areas or abstain from competing in anticipated domains to divert attention.
Passive crypsis	Businesses can gain advantages by adopting a passive crypsis state, which allows them to lower their visibility in challenging environments even in the absence of immediate threats. This diminishes the necessity for continuous vigilance in monitoring the surroundings for potential risks.

Flex Ltd have integrated a robust internal business intelligence dataset with extensive real-time market data to create a synthesized network of supply chain decision signals for their corporate leaders.[39] Their Pulse center has been showcased in numerous articles, videos, and books as an exemplar of sensory intelligence in the business world.

Similar to the octopus, local scanning can aid in taking less risky, reflexive actions with minimal input, while global scanning is more effective for riskier, deliberative actions involving multiple inputs. Sensory mechanisms can detect subtle changes over a wide area. Well-developed sensing mechanisms are pivotal for achieving P-adaptability, and cephalopods are renowned for their vision, featuring eyes astonishingly similar in design to humans. Cuttlefish eyes can distinguish variations in the polarization of light. Large eyes in giant cephalopods may enable them to detect substantial predators, like the sperm whale, from a distance and take precautionary measures without getting too close to the whale's sonar system. Cephalopods can spot prey through sight, scent, and distant touch. They also possess distributed light-sensing systems, and their statocysts, situated below the brain, offer information about gravity and acceleration while detecting infrasound. Cephalopods also employ vigilance strategies to aid in their environmental adaptation. The crucial lesson for businesses is that a well-developed sensing mechanism is indispensable for P-adaptability. Businesses should invest in both centralized and distributed sensing mechanisms to monitor both the internal and external environment and respond with reflexive and deliberative actions accordingly.

Attribute Adaptation

Cephalopods benefit from the capability to adjust multiple attributes at different rates, and prominence is linked to both attribute contrast and changes in attributes. If an organism aims to enhance its prominence, it can alter its attributes at a faster or slower pace than the surrounding environment. Consequently, organizations can gain advantages by having the flexibility to change quickly or gradually according to their desired prominence. Depending on the context, rapid blending may be necessary to avoid detection, while in other scenarios, a gradual alignment with the environment or changes at rates similar to other entities can be beneficial. This concept also applies to change management within organizations, where businesses can benefit from both swift and gradual adjustments that align with the changes in the business environment around them. A relevant example is price adjustments in marketing, where a business may choose to draw attention to its pricing changes by modifying the rate of change relative to competitors. Features related to attribute modification include the ability to swiftly adapt attributes and adjust the rate of changes in attributes. Social media has furnished organizations with copious data regarding the range of P-adaptability necessary to meet customer expectations and desires.

Flexible Form

As invertebrates, cephalopods possess the capability to easily modify their shape, enabling them to conceal themselves in small spaces, which is a valuable survival mechanism, particularly when facing threats from predators. Similarly, business organizations that exhibit modularity and flexibility in their structure can also leverage this concealment ability by adjusting their size and form. For instance, if an organization seeks to evade attention from a larger competitor, having fewer warehouses in place of a single large warehouse can enhance their nimbleness and adaptability, making it more difficult for the larger competitor to locate and target them.

Life-Cycle Changes

Cephalopods undergo significant changes in their prominence mechanisms throughout their lives. What works for them as adults may not work for juveniles, and their relevant predators and prey also change over time. For instance, the Piglet Squid alters its deep-sea location as it matures to adjust its prominence concerning predators, prey, and mates. This principle can be readily applied to businesses. As a company expands, the types of entities observing it will evolve. Thus, it's essential for firms to develop competence in managing prominence that adapts over time. Sometimes, changes in observers are triggered by a business action, making it necessary to make immediate adjustments related to prominence. Many successful large businesses follow this example as they grow. For example, Facebook rebranded itself to Meta in 2021 as part of an effort to signal its ambition to be more than just a social media company and to establish a presence in the metaverse (3D Internet).[40]

Differential Prominence

One essential aspect of P-adaptability observed in cephalopods is differential prominence, which entails the ability to exhibit varying levels of prominence within a brief timeframe. The mimic octopus serves as a notable illustration of P-adaptability through the utilization of differential prominence. This cephalopod species can alter its color, shape, and behavior to imitate diverse organisms in its environment, effectively evading predators. In a similar vein, it employs social mimicry by swimming with other fish groups, like the small grouper, to avoid detection. In the realm of business, a highly P-adaptable company should possess the capacity to strategically showcase its activities to specific groups while concealing them from others. For instance, a company might wish to disclose its new product development projects to investors while keeping them concealed from competitors. Achieving this requires a delicate balancing act where the company must strike the right balance of visibility with the appropriate groups.

Distraction

One of the most sophisticated prominence-related abilities among cephalopod species is their distraction mechanisms. Octopuses and squids are particularly well known for employing ink as a distraction mechanism. When confronted by a predator, these cephalopods release ink, creating a dense cloud that bewilders their pursuers and facilitates their escape. This distraction technique is not only advantageous for cephalopods but can also find applications in the business world. In the face of a hostile takeover attempt, a company can devise emergency distraction methods for use in critical situations. These methods might involve creating a smoke screen or deploying pseudomorphs acting as decoys to divert the predator's attention. Pseudomorphs, also referred to as "false forms," closely resemble the squid that produced them, making it challenging for the predator to distinguish between the real and imitation creatures. Besides ink and pseudomorphs, cephalopods use deflective marks on their bodies to direct attacks away from vulnerable areas, making it more difficult for predators to land successful blows. Businesses can similarly employ these techniques to shift the focus of potential threats, such as by highlighting a less valuable aspect of the company or redirecting attention to less vulnerable segments of the market.

Passive Crypsis

Passive crypsis is a survival strategy employed by octopuses and other cephalopods to elude detection by predators or prey. It encompasses the act of blending into the surroundings or mimicking less menacing elements of the environment, even when not under direct threat or in the presence of a predator. When in transit, octopuses frequently take on an appearance resembling flounders, even in the absence of an immediate threat. This form of mimicry can prove advantageous for businesses too, particularly when companies are venturing into new markets and aim to remain inconspicuous until they are firmly established, even when there is no immediate predatory threat.

P-adaptability, Efficiency, and Resilience

Cephalopods offer valuable insights into developing P-adaptability for businesses operating in highly dynamic environments. Beyond prominence, organizations must also prioritize resource conservation, waste reduction, and addressing environmental fluctuations to enhance efficiency and resilience. The correlation between efficiency, resilience, and prominence (ERP) factors and variability levels among cephalopod species imparts crucial lessons for organizations and their ideal survival environments. Typically, larger firms display lower levels of P-adaptability and thrive in stable, less variable environments, whereas species inhabiting complex environments demand elevated P-adaptability and resilience to cope with changes.

Nonetheless, attaining elevated levels of P-adaptability comes at a cost. The necessary degree of P-adaptability hinges on the extent of variation an entity encounters. Consequently, compensation mechanisms can be devised, and the correlation between P-adaptability and ER-adaptability can be leveraged to ascertain the optimal strategy. In environments characterized by high variability, both high resilience and P-adaptability are essential, although this entails a trade-off in efficiency. Lower resilience can be offset by heightened P-adaptability, and vice versa. The energy expended on high-prominence actions means that low-prominence strategies may be more appropriate in energy-constrained environments. Nonetheless, high-prominence actions, such as startle behaviors, can prove efficient in the long term if they lead to a reduction in intensive engagement with observers.

P-adaptability is indispensable for startups and smaller firms that must distinguish themselves based on subtle, agile, and precise attributes. The ability to have visibility in the supply chain has become a substantial differentiator, allowing companies to position themselves as astute specialists in detecting subtle signals within complex supply networks. The persistence and dissemination of prominence can influence P-adaptability and should be taken into account. Prominence may endure even after reaching its peak and can either benefit or harm the entity, while activation may require time to diffuse and reach the intended observer, as observed in the use of inking by cephalopods.

Prominence Strategies Using Generative AI

The incorporation of large language models like GPT, as well as text-to-image generative models such as Stable Diffusion and Midjourney, has revolutionized the way organizations can approach strategy. Generative AI has the potential to democratize innovation and significantly enhance our capacity to formulate strategies through natural analogies.[41] For instance, we introduced our definition of "P-adaptability" to ChatGPT and posed a series of questions aimed at assisting a small advisory firm in developing its strategies for gaining prominence. We tasked ChatGPT with evaluating the novelty, feasibility, and resource requirements of each strategy it generated. The responses are provided below and have been slightly edited for clarity and conciseness.

ChatGPT Response: Prominence Strategies

In response to our prompt, the following is the output provided by a large language model (LLM; ChatGPT), which is summarized in Table 3.13. This was followed by a brief description of each of the strategies.

Camouflage Marketing

- Natural Analogy: Chameleon
- Description: The firm can adopt a flexible and adaptive marketing approach that blends into the competitive landscape while still maintaining a distinctive presence. This strategy involves carefully analyzing competitors' positioning and messaging and then adjusting the firm's own marketing efforts to highlight unique value propositions.
- Novelty: High

Table 3.13 Evaluation of Prominence Strategies by an LLM

P-Adaptable Strategy	Natural Analogy	Novelty	Feasibility	Resource Intensity
Camouflage marketing	Chameleon	High	High	Low
Swarm collaboration	Bird flocking	Medium	Medium	Medium
Coevolutionary partnerships	Symbiotic relationships	High	High	High

- Feasibility: High
- Resource Intensity: Low

Swarm Collaboration

- Natural Analogy: Bird Flocking
- Description: The firm can establish collaborative partnerships with other complementary organizations or experts in the innovation ecosystem. This strategy involves forming alliances and networks that allow for the collective sharing of knowledge, resources, and opportunities. By working together as a cohesive unit, the firm can adapt quickly to market changes and enhance its competitive edge.
- Novelty: Medium
- Feasibility: Medium
- Resource Intensity: Medium

Coevolutionary Partnerships

- Natural Analogy: Symbiotic Relationships
- Description: The firm can cultivate strategic partnerships with key clients or organizations to create mutually beneficial relationships. This strategy involves deepening connections with clients, understanding their evolving needs, and coevolving innovative solutions together. By aligning their goals and collaborating closely, the firm can adapt its services to meet the changing demands of its clients, while also fostering loyalty and long-term success.
- Novelty: High
- Feasibility: High
- Resource Intensity: High

Among the three strategies mentioned, ChatGPT recommended the "Coevolutionary Partnerships" strategy for the small advisory firm and provides the following reasons:

Why I (ChatGPT) Recommend It

- Novelty: This strategy offers a high level of novelty as it emphasizes a deep, evolving relationship between the firm and its clients, rather than traditional transactional interactions.

- Feasibility: Establishing coevolutionary partnerships is feasible for a small advisory firm, as it primarily requires fostering strong client relationships and aligning goals.
- Resource Intensity: While this strategy may require a moderate level of resources, such as time and effort dedicated to building and maintaining partnerships, the potential long-term benefits outweigh the investment.

Additional Reasons

- Client-Centric Approach: By coevolving with clients, the firm can better understand and meet their changing needs, enhancing customer satisfaction and loyalty.
- Competitive Advantage: The firm can differentiate itself by offering tailored solutions and deep expertise gained from close collaboration with clients.
- Network Expansion: Through partnerships, the firm can tap into the networks and resources of its clients, accessing new opportunities and expanding its reach within the innovation ecosystem.
- Sustainability: Coevolutionary partnerships foster long-term relationships, which can lead to stable revenue streams and a sustainable business model.

According to ChatGPT, it recommended "Coevolutionary Partnerships" due to the strategy's unique combination of innovation, client centricity, and strategic collaboration, offering an adaptive approach that aligns with the advisory firm's competitive market goals.

Exercises

1. Suppose your organization is preparing to introduce a new product in a market with established competitors. You have concerns that your actions might provoke a predatory response from the existing market players. Describe how you can employ principles from any two camouflage strategies outlined in this chapter to assist your company in avoiding detection. Furthermore, outline three strategies for utilizing the concept of nocturnality to bolster your market share in the new market.

2. Imagine you are the CEO of a startup business in the medical devices industry, and you are preparing to introduce a marketing program in a new market. How can you apply the prominence strategies of cephalopods to capture the interest of investors and customers while evading potential competitors' detection?

3. Your firm produces products that rely on materials and parts from a complex, multi-national supply chain. What strategies inspired by nature can you implement to improve your network's P-adaptability during various contingencies?

4. Examine the prominence strategies of a company of your choosing. Assess its degree of P-adaptability when dealing with customers, competitors, and potential collaborators. In your opinion, what is the ideal level of P-adaptability the company should strive for with each of these target observers? Additionally, suggest principles derived from biological organisms that the company could employ to enhance its level of P-adaptability to meet your ideal standard.

Notes

1. Nordell, S. E., & Valone, T. J. (2021). *Animal Behavior: Concepts, Methods, and Applications.* Oxford University Press.
2. Jablonski, P. G., & Lee, S. I. (2018). Painted redstarts (*Myioborus pictus*) attack larger prey when using the flush-pursue strategy. *The Open Ornithology Journal*, 11(1).
3. Corruption in Conflict. (2016, September). SIGAR | Special Inspector General for Afghanistan Reconstruction. https://www.sigar.mil/interactive-reports/corruption-in-conflict/index.html.
4. Global Trends | The Future of Public Activism: Populations Poised to Increase Pressure Worldwide (2021). In *Office of the Director of National Intelligence.* National Intelligence Council | Strategic Futures Group. https://www.dni.gov/files/images/globalTrends/GT2040/NIC-2021-02495-Future-of-Public-Activism_18Nov21_UNSOURCED.pdf.
5. Parsons, D. (2017, October 10). *Army Considers Punishing Industry for "Frivolous" Protests.* Defense Daily. https://www.defensedaily.com/army-considers-punishing-industry-frivolous-protests/army/.
6. Wirsching, E. (2018). The revolving door for political elites: Policymakers' professional background and financial regulation. *EBRD Working Paper No. 222.* https://doi.org/10.2139/ssrn.3280933.
7. Kelly, C. (2022, May 17). *Burger Wars: How Burger King's Rivalry with McDonald's Reverberates Through Adland.* Marketing Dive. https://www

.marketingdive.com/news/mcdonalds-burger-king-brand-rivalry-burger-wars/621713/.

8. Cott, H. B. (1940). *Adaptive Coloration in Animals*. Methuen.

9. Holmes, G. G., Delferrière, E., Rowe, C., Troscianko, J., & Skelhorn, J. (2018). Testing the feasibility of the startle-first route to deimatism. *Scientific Reports*, 8(1), 1–8.

10. Rosier, R. L., & Langkilde, T. (2011). Behavior under risk: How animals avoid becoming dinner. *Nature Education Knowledge*, 2(8).

11. *Bear Attacks*. (2019). National Park Service. https://www.nps.gov/articles/bearattacks.htm.

12. Hausheer, J. E. (2020, January 27). *Shrikes: Meet the Bird That Impales Prey on Spikes*. Cool Green Science. https://blog.nature.org/science/2020/01/27/shrikes-meet-the-bird-that-impales-prey-on-spikes/.

13. Lynch, W. (2007). *Owls of the United States and Canada: A Complete Guide to Their Biology and Behavior*. The Johns Hopkins University Press.

14. Zanette, L. Y., & Clinchy, M. (2019). Ecology of fear. *Current Biology*, 29(9), R309–R313.

15. Forbes, P. (2011). *Dazzled and Deceived: Mimicry and Camouflage*. Yale University Press.

16. Thayer, A. H. (1896). The law which underlies protective coloration. *The Auk*, 13, 477–482.

17. Cott (1940).

18. Mills, L. S., Zimova, M., Oyler, J., Running, S., Abatzoglou, J. T., & Lukacs, P. M. (2013). Camouflage mismatch in seasonal coat color due to decreased snow duration. *Proceedings of the National Academy of Sciences*, 110(18), 7360–7365.

19. Duarte, R. C., Flores, A. A. V., & Stevens, M. (2017). Camouflage through colour change: Mechanisms, adaptive value and ecological significance. *Philosophical Transactions of the Royal Society B: Biological Sciences*, 372(1724), 20160342.

20. Hall, J. R., Cuthill, I. C., Baddeley, R., Shohet, A. J., & Scott-Samuel, N. E. (2013). Camouflage, detection, and identification of moving targets. *Proceedings of the Royal Society B: Biological Sciences*, 280(1758), 20130064.

21. Lev-Yadun, S., Dafni, A., Flaishman, M. A., Inbar, M., Izhaki, I., Katzir, G., & Ne'eman, G. (2004). Plant coloration undermines herbivorous insect camouflage. *BioEssays*, 26(10), 1126–1130.

22. Justh, E. W., & Krishnaprasad, P. S. (2006). Steering laws for motion camouflage. *Proceedings of the Royal Society A: Mathematical, Physical and Engineering Sciences*, 462(2076), 3629–3643.

23. Hughes, A., Liggins, E., & Stevens, M. (2019). Imperfect camouflage: How to hide in a variable world? *Proceedings of the Royal Society B*, 286(1902), 20190646.

24. Stokel-Walker, C. (2022, September 26). *This Company Says It's One Step Closer to an Invisibility Cloak*. Wired UK. https://www.wired.co.uk/article/vollebak-invisibility-cloak.

25. Templeton, S., Bishop, M., Levitt, K., & Heckman, M. (2019). A biological framework for characterizing mimicry in cyber-deception. In *European Conference on Cyber Warfare and Security*, 508–517. Academic Conferences International Limited.

26. Skelhorn, J., & Rowe, C. (2016). Cognition and the evolution of camouflage. *Proceedings of the Royal Society B: Biological Sciences*, 283(1825), 20152890.

27. Vranica, S., & Bruell, A. (2021, October 30). Supply-chain crisis has companies asking: Should we still advertise? *Wall Street Journal*. https://www.wsj.com/amp/articles/supply-chain-crisis-has-companies-asking-should-we-still-advertise-11635599386.

28. Kumar, N., & Steenkamp, J. B. E. M. (2007). *Private Label Strategy: How to Meet the Store Brand Challenge*. Harvard Business Press.

29. Humphries, D. A., & Driver, P. M. (1970). Protean defence by prey animals. *Oecologia*, 5(4), 285–302.

30. Malnes, R. (1983). OPEC and the problem of collective action. *Journal of Peace Research*, 20(4), 343–355.

31. Champion, B. (2008). Spies (look) like us: The early use of business and civilian covers in covert operations. *International Journal of Intelligence and Counter Intelligence*, 21(3), 530–564.

32. Brepson, L., Troïanowski, M., Voituron, Y., & Lengagne, T. (2012). Cheating for sex: Inherent disadvantage or energetic constraint? *Animal Behaviour*, 84(5), 1253–1260.

33. Freeman, A. R., & Hare, J. F. (2015). Infrasound in mating displays: A peacock's tale. *Animal Behaviour*, 102, 241–250.

34. Hanlon, R. T., Vecchione, M., & Allcock, L. (2018). *Octopus, Squid & Cuttlefish: A Visual, Scientific Guide to the Oceans' Most Advanced Invertebrates*. Chicago: University of Chicago Press.

35. Livni, E. (2018, May 19). *A Controversial Study Has a New Spin on the Otherworldliness of the Octopus*. Quartz. https://qz.com/1281064/a-controversial-study-has-a-new-spin-on-the-otherworldliness-of-the-octopus.

36. Hanlon, R. T., & Messenger, J. B. (2018). *Cephalopod Behaviour*. Cambridge University Press.

37. Wood, J. (2023, November 3). *Octopus, Squid, Cuttlefish, and Nautilus*. The Cephalapod Page. https://www.thecephalopodpage.org/.

38. Hanlon, R. T. (2007). Cephalopod dynamic camouflage. *Current Biology*, 17(11), R400–R404.

39. *How We Make: Flex Pulse® Supply Chain Visualization | Flex*. (2022, November 15). Flex.com. https://flex.com/resources/how-we-make-flex-pulse-supply-chain-visualization.

40. Wertenbroch, K. (2022, January 24). *Why Facebook Is Rebranding Itself as Meta*. INSEAD Knowledge. https://knowledge.insead.edu/marketing/why-facebook-rebranding-itself-meta.

41. Eapen, T. T., Finkenstadt, D. J., Folk, J., & Venkataswamy, L. (2023). How generative AI can augment human creativity: Use it to promote divergent thinking. *Harvard Business Review*, 101(4), 56–64.

References

Brepson, L., Troïanowski, M., Voituron, Y., & Lengagne, T. (2012). Cheating for sex: Inherent disadvantage or energetic constraint? *Animal Behaviour*, 84(5), 1253–1260.

Champion, B. (2008). Spies (look) like us: The early use of business and civilian covers in covert operations. *International Journal of Intelligence and Counter Intelligence*, 21(3), 530–564.

Cott, H. B. (1940). *Adaptive Coloration in Animals*. Methuen.

Duarte, R. C., Flores, A. A. V., & Stevens, M. (2017). Camouflage through colour change: Mechanisms, adaptive value and ecological significance. *Philosophical Transactions of the Royal Society B: Biological Sciences*, 372(1724), 20160342.

Eapen, T. T., Finkenstadt, D. J., Folk, J., & Venkataswamy, L. (2023). How generative AI can augment human creativity: Use it to promote divergent thinking. *Harvard Business Review*, 101(4), 56–64.

Forbes, P. (2011). *Dazzled and Deceived: Mimicry and Camouflage*. Yale University Press.

Freeman, A. R., & Hare, J. F. (2015). Infrasound in mating displays: A peacock's tale. *Animal Behaviour*, 102, 241–250.

Hall, J. R., Cuthill, I. C., Baddeley, R., Shohet, A. J., & Scott-Samuel, N. E. (2013). Camouflage, detection, and identification of moving targets. *Proceedings of the Royal Society B: Biological Sciences*, 280(1758), 20130064.

Hanlon, R. T. (2007). Cephalopod dynamic camouflage. *Current Biology*, 17(11), R400–R404.

Hanlon, R. T., & Messenger, J. B. (2018). *Cephalopod Behaviour*. Cambridge University Press.

Hanlon, R. T., Vecchione, M., & Allcock, L. (2018). *Octopus, Squid & Cuttlefish: A Visual, Scientific Guide to the Oceans' Most Advanced Invertebrates*. Chicago: University of Chicago Press.

Holmes, G. G., Delferrière, E., Rowe, C., Troscianko, J., & Skelhorn, J. (2018). Testing the feasibility of the startle-first route to deimatism. *Scientific Reports*, 8(1), 1–8.

Hughes, A., Liggins, E., & Stevens, M. (2019). Imperfect camouflage: How to hide in a variable world? *Proceedings of the Royal Society B*, 286(1902), 20190646.

Humphries, D. A., & Driver, P. M. (1970). Protean defence by prey animals. *Oecologia*, 5(4), 285–302.

Jablonski, P. G., & Lee, S. (2018). Painted redstarts (*Myioborus pictus*) attack larger prey when using the flush-pursue strategy. *The Open Ornithology Journal*, 11(1), 34-38.

Kumar, N., & Steenkamp, J. B. E. M. (2007). *Private Label Strategy: How to Meet the Store Brand Challenge*. Harvard Business Press.

Lev-Yadun, S., Dafni, A., Flaishman, M. A., Inbar, M., Izhaki, I., Katzir, G., & Ne'eman, G. (2004). Plant coloration undermines herbivorous insect camouflage. *BioEssays*, 26(10), 1126–1130.

Lynch, W. (2007). *Owls of the United States and Canada: A Complete Guide to Their Biology and Behavior.* The Johns Hopkins University Press.

Malnes, R. (1983). OPEC and the problem of collective action. *Journal of Peace Research*, 20(4), 343–355.

Mills, L. S., Zimova, M., Oyler, J., Running, S., Abatzoglou, J. T., & Lukacs, P. M. (2013). Camouflage mismatch in seasonal coat color due to decreased snow duration. *Proceedings of the National Academy of Sciences*, 110(18), 7360–7365.

Nordell, S. E., & Valone, T. J. (2021). *Animal Behavior: Concepts, Methods, and Applications.* Oxford University Press.

Rosier, R. L., & Langkilde, T. (2011). Behavior under risk: How animals avoid becoming dinner. *Nature Education Knowledge*, 2, 8.

Skelhorn, J., & Rowe, C. (2016). Cognition and the evolution of camouflage. *Proceedings of the Royal Society B: Biological Sciences*, 283(1825), 20152890.

Templeton, S., Bishop, M., Levitt, K., & Heckman, M. (2019). A biological framework for characterizing mimicry in cyber-deception. In *European Conference on Cyber Warfare and Security*, pp. 508–517. Academic Conferences International Limited.

Thayer, A. H. (1896). The law which underlies protective coloration. *The Auk*, 13, 477–482.

Wirsching, E. (2018). The revolving door for political elites: Policymakers' professional background and financial regulation. EBRD Working Paper No. 222. https://doi.org/10.2139/ssrn.3280933

Zanette, L. Y., & Clinchy, M. (2019). Ecology of fear. *Current Biology*, 29(9), R309–R313.

Chapter 4
Natural Design Heuristics

Heuristic is an algorithm in a clown suit. It's less predictable, it's more fun, and it comes without a 30-day, money-back guarantee.

–Steve McConnell

DOI: 10.4324/9781032715315-5

Heuristics are approximate strategies that aid in decision-making.[1] Many refer to heuristics as "rules of thumb." Heuristics can assist in achieving goals in uncertain conditions in various contexts, including computer problem-solving,[2] organizational decision-making,[3] military strategy,[4] and product design.[5] In this book, we use the term "heuristics" in a positive sense,[6] rather than as biases that hinder decision-making.[7]

In this chapter, we identify and describe seven "natural" design heuristics that can be employed to identify potential actions for enhancing the ERP (efficiency, resilience, and prominence) factors of a system in favorable ways. These natural heuristics include (1) combination (Com), (2) removal (Rem), (3) separation (Sep), (4) segmentation (Seg), (5) replication (Rep), (6) dynamics (Dyn), and (7) maximization (Max).

These seven natural heuristics represent common patterns of adaptation and strategies observed in natural and biological systems. They also correspond to basic mathematical operations, including addition/union, subtraction, intersection, division, multiplication, mapping, and functional optimization. Additionally, the seven heuristics overlap with several of the inventive principles identified by Genrikh Altshuller as part of the Theory of Inventive Problem Solving (TIPS), which is better known as TRIZ based on its Russian name.[8] These heuristics can be applied to various systems, including individuals (e.g., employees), living organisms, business organizations, and countries, as well as aggregate systems with multiple decision-making entities, such as employee teams, herds, business conglomerates, or intergovernmental organizations. They are also useful for examining how external entities, like product designers, can enhance or redesign existing human artifacts, such as products.

Our primary goal in this chapter is to identify how these natural heuristics correspond to and relate to the survivability health/capability ERP factors of efficiency, resilience, and prominence. We aim to explore how these heuristics can be used to identify strategies and designs that enhance the overall system design along the ERP dimensions. In Table 4.1, you'll find a brief definition of the seven natural heuristics, along with illustrative cases from biological systems where these principles are observed.

Natural Design Heuristics and ERP Factors

The seven natural heuristics enhance system survivability by positively modifying ERP factors. Understanding the relationship between heuristics and

Table 4.1   Definitions and Illustrations of the Natural Design Heuristics

Design Heuristics	Summary and Illustration
Combination (Com)	Combination, connection, or integration of two or more entities or components of entities. For example, symbiotic relationships between different species, such as clownfish and anemones or oxpecker birds and rhinoceroses.
Removal (Rem)	Removing an entity or a part of an entity from a unified whole, as seen in the shedding of leaves by deciduous trees in the fall to conserve resources during the winter.
Separation (Sep)	Separating an entity into two or more parts that are dissimilar in nature but continue to function together in distinct roles. An illustration of this is found in ant colonies, which consist of various specialized groups, including worker ants, soldier ants, and queen ants, each performing distinct functions.
Segmentation (Seg)	Dividing an entity into two or more parts that share similar nature or features, enabling them to cooperate while performing different functions. For example, earthworms have segments along their bodies that allow them to move efficiently and dig through the soil.
Replication (Rep)	Replicating an entity, its component, or function in a way that a new co-existing entity is created, bearing some of the characteristics of the original entity. This principle is observed inside a beehive, where numerous identical honeycomb cells are used by bees to store honey, pollen, and raise their young.
Dynamics (Dyn)	Dynamically changing a part of the entity, like a component, attribute, or function, which was previously static, in response to specific inputs. For instance, sunflowers display heliotropism, a dynamic response where they adjust the orientation of their flowers to face the sun throughout the day, ensuring optimal sunlight exposure for photosynthesis.
Maximization (Max)	Adjusting an attribute of an entity to its minimum, maximum, extreme, or optimal level. For instance, male peacocks have vibrant, elaborate feathers that are maximized in size and coloration, serving to attract mates and enhance the possibility of reproductive success.

ERP factors offers several benefits. Firstly, it helps identify strategies for each ERP factor as needed. For example, relevant heuristics can serve as starting points for identifying specific strategies to improve efficiency in particular circumstances. Secondly, certain heuristics are strongly linked to specific factors, making it easier to quickly evaluate the potential effects of strategic actions. For instance, employing the replication heuristic can enhance redundancy and resilience. Thirdly, the heuristics enable a systematic approach to managing trade-offs involving multiple ERP factors in a dynamic environment. In a turbulent environment, a system may choose to segment (Seg) into smaller units and later combine (Com) when the threat subsides. Recognizing the underlying heuristics helps efficiently identify ERP trade-offs in decision-making.

The design heuristics also serve as mechanisms for generating novelty. In other words, they create a perception of novelty for a user or observer. This perception arises when a target observer compares the current state to a former state or other comparable entities in the surrounding environment. Novelty is also commonly effective in increasing prominence. The use of design heuristics often results in a change in the entity's appearance, creating a contrast with its former state. Therefore, if the target observer remembers the former state, the new state often appears novel. Novelty can be employed to attract, distract, or repel an observer and can be effective with various types of observers, including predators, prey, and potential mates. Next, we will delve into a detailed discussion of each of the seven natural heuristics in turn. Our goal is to understand the nature of each heuristic and its application in designing and improving survivable systems. To illustrate the heuristics, we will provide examples from living systems and human organizations.

Heuristic 1: Combination

The first natural design heuristic we consider is called combination. An expanded definition of this heuristic is as follows:

> An approximation planning method used by organisms or organizations that merges two distinct and independent entities to increase the relative worth of their functions (purposes). For combination to occur there must be two or more independent entities whose functions are merged with the intent to increase the total value obtained by increasing efficiency or resilience and/or optimizing attention to meet strategic ends.

This heuristic involves merging a plurality of elements related to an activated entity into a singularity with the objective of providing benefits, such as increased efficiency, resilience, or attention from a receiver entity. The combination heuristic is an approximation planning method used by organisms or organizations to merge two independent entities, thereby increasing the relative worth of their functions or purposes. To facilitate combination, there must be two or more independent entities whose functions are merged to increase efficiency, resilience, and/or optimize prominence to achieve strategic ends. Combination is related to concepts such as addition, association, joining, merging, unification, mixing, coordination, and cooperation. Here are some examples of the Combination (Com) heuristic found from nature, product design, business, and military strategy:

1. In nature, organisms often form symbiotic relationships, such as lichens.[9] Lichens are a combination of fungi and algae, where the fungus provides a protective structure, while the algae perform photosynthesis. This combination allows both entities to thrive in environments where they couldn't survive alone.
2. Smartphone applications combine camera functionality with GPS technology. This integration allows users to capture photos and immediately tag them with geolocation information. It enhances the user experience by enabling easy photo organization and sharing while providing context about the location where the photo was taken.
3. Companies often form strategic alliances to combine their strengths and resources.[10] For instance, a technology company might partner with a manufacturing company to create innovative products. By combining their expertise, they can develop and deliver better solutions, expanding their market reach and increasing competitiveness.
4. During major conflicts, countries often form military alliances to combine their forces.[11] By pooling resources, sharing intelligence, and coordinating strategies, these alliances achieve greater military power and enhance their likelihood of success in a conflict.

Next, let us consider the relationship between the combination (Com) heuristic and the ERP factors of efficiency, resilience, and prominence. By doing so, we can identify how the combination heuristic can be used to identify strategic actions to improve or modify the ERP factors in various situations. While the combination heuristic (Com) is most closely associated with efficiency, it can be used to modify all three ERP factors, as seen in the following cases:

1. Efficiency: Smart grid systems integrate sensors, sophisticated communication networks, and advanced data analytics to optimize electricity distribution.[12] This seamless integration enables the system to continuously monitor real-time energy consumption, promptly identify areas with high demand or wastage, and expertly recalibrate resource allocation in response. This multifaceted synergy significantly enhances overall grid efficiency, substantially reducing energy losses, and promoting superior resource management.

2. Resilience: Natural ecosystems often exhibit high biodiversity, where multiple species coexist and interact in a complex web of relationships. This combination of diverse species provides resilience against future environmental disturbances.[13] For example, a diverse forest ecosystem with various tree species can better withstand pests, diseases, or natural disasters, as the impact on one species is buffered by others. The combination of different species enhances the ecosystem's resilience to external environmental forces.

3. Prominence: In marketing, combining the popularity and attention surrounding a celebrity with a brand's products or services can enhance prominence.[14] By associating with a well-known figure, a brand can attract attention from a broader audience and increase its visibility. This combination leverages the attention that the celebrity receives to elevate the brand's prominence and create a positive association in the minds of consumers.

A well-developed understanding of the relationship between the ERP factors and the combination heuristic can be helpful in making decisions about whether to join a group or connect one entity with another. Examples of such decisions include (1) whether a wandering animal is deciding whether it should remain alone or join a herd, (2) if a product designer should integrate products to create a multi-functional device or keep them separate, and (3) whether a food company should merge with its main competitor to create a market leader.

In making these decisions, it is important to consider trade-offs when using the combination heuristic in relation to the other ERP factors. For example, in the case of the wandering animal, joining a herd may increase efficiency and resilience, but it may also decrease the animal's prominence in the eyes of a mate from outside the herd. In product design, combining products may increase efficiency, but it may also result in reduced attention from consumers if the product is too complex or unfamiliar. In business mergers, combining two firms can enhance efficiency and prominence, but it may also lead to cultural clashes among employees, ultimately resulting in reduced resilience.

Heuristic 2: Removal

The strategy of removal is a common heuristic-based approach that involves eliminating or removing a part of an entity to provide benefits that increase its chances of survival or efficiency. An expanded definition of this heuristic is as follows:

> An approximation planning method used by organisms or organizations intentionally omits or discards a prominent yet unnecessary attribute to enhance efficiency or alter their ability to be noticed or discovered. For removal to occur, there must be an independent entity whose functions are cast off with the intent to increase the total value obtained by increasing efficiency and/or optimizing attention to meet strategic goals, often at the expense of the entity's ability to respond and recover from disruptive situations.

When a feature or function becomes superfluous or unnecessary, it may be removed, and the entity may shift its resources and energies toward other parts that compensate for the loss. A classic example of such removal is the blind cavefish, which have lost their vision because there was no need for it in their environment.[15] During times of crisis, organizations may seek to decrease redundancy to improve efficiency. However, the removal of parts can often lead to lower levels of resilience, as the eliminated part may have played an essential role during uncommon or rare settings. For instance, a business may decide to eliminate a less profitable product line during good times. While such removal may offer a foundation for improved efficiency in the short run, it may also result in reduced resilience, as the product may experience increased demand during an economic downturn. Here are some examples of the removal (Rem) heuristic found in nature, product design, business, and military strategy:

1. Proteasomes, as cellular complexes, exemplify the removal (Rem) heuristic in living systems. The fundamental role of proteasomes is the degradation of proteins.[16] They selectively eliminate and break down

damaged or misfolded proteins within cells. Through the elimination of these aberrant proteins, proteasomes contribute to the preservation of cellular integrity and the prevention of the accumulation of potentially detrimental substances, thereby ensuring the efficient functionality of the cell.

2. In product design, removal (Rem) is often employed to create minimalist aesthetics and streamline functionality. For instance, minimalist architecture may involve eliminating unnecessary ornamentation, reducing the number of components, and focusing on clean lines and simplicity.[17] This intentional removal of non-essential elements aims to enhance user experience, increase efficiency, and create a visually appealing design.

3. Marketers also use removal as a heuristic to optimize attention and increase the perceived value of a product. For instance, in 2021, as part of its "Open to Better" campaign, Coca-Cola removed its iconic logo from its cans to encourage customers to share pictures of their cans on social media.[18]

4. One notable example of removal (Rem) in military strategy is the concept of a strategic retreat or withdrawal.[19] In certain situations, armies may purposefully remove themselves from a battle or territory to regroup, preserve resources, or lure the enemy into a disadvantageous position.

How does the removal heuristic impact the ERP factors? While the removal heuristic (Rem) is primarily associated with efficiency and prominence, it can be applied to modify all three ERP factors, as demonstrated in the following cases:

1. Efficiency: The removal (Rem) heuristic can enhance efficiency by eliminating unnecessary components or processes within a system, allowing resources to be allocated more effectively. In software development, the practice of "code refactoring" involves removing redundant or inefficient code segments. This process optimizes the software's performance, reduces resource consumption, and enhances the overall efficiency of the system.

2. Resilience: While removal has the potential to bolster efficiency, it can, at times, entail a trade-off with resilience. Take, for instance, the scenario where removing backup power supplies from a data center may trim operational expenses but concurrently elevate the vulnerability to downtime during power outages. Nevertheless, in specific contexts,

removal can bolster resilience, as demonstrated by the destruction or elimination of a conduit (e.g., a bridge or window) that could serve as a potential ingress point for external threats.

3. Prominence: In marketing, the removal heuristic can be employed to create a sense of exclusivity and generate attention. Limited-edition products or time-limited offers are designed to give the impression that something is being removed or unavailable soon.[20] This scarcity can attract attention, create a sense of urgency, and drive customer engagement.

In certain instances, the act of eliminating undesirable elements or activities can yield remarkable enhancements in efficiency, as discerned in heuristic-driven strategies for refining business processes, such as the Toyota Production System. This approach is rooted in the elimination of various types of waste, collectively referred to as "muda," encompassing elements like transportation, inventory, motion, waiting, overproduction, overprocessing, and defects. Additionally, the concept of removal extends to marketing tactics, as exemplified by Remilk, a company offering "dairy-free milk" or "cow-free milk." Similarly, some companies are positioned as "logo-free" or "brand-free," strategically tapping into the notion that the elimination of undesirable components can heighten efficiency and appeal to particular consumer segments. One example of this strategy was employed by a company called Brandless, which shut down in 2020 and was subsequently revived in 2022.[21]

In certain instances, the act of elimination can boost resilience, even though it may appear counterintuitive. This occurs because the removal of specific components can pave the way for the introduction of slack or redundancy in other domains, ultimately resulting in an overarching enhancement of resilience. Moreover, the elimination of functions or features that function as liabilities for an entity can also foster increased resilience. Take, for example, a news broadcasting network or a sports team's decision to eliminate highly talented human resources, such as anchors, players, or managers, when they present a public relations risk that could potentially harm attention and, consequently, revenue. This might seem detrimental to the financial resilience of the organization as a whole. Nevertheless, by eliminating these individuals, the organization can redirect resources toward other areas, such as investing in fresh talent or refining operations, thereby augmenting overall resilience. Similarly, certain government surveillance programs have been terminated to safeguard political capital and maintain public trust. While these programs may have originally been instituted to bolster security and intelligence gathering, their continuation can transform into a liability for the government if they become public knowledge or are perceived as unethical. In such scenarios, discontinuing these programs can indeed heighten the resilience of the government by preserving public trust and credibility.

Eliminating a constituent from a system or entity can introduce diverse consequences for its prominence and the attention it garners from external observers. As previously alluded to, adverse attention can be mitigated by the removal of specific functions, components, or individuals from an entity. Nevertheless, removal can also precipitate a reduction in attention through three principal avenues: (1) a decline in size or importance, (2) the elimination of a conspicuous attribute, and (3) the eradication of a classifying trait. Firstly, the size and magnitude of an entity frequently serve as magnets for attention from observers. The removal of a portion of the entity can result in an overall reduction in its size and significance, leading to an associated reduction in external attention. For example, a corporation might divest itself of a non-core business unit to streamline its size and concentrate on primary operations. This, in turn, can diminish the overall attention directed toward the company, as it is no longer perceived as a conglomerate operating across multiple industries.

Secondly, the elimination of a salient feature can render an entity less conspicuous, enabling it to evade the scrutiny of rivals or predators. For instance, a company operating covertly might opt not to maintain a registered name or website, rendering it more challenging for competitors to pinpoint. In certain instances, a company might even dispense with its logo or branding to assimilate into the surroundings and avoid attracting attention. Lastly, the removal of marker entities that facilitate the classification of an entity as part of a specific group can yield a reduction in attention. Assume that a particular set of distinctive traits is requisite for an entity to be designated as a member of a group it aligns with. If one of these traits is excised, the entity may find itself less readily identified as a part of that group, thereby allowing it to seamlessly blend into its surroundings and elude detection. This strategy is frequently employed in the context of military or intelligence operations, where the elimination of specific markers can decrease the probability of detection by hostile forces.

The process of removal can also have a notable impact on the level of attention it garners, particularly if it engenders a sense of novelty in the mind of the observer. This sense of novelty tends to emerge when a specific feature or component is extracted, resulting in the entity appearing distinct from its prior state or when compared to other entities within the same category. For instance, when a leading car manufacturer opts to eliminate the conventional gear stick and opts for a cutting-edge push-button gear selector, this can elicit a perception of novelty, thereby capturing more attention. Another facet through which removal heightens attention is by means of stark contrast with the prevailing environment. If an entity is relocated from its customary surroundings or context, it can promptly stand out and draw attention. Consider, for example, when a high-end hotel chain decides to remove all in-room televisions, this departure from the norm can kindle a perception of novelty and attract both the patrons and the media. Furthermore, removal can cultivate a sense of improvement over the previous status quo. For instance, a company might choose to eliminate a business segment tainted by a subpar reputation in order to enhance its overall image and, consequently, attract a larger customer and investor base. The process of product innovation frequently involves the removal of superfluous or vestigial components to render the product more efficient, user-friendly, or aesthetically pleasing. The poem "The March of Science" by Arthur Guiterman suggests that technological innovation often entails the elimination of both desirable and undesirable components.[22]

Heuristic 3: Separation

Separation is a heuristic strategy that involves dividing an entity into isolated and dissimilar parts. An expanded definition of this heuristic is as follows:

> An approximation planning method used by organisms or organizations that divides itself into two or more distinct parts/groups/categories. This strategy sets these divided, dissimilar parts away from each other to direct attention away from and impacts of conditions or other entities that may harm or exploit the whole. Separate parts are differentiated for the purpose of consolidating harm/exploitative impacts to the most minimal area possible. Highly specialized parts may also enjoy greater efficiencies related to differentiated resource management.

For instance, consider a system with two sub-components, A and B, that have different functions. Separation involves making A and B independent entities that remain related to each other. This strategy also represents the idea of specialization and implies creating a distance or relative isolation between the divided entities in time, space, or communication (information exchange). The basis for separation is that an entity is more likely to achieve its survival-related goals as separated units rather than as a unified entity. Separation divides a component into two separate dissimilar entities. In biology, separation is represented by autotomy, which is often used as a distraction mechanism.[23] For instance, predators are forced to chase after one of the separated units, providing the ability for the other unit to survive. Similar to the distraction strategy seen in autotomy, a firm faced with a hostile takeover may decide to separate out part of its assets or business that is most attractive to the predator in the hopes that the remaining entity will be allowed to survive. In business contexts, separation occurs in the form of spin-offs, where a part of the business develops an individual identity. For example, IBM was split into two companies in 2021 that focus on different lines of business.[24] Here are some other examples of the separation (Sep) heuristic found from nature, product design, business, and military strategy:

1. The human immune system also demonstrates the separation (Sep) heuristic. It employs specialized cells and tissues, such as lymph nodes and spleen, which are strategically separated throughout the body. These components work together to identify and eliminate pathogens or harmful entities.[25] By distributing these defense mechanisms throughout the body, the immune system efficiently manages resources and increases its resilience by targeting potential threats in different areas simultaneously.

2. In industrial design, separation can be applied to improve functionality and user experience. Consider a smartphone with separate physical buttons for volume control or power on/off. This separation helps users locate and interact with specific functions easily, reducing the chances of accidental actions and enhancing usability.

3. In the realm of business and organizational strategy, the separation (Sep) heuristic can be observed in the creation of different departments or divisions within a company. Each division focuses on a specific area, such as sales, marketing, or research and development, and operates relatively independently. This separation allows for greater efficiency in managing resources, as each division can allocate its resources optimally for their specialized tasks.

4. In military history, separation has been used to divide and conquer opponents. Hannibal, the Carthaginian general, employed the strategy of separating Roman armies by luring them into unfavorable terrains, isolating them from reinforcement and supply lines. This separation weakened the Roman forces and allowed Hannibal to defeat them in individual engagements. Another well-known example is Hannibal's capture of the village of Cannae in 216 BC, which effectively isolated the Romans from their essential supply sources.[26]

Separation (Sep) can result in an increase in efficiency, particularly if the separated entities can better manage resources in different conditions. For example, separation of concern models in computer science, such as the Model-View-Controller model (MVC), involves different parts of the computer program designed to address separate concerns through the process of encapsulation.[27] Separation can lead to increased resilience if the separated entities are able to better withstand external forces or threats compared to the united entity. Here are some ways that Separation (Sep) impacts the ERP factors:

1. Efficiency: The Separation heuristic can enhance efficiency by enabling specialized management of resources within various components of a system. Each distinct component can concentrate on particular tasks, thereby optimizing the utilization of resources. For example, in a manufacturing facility, the separation of different assembly lines for distinct products permits the allocation of dedicated resources, special tools, and skilled personnel. In a computer system, the separation of processes into distinct threads enables parallel processing, leading to quicker execution of jobs. Each thread or core can dedicate itself to a specific task, mitigating bottlenecks and ultimately improving the overall system's efficiency.

2. Resilience: The Separation heuristic can be used to identify strategic actions that bolster resilience by minimizing the adverse effects of harmful conditions on the entire system. By segregating system components, it becomes possible to isolate and mitigate potential risks. In the realm of computer networks, the deployment of firewalls effectively separates various sections of the network, thereby curbing the propagation of malware.[28] In the event of one part being compromised, this separation strategy limits the impact on the remainder of the network. Similarly, in ecosystems, biodiversity acts as a form of separation. A

diverse array of species, each performing distinct roles and occupying different niches within the ecosystem, contributes to increased resilience.

3. Prominence: By deliberately segregating components or data, the system can effectively selectively steer attention, exerting an impact on how perceptions and interactions unfold. In the realm of product design, the act of partitioning vital features or controls from less crucial elements can serve as a navigational aid for users, shining a spotlight on essential functionalities. This expedites users' comprehension and engagement with the core facets of the product, ultimately heightening its visibility. Within the sphere of public relations and marketing, businesses frequently opt to segregate their brands into discrete product lines or campaigns, tailored to suit diverse target demographics. This strategic separation allows them to wield control over the attention of specific customer segments, ensuring that their brand messages and offerings attain prominence within the intended audience.

The separation principle is observed in the behavior of a herd of animals or a shoal of fish when confronted by a predator. In such situations, group members tend to disperse to reduce overall risk and increase survival chances. By spreading out, they can cover more ground and explore various escape routes efficiently. This optimizes the use of available space and resources. Each member of the group can independently assess the situation and respond accordingly, enhancing their chances of survival. Separation from the main group also helps protect the herd or shoal's resilience. Even if the predator captures a few individuals, the separation prevents the entire group from harm. Separated individuals can regroup or join other herds or shoals later, ensuring the survival of the species.

Heuristic 4: Segmentation

In contrast to separation, segmentation involves dividing an entity into similar or comparable parts. An expanded definition of this heuristic is as follows:

An approximation planning method used by organisms or organizations that divides itself or its processes into two or more distinct parts/groups/categories that are alike in nature. Process steps may be temporally separated into batches of similar actions, versus discrete steps of dissimilar actions. This strategy sets these divided, similar parts away from each other to direct attention away from and impacts of conditions or other entities that may harm or exploit the whole. This division can be caused by internal or external factors. This strategy may also increase entity agility and response to changed conditions.

Segmentation is observed in organisms like starfish, where fragmentation into smaller parts increases the likelihood of survival compared to a single large entity. The rationale behind segmentation is that smaller entities are more likely to be agile and flexible, providing the organism with the ability to act differently in different situations. For instance, when a herd is attacked, the segmentation of the herd into smaller units increases the chances of at least some parts surviving. Segmentation is particularly helpful in situations where being smaller or nimble is advantageous in evading detection or escaping from predators. The choice between segmentation and separation as a survival strategy depends on whether size or function plays a role in survival. In business environments, segmentation may be the result of an endogenous action, such as when a firm decides to divide itself or its resources into similar entities. In other cases, segmentation is exogenous and imposed on it by an external entity such as the government. For instance, AT&T Bell was broken up into smaller entities that continued to provide similar telecommunication services.[29] Segmentation may be used in a search/discovery-oriented process in businesses, where smaller units may be allowed to pursue different strategies. Here are some examples of the Segmentation (Seg) heuristic found in nature, product design, business, and military strategy:

1. In nature, living organisms frequently showcase segmentation as a key strategy for enhancing their chances of survival. An illustrative instance can be found in the segmentation observed in earthworms. These organisms possess a body divided into multiple segments, and each of these segments houses its distinct array of muscles and fine bristles known as setae.[30] This intricate segmentation affords them the ability to navigate through the soil with remarkable efficiency. Earthworms can selectively contract and expand individual segments, enabling them to exert precise force against the soil and, in turn, minimize friction. Furthermore, in situations where one of these segments sustains

damage, the remaining segments can carry on their functions independently, significantly bolstering the organism's overall resilience.

2. UX designers often segment their prototyping process into separate stages, which may include low-fidelity wireframing, mid-fidelity design, and high-fidelity prototyping. This segmentation enables them to iteratively assess and enhance product concepts. Each stage incorporates varying levels of detail and functionality, enabling designers to concentrate on specific aspects of the user experience.

3. In marketing, segmentation is a fundamental concept for targeting specific customer groups effectively. For instance, a beverage company may segment its target market based on age demographics, offering energy drinks for younger consumers and low-sugar beverages for health-conscious individuals. By segmenting their marketing efforts, companies can tailor messages that are consistent with each group's preferences.

4. Throughout history, military strategists have employed segmentation as a tactical approach. An illustrative example is the Roman military formation called the Testudo, or "tortoise." Soldiers would align their shields in a segmented manner, forming a protective barrier above them and on the sides.[31] This segmentation offered enhanced defense against projectiles, allowing the soldiers to advance or hold their ground amidst enemy attacks while minimizing casualties.

Segmentation can sometimes appear similar to replication and provide similar benefits to the entity. However, there is a key difference between the two – segmentation involves splitting of an existing entity, while replication involves creating a new entity. Here are some ways that segmentation (Seg) influences the ERP factors:

1. Efficiency: When the system or its processes are partitioned into discrete parts or groups sharing common characteristics, resource allocation becomes more efficient. Consider a manufacturing facility, where production lines can be segmented according to product types or different stages of production. This approach facilitates the allocation of specialized resources, such as dedicated equipment or personnel, to enhance efficiency and minimize bottlenecks. Each segment can be autonomously managed, ensuring optimal resource utilization within its unique context.

2. Resilience: When a system is partitioned into discrete parts or groups, it gains greater resilience against external disturbances or threats. Take,

for example, computer networks, where dividing networks into various subnets with individualized security measures can effectively mitigate the consequences of potential cyberattacks. Should one segment fall victim to a breach, it can be isolated to prevent further harm and safeguard the overall system. This segmentation approach aids in the proactive management and containment of external threats, thereby upholding the system's stability and sustained functionality.

3. Prominence: Through the strategic segmentation of a system into distinct parts or groups, focus can be diverted from specific components or processes that could potentially draw unwarranted attention or exploitation. In military operations, for instance, pivotal assets or high-value targets can be segmented and concealed to decrease their exposure to potential adversaries. By maintaining separation among these segments and employing camouflage techniques, the overall system's prominence is diminished, rendering it more challenging for hostile observers to discern and pinpoint specific vulnerabilities.

Segmentation is observed in product partitions where it enables flexibility and easier storage. It can also be a resource-saving (efficiency-increasing) strategy. As an illustration, consider the design of product packaging, where segmentation allows for the selective opening of only a portion of the product, preserving the remainder without risk of damage or spoilage. Furthermore, segmentation can include actions distributed across time, with one part of an action executed at one time and the remaining part completed at a later juncture. This multidimensional concept of segmentation underscores its multilayered utility.

Heuristic 5: Replication

Replication is a heuristic strategy that involves repeating an entity or a part of it to create redundancy or introduce a new function into the system. An expanded definition of this heuristic is as follows:

> An approximation planning method used by organisms or organizations that creates duplicated/multiplied forms or functional capabilities to prevent failure, allow for multi-tasking, or generate new capabilities. Replication can occur as an exact replication of form or duplication of functional capability or purpose.

Although replication has the potential to bolster system resilience, it can simultaneously introduce complexities that impede overall efficiency. Yet, intriguingly, there exist select scenarios where replication can enhance efficiency. One of the foremost advantages of replication is its ability of a replicated unit to assume control when the primary entity is compromised or engaged elsewhere. Furthermore, the primary and its replica can collaboratively yield novel advantages that were hitherto unachievable. Replication may also address unique situations that the primary entity struggles to handle adequately. Nevertheless, it's important to acknowledge that replication naturally demands additional components, which can incur considerable maintenance costs, particularly when the redundant entity is infrequently utilized. This intricate interplay between replication, efficiency, and resilience underscores the nuanced dynamics of this approach.

In biological systems, redundancy and duplication also play an important role in achieving resilience, safety, and robustness. Replication in biological systems may not always be an exact replication, but rather an abstracted or functional replication where the entity replicates a function that is performed using a component that may be very different in structure compared to the original. This replication can manifest in various forms, including the replication of form without replicating function or replication in varying sizes. In the realm of products, the provision of spare parts, like spare tires for vehicles, exemplifies a common form of replication. Business organizations, as part of their risk management strategy, frequently leverage replication. For instance, a company might sustain relationships with multiple suppliers for critical components or engage multiple advertising agencies to access diverse creative options. Similarly, in high-stakes projects where failure is not an option, companies may commission multiple teams to compete, employing replication as a strategic measure to ensure success.

1. Within living organisms, replication is crucial for cellular function. DNA replication is a critical biological process in which DNA molecules are accurately duplicated, enabling the transmission of genetic information during cell division.[32] This process ensures that each daughter cell receives the exact replica of the genetic blueprint, maintaining genomic integrity and enabling the growth and development of multicellular organisms.
2. Replication is used in product design to enhance functionality and reliability. For instance, in the aerospace industry, redundant systems are incorporated into aircraft to ensure safety. Critical components like

engines, control systems, and navigation instruments are often replicated, allowing the aircraft to continue functioning even if one system fails. Aircraft also incorporate redundancy-based strategies to monitor and supervise the integrity of in-flight systems.[33] This redundancy minimizes the risk of catastrophic failures and improves overall system resilience.

3. The principle of replication is often utilized in business and organizational strategy to scale operations and increase efficiency. One prominent illustration of this concept is franchising, a strategic approach in which a thriving business model is duplicated through the issuance of licenses to independent operators.[34] This enables the original company to expand its reach and replicate its success in different locations, while franchisees benefit from a proven business model and established brand.

4. Historical military strategies have employed replication to gain a tactical advantage. The "double envelopment," also known as the pincer movement strategy, serves as a classic example.[35] In this tactic, an army divides itself into two or more units to surround and attack an enemy from multiple directions. This replication of forces prevents the enemy from concentrating their defenses effectively and increases the likelihood of victory by exploiting vulnerabilities and achieving numerical superiority.

Skydivers have backup parachutes that serve as a redundant safety measure in case the main parachute fails to deploy. These backup parachutes are designed to be essentially the same in form and function as the main parachute but may use slightly different materials. Similarly, cars often carry spare tires that are either exact replicas of the main tires or short-term use "donut" tires, which are easy to store for gas mileage and space-saving reasons but are still adequate to get someone to a garage should their main tires be damaged. Here are some ways that the replication (Rep) principle relates to the three ERP factors:

1. Efficiency: Replication finds versatile application in optimizing efficiency across various domains. Data centers, for instance, harness the power of server virtualization to replicate servers, thus curbing hardware expenses and conserving energy resources while concurrently fortifying operational efficiency and resilience. The replication of renewable energy sources, such as solar panels and wind turbines, serves to

fine-tune resource utilization, leading to heightened energy generation efficiency. Furthermore, within computer networks, the strategic replication of computational tasks across multiple nodes paves the way for parallel processing, effectively curtailing overall computation time and bolstering computational efficiency.

2. Resilience: Replication is commonly employed to improve the resilience of systems. In natural systems, some species can replicate their genetic material to adapt to changing environmental conditions or resist disease. This replication enhances the resilience of the species by increasing genetic diversity. Critical infrastructure systems like power grids or transportation networks replicate components to withstand disruptions. Through the duplication of key elements, such as power generators or the creation of alternative routes, resilience is substantially elevated, ensuring the continued functionality and stability of these vital systems.

3. Prominence: Replication can be used to both increase and decrease prominence. Companies replicate their brand identity across various channels and touchpoints to increase recognition and prominence among consumers. In military strategy, tactics such as decoys or false targets can replicate the appearance or behavior of a real target.[36] This replication can divert attention from the real target and enhance the prominence of the decoy, creating a strategic advantage. In marketing and pricing strategies, offering a replicated product option with minor variations can influence consumer choices. By replicating options, businesses can steer attention toward preferred choices. This is referred to as the decoy effect.

In government contracting, the use of duplication and redundancy is also common as a risk management strategy. For example, supplier down-selects may be conducted for the product development of new or emerging technology, especially when the chances of success are low. The goal is to bring suppliers to a point in the design and development stage where a clearly superior offering emerges and then continue through to production with that selected supplier. Alternatively, multiple-award type contracts may be established to accommodate future contract needs for supplies or services. This approach helps prevent the risk of adverse selection (choosing a supplier with asymmetric information about their capabilities) and moral hazard (choosing a supplier with asymmetric information about their post-award behaviors). The presence of additional awardees enables the customer to have other options for future work or easily cancel current work and shift to another supplier if the first choice is found to be inadequate or unsatisfactory.

Replication can also serve to create new functions. For example, one can duplicate a robotic arm. The original arm might have been used for welding two pieces of metal together. However, a second arm can be added to facilitate material rotation during welding, a task that previously required manual intervention by a technician. Consequently, the duplicate arm is employed to introduce a new function. Instead of its original function being solely "welding," it now encompasses "welding, rotating, welding."

Heuristic 6: Dynamics

The dynamics heuristic strategy is a method in which an entity adjusts its functions or attributes based on internal or external environmental changes. An expanded definition of this heuristic is as follows:

> An approximation planning method used by organisms or organizations that leverages an existing, essential ability to alter or regulate an existing attribute, quality, or characteristic for the purpose of conforming to or accommodating interrelated environmental conditions as they change. It may also be used to evoke change in the environment. Regulation can be used for resilience and efficiency purposes, and alteration may be used to increase or decrease attention, in addition to resilience and efficiency purposes. Generally, such methods include a feedback sensor to transmit evaluative or corrective information about an action, event, or process to the original or controlling source, to continue altering, stop altering, or revert back to the entity's original state.

This approach is observed in both biological systems and human-made artifacts. The ability of a cephalopod to alter its attributes serves as an excellent example of this strategy. To represent dynamics, the equation $A(t) = F(S, X, A(t-1), t)$ is employed. This equation illustrates that an entity's attribute, A, at any given time, t, depends on an external stimulus, S, in a time-dependent manner, with $A(t-1)$ representing the previous state of the attribute before the stimulus. This attribute can be controlled or switched on and off by a signal. It may also possess memory, depend on past values, and potentially vary in magnitude or direction with time.

One method for generating novel product concepts involves exploring how a system with a static attribute can be transformed into a dynamic one. This transformation can be achieved through the introduction of fresh stimuli, adjustments to the link function, or alterations to the controller. The dynamics can be initiated or sustained either by the entity itself or by an external triggering entity. For instance, the adaptability of a hammer can be achieved by adjusting the length of its handle or the relative positioning of the hammer head. Various types of dynamics exist and can be categorized based on several factors. First, dynamics can be locally controlled or centrally coordinated. Second, the nature of the link function connecting input and output can be linear, continuous, monotonic, or step-function. Third, the quantity of stimuli and their interrelations can vary. Fourth, the activation signal may originate directly from the stimuli, from a sensor, or from a third catalyst entity that signals the presence of stimuli. Fifth, there may be a stable state to which the product returns after the activation of dynamics, as opposed to continuous change. Sixth, the nature of the link can change, including increases, decreases, or changes in direction. Finally, feedback signals can also influence the dynamics. Here are some additional examples of the dynamics (Dyn) heuristic found in nature, product design, business, and military strategy:

1. Living organisms frequently employ dynamic adjustments in response to changing environmental conditions. The human body exemplifies the dynamics heuristic through a range of intricate biological processes. Take, for instance, the intricate regulation of body temperature. When the external environment becomes excessively hot, sweat glands are activated to facilitate body cooling through evaporation.[37] Conversely, when it becomes excessively cold, the body employs the strategy of constricting blood vessels to reduce heat loss. These dynamic adaptations play a pivotal role in maintaining the body's homeostasis. Enzymes, on the other hand, exhibit allosteric regulation, a mechanism whereby their activity can be finely modulated through the binding of specific molecules at sites distinct from the active site. This remarkable feature allows the enzyme to adeptly respond to fluctuations in substrate or product concentrations, thereby efficiently regulating metabolic pathways.
2. The dynamics heuristic can be applied to product design to enhance user experience. Consider a smart thermostat, such as Sensi by Copeland,[38] that dynamically adjusts room temperature based on

occupancy and user preferences. By monitoring inputs such as motion sensors and user feedback, the thermostat adapts its behavior to maintain optimal comfort and energy efficiency.

3. Dynamic pricing models adjust prices based on factors like demand, competitor pricing, or time of day, allowing businesses to optimize revenue and respond to market conditions promptly.[39] Dynamic marketing strategies also leverage the dynamics heuristic to engage and retain customers. Personalized recommendations on e-commerce platforms dynamically adjust based on a user's browsing history and preferences. By tailoring product suggestions in real time, companies can increase customer satisfaction and drive sales.

4. Successful military leaders have employed dynamic tactics, such as flanking maneuvers or adjusting formations on the battlefield, to respond to changing enemy positions or exploit weaknesses.

Dynamics can play a pivotal role in the functioning of organisms and systems as they adapt to their surroundings. By adjusting their attributes in response to external or internal stimuli, dynamics can lead to striking variations or facilitate seamless blending with the environment. For example, some organisms alter their color or texture to either attract prey or elude predators, while others employ camouflage techniques to diminish their visibility. In addition to enhancing or reducing attention, dynamics can optimize system efficiency by seamlessly transitioning between various modes. This may involve mechanisms that automatically deactivate internal resources like heat or light when external sources are readily available, contributing to energy conservation and resource preservation. Furthermore, dynamics can foster resilience within systems by enabling components to dynamically assume new roles in response to changing conditions. For instance, an organism can trigger body armor in response to a threat without requiring conscious decision-making. This automatic response mechanism is often vital for the organism's survival. Here are some ways that the dynamics (Dyn) principle relates to the ERP factors:

1. Efficiency: The dynamics heuristic can improve efficiency by dynamically modifying system attributes to optimize resource utilization without having to incur unnecessary costs to purposely modify a system after it has experienced an impact from an environmental stimulus such as long delays or damage. In a smart energy grid, the system can dynamically adjust power distribution based on real-time demand and

availability, ensuring efficient allocation of resources and minimizing waste.[40] In a manufacturing process, the system can dynamically adjust production rates and allocate resources to meet changing demand, optimizing productivity while avoiding overproduction or underutilization.

2. Resilience: The Dyn heuristic contributes to resilience by enabling a system to dynamically adapt to external environmental forces or disturbances. In ecological systems, some plant species exhibit phenotypic plasticity, where they dynamically adjust their growth patterns, leaf morphology, or root systems in response to changing environmental conditions like light availability or nutrient levels.[41] This adaptive behavior enhances their resilience to varying habitats. In computer networks, dynamic routing protocols enable the system to adjust network paths in real-time based on traffic congestion or link failures. This allows the system to quickly adapt and reroute data, maintaining connectivity and resilience in the face of network disruptions.

3. Prominence: In social media platforms, algorithms can dynamically adjust the visibility and prominence of user-generated content based on factors like engagement, relevance, or user preferences. This ensures that content with high visibility receives more attention from users, contributing to the prominence of the system. In military operations, deception strategies involve dynamically altering troop movements, equipment positions, or communication patterns to mislead or divert attention from enemy observers.[42] This dynamic manipulation of information and actions aims to enhance the prominence of friendly forces while confusing and distracting adversaries.

Dynamics serves as a pivotal mechanism for organisms to adeptly adapt and swiftly respond to dynamic alterations within their surrounding environment. These fluctuations encompass diverse variables such as temperature shifts, alterations in illumination, shifts in food availability, and the looming specter of threats posed by predators and other perilous hazards. One of the ways in which dynamics proves beneficial is by optimizing efficiency, notably through the precise regulation of an organism's internal body temperature. To illustrate, certain animals exhibit the remarkable capacity to modulate their metabolic rate, thus conserving precious energy resources in times of food scarcity while ramping up metabolism when sustenance abounds. Furthermore, dynamics can confer advantages by heightening or diminishing an organism's vigilance. Take, for instance, the ability of select animals to morph their coloration or patterns to seamlessly blend into their surroundings, thereby eluding the watchful eyes of both predators and prey. A well-documented exemplar of this phenomenon can be found in the cuttlefish, which adeptly alters its texture and hue to mimic its immediate environment, whether for the purpose of attracting prey or sidestepping unwanted attention. Dynamics also double as a formidable defense mechanism, allowing organisms to alter their shape or form when facing threats. The *Armadillidium vulgare*, commonly known as the pill bug, epitomizes this strategy by expertly curling itself into a protective ball when confronted by danger, rendering it impervious to predators and ensuring its safety.

Dynamics are frequently integrated into products to enable variations relevant to the user or the environment. One such example is a smart textile suit that adjusts its temperature based on external temperature or weather. Products that incorporate dynamics help accommodate variations in a customer's preference for product attributes or changes over time, such as when users age. For instance, Petit Pli clothing can adjust to the size of growing children.[43] DeepOptics has developed electronic lenses that can adjust their focal length based on the object being viewed.[44] Dynamics can also be used to accommodate differences among multiple users of the same product. For example, the size of a theater seat might be adjusted based on the immediate user. In some cases, dynamics in products involve a feedback process that utilizes sensors. The Ember coffee cup is an example of such a product that adjusts the temperature of the drink to maintain it at an appropriate level for consumption.

Dynamics, as a heuristic design strategy, can be observed at multiple levels within business organizations. At the product level, a firm might offer different products or offerings in different countries based on cultural or market-specific needs. At the process level, businesses may adapt their production lines or business relationships based on external conditions such as market demand or supply chain disruptions. Similarly, businesses might explore joint ventures or partnerships with competitors in certain markets while competing as rivals in others. Military strategists employ dynamic formations as a tactical response to adapt swiftly to evolving scenarios on the battlefield, ensuring a vital edge in the face of unforeseen shifts. This adaptive approach enables military forces to counter unexpected developments and maintain a tactical advantage. In the realm of marketing, firms adeptly tailor their positioning to mirror the unique character of different markets. For example, a quick-service restaurant might brand itself as a premium restaurant chain in a particular market to cater to local preferences.

Heuristic 7: Maximization

Maximization is a biological phenomenon where an organism achieves a survival-related goal by maximizing a certain component or function to a very high level compared to what is observed normally in other organisms. An expanded definition of this heuristic is as follows:

> An approximation planning method employed by organisms or organizations that seeks to maximize, extremize, or exaggerate a critical aspect of functionality through the reallocation of resources. This exaggeration can manifest in terms of physical size, function, attribute or the quantities of supplies, support, or information. It may involve significant increases or decreases in these resources within a vital or primary domain, all with the ultimate goal of enhancing survival.

The Max heuristic is often employed when a single property takes center stage as the primary determinant for an entity's survival, leading to either an increase or reduction of a functional or componential attribute to an extreme level. For instance, consider the scenario where animals increase their size in response to the presence of predators, as seen in the deimatic response of creatures like the frilled-neck lizard or puffer fish, which inflate their bodies to deter potential threats.[45] In such situations, these organisms maximize their size as a survival strategy. Maximization also manifests in critical survival functions, such as the fight or flight response, where, when threatened, organisms redistribute all their resources to enhance their chances of survival, including the release of adrenaline and increased blood flow, exemplifying the concept of maximizing a function to achieve a survival-oriented objective. Another instance of maximization can be observed in cases of suspended animation, hibernation, dormancy, or anabiosis in animals. In these scenarios, entities minimize their activity to maximize available energy resources over time, given the constraints of limited calories, thereby representing a minimization of movement and metabolism but a maximization of energy efficiency.

In the context of products, maximizing specific attributes can provide products with an advantage over competitors. Companies frequently promote their products based on maximized features or attributes that distinguish them in the market. In a business environment, organizations might opt to maximize a crucial product attribute, even at the expense of others, to attain a competitive edge. For instance, during a crisis, a business may implement aggressive cost-cutting measures, even if this entails compromising quality or shortening production time. Here are some examples of the maximization (Max) heuristic found from nature, product design, business, and military strategy:

1. During mating season, male deer grow large and intricate antlers to maximize their attractiveness to females and establish dominance among other males. Enzymes play a crucial role in biological processes, and their activity can be maximized by increasing their concentration or optimizing their structure. This allows for efficient catalysis of chemical reactions and faster metabolic pathways.

2. Companies often employ the Max heuristic by emphasizing unique features or qualities of their products or services. By maximizing these distinctive attributes, businesses aim to differentiate themselves from competitors and attract customers. For example, Apple maximizes product design and user experience to set their devices apart from competitors. In product design, the Max heuristic can be used to optimize the performance of a product. For example, a smartphone manufacturer may maximize the battery life of its product by increasing its capacity or optimizing the software to consume less power. High-performance sports cars utilize the Max heuristic by pushing the limits of speed and power, maximizing the thrill and performance experienced by the driver.

3. The Max heuristic can be seen in market penetration strategies, where businesses aim to maximize their market share by aggressively capturing a larger portion of the market. This can involve tactics like predatory pricing strategies, aggressive advertising campaigns, or offering extreme discounts to attract customers and gain a competitive edge. In digital marketing, the Max heuristic is employed to maximize the reach and visibility of content through various channels. Companies that prioritize exceptional customer service employ the Max heuristic by maximizing their efforts to create positive customer experiences. By providing personalized support, quick response times, and going above and beyond customer expectations, businesses aim to maximize customer satisfaction, loyalty, and advocacy.

4. In World War I, both sides employed massed artillery barrages as a Max heuristic. By concentrating a large number of artillery pieces and bombarding enemy positions simultaneously, they sought to maximize

the destructive power and psychological impact on the opposing forces. The goal was to weaken defenses, create openings, and pave the way for infantry assaults. During the Napoleonic Era, cavalry charges were often employed as a Max heuristic. By gathering large numbers of mounted soldiers and charging at high speed, commanders aimed to maximize the shock and disruption caused to enemy formations. The intention was to break their ranks, create disorder, and exploit the resulting chaos for a decisive victory. The principle is also famously evident in the Blitzkrieg strategies employed by the Germans during World War II, as well as in other "Shock and Awe" tactics.[46]

In the context of business, maximization is seen in product differentiation. A maximized attribute often serves to attract the attention of potential customers. Companies may choose to maximize certain attributes in response to known threats, such as adding stronger encryption to a product in response to a data breach, but new threats can create widespread damage. For example, dependence on a single cultivar of bananas (Cavendish) potentially can lead to large-scale crop losses if attacked by fungus.[47] However, maximizing a certain attribute of a product can also have unintended consequences. For example, a product that maximizes speed may sacrifice durability or safety. Here are some ways that the maximization (Max) principle relates to the ERP factors:

1. Efficiency: The maximization heuristic can be effectively applied to optimize the efficient management of resources within a system. Through the amplification of resource allocation and utilization to their peak levels, a system can attain heightened productivity and enhanced cost-effectiveness. In the realm of energy management, the pursuit of maximum efficiency in power generation processes via cutting-edge technologies and streamlined operations serves as a pivotal strategy for optimizing resource utilization while concurrently curbing wastage.

2. Resilience: The Max heuristic can be utilized to increase the resilience of a system in the face of external environmental forces or disruptions. By exaggerating certain attributes, a system can enhance its ability to adapt, recover, and withstand adverse conditions. Urban planning may involve maximizing green spaces, permeable surfaces, and natural drainage systems to enhance a city's resilience against extreme weather events like floods or heat waves. In disaster management, emergency response systems may maximize their preparedness by exaggerating

resource stockpiling, training exercises, and communication networks to better handle large-scale crises.

3. Prominence: The maximization heuristic can also be employed to modify the prominence and management of attention from both friendly and unfriendly observers. By amplifying certain attributes, a system can attract attention, influence perceptions, and effectively manage the attention it draws from observers. Public relations and marketing strategies often employ the Max heuristic to maximize the impact of promotional campaigns, brand activations, or celebrity endorsements to gain widespread attention and positive perception.

In certain scenarios, the hyper-focus on a specific attribute can result in a product becoming ill-suited for particular market segments. Take, for instance, the case of a high-performance sports car, which may lack practicality for a family with young children. Another non-biological illustration of maximization can be found in the utilization of tourniquets to manage bleeding in a trauma situation. In this particular context, a tourniquet is meticulously applied to the affected limb, effectively halting the blood flow and redirecting it toward functions of greater urgency. This inverted variant of maximization centers on the complete elimination of a function to achieve a survival-oriented objective, specifically, ensuring the overall survival of the individual.

Natural Design Heuristics for Product Design

Natural heuristics can also be effectively employed in the generation of product design concepts (Table 4.2). To illustrate the application of the seven natural heuristics to a product design case, we define the heuristics in the context of products and then demonstrate their application for a basic product, a rudimentary mallet composed of two cylinders (Table 4.3).

Heuristic Ideation Using Generative AI

In this section, we will explore how large language model (LLM) tools, such as ChatGPT and Google Bard (Gemini), can support a systematic idea-generation process that leverages creativity heuristics to steer divergent thinking. Initially, we instruct the LLM to function as a general-purpose ideator that incorporates all seven design heuristics. The following prompt was employed.

Table 4.2 Natural Design Heuristics for Product Design

Heuristic	Illustration
Combination	Two different functions previously found in multiple products combined into a single component or product
Removal	Removal of a key component or attribute in a prototypical product
Separation	Separating two functions or attributes found in the prototypical attribute
Segmentation	Segmenting an attribute or function in a product into smaller units
Replication	Replicating an attribute or function in a product
Dynamics	Modifying a function or attribute of a product such that it is dynamic
Maximization	Maximizing (or minimizing) an attribute or function of a product

You will play the role of an idea generator. For every target system such as product, process or business that I tell you, you will give me an idea that involves (1) Combination (Com): combining two components of the target system (2) Removal (Rem): removing or eliminating a component of the target system (3) Separation (Sep): separating components or processes of the target system in space or time (4) Segmentation (Seg): segmenting, dividing, or modularizing the target system or its components (4) Replication (Rep): copying, replicating or adding redundancy to the target system or its components (5) Dynamics (Dyn): varying or modifying a feature or process of the target system or its component dynamically based on some external input (7) Maximization (Max): maximizing, minimizing, optimizing or extremizing any attribute or process of the target system. If a target goal is specified along with the target system, the ideas should be aimed at meeting the target goal. Also provide a unique and interesting name for the idea and identify the benefit of the idea. At every turn, ask me for the name and description of the target system, and the target goal if applicable.

Next, we can utilize the heuristic to generate new ideas or address a particular challenge. To demonstrate, let's explore how the prompt can be applied to redesign a hospital bed. By employing the prompts with ChatGPT and Google Bard, we were able to identify the following innovative ideas (Table 4.4).[48]

Table 4.3   Natural Design Heuristics Applied to a Basic Product

Heuristic	Illustrative Concept
Combination	Two cylindrical objects that can be united to form a mallet. The combination could yield a tool with the weight and balance of a mallet, coupled with a distinctive cylindrical shape that might serve various functions.
Removal	A section of the handle grip is removed to reduce the mallet's weight. By eliminating superfluous components, the tool can become lighter, more ergonomic, and potentially more efficient. In the case of the mallet, reducing its weight could enhance ease of handling and mitigate the risk of injury or fatigue.
Separation	The mallet can be separated into two different parts for convenient storage. Breaking down the mallet into smaller parts facilitates storage and transportation, particularly advantageous for individuals or organizations with limited space. Furthermore, disassembling the mallet might simplify cleaning or maintenance of individual components.
Segmentation	The mallet can be segmented into two similarly sized hammers. Dividing the mallet into two hammers provides two separate tools that can be used independently or collaboratively, improving job site efficiency. Additionally, two people can simultaneously wield the two hammers, further enhancing work productivity.
Replication	Replicate the handle to create a dual-ended mallet. This design feature would enable more efficient utilization of the mallet as the user can switch between the two ends without constant grip adjustments. Additionally, the two ends can be tailored for distinct purposes, such as one end for striking and the other for precision work.
Dynamics	Design the mallet with a telescoping handle that can be extended or retracted to adjust its length. Such a feature proves beneficial in situations where different lengths are required for various tasks or when accommodating users of varying heights. The telescoping mechanism can be fashioned from durable materials like aluminum or steel, ensuring strength and longevity.
Maximization	Fashion a mallet with an exceptionally lengthy handle, enabling its use as a lever for heavy-duty prying or lifting. Conversely, shortening the handle creates a more compact and portable mallet, ideal for toolbox storage or on-site transportation. Similarly, enlarging the mallet face area yields a larger striking surface, valuable for tasks demanding greater impact force.

Table 4.4   Natural Design Heuristics with Generative AI

Heuristic	OpenAI ChatGPT	Google Bard
Com	Integrate a built-in vital signs monitoring system into the hospital bed. This combines the functionalities of the bed and a separate monitoring device, allowing healthcare providers to continuously monitor patients' vital signs such as heart rate, blood pressure, and oxygen saturation without the need for additional equipment.	Combine a hospital bed with a toilet and sink to create a self-contained unit that can be used in patient rooms. This would eliminate the need for patients to leave their rooms to use the bathroom, which can be difficult or impossible for some patients.
Rem	Eliminate the need for manual bed adjustments by implementing an automated bed positioning system. This removes the manual crank or lever mechanism typically found in hospital beds and replaces it with a motorized system controlled through a user-friendly interface. Patients or healthcare providers can easily adjust the bed's height, incline, and other parameters with the push of a button.	Remove the headboard from a hospital bed to create more space in the room. This would make it easier for caregivers to move around the room and provide care to patients.
Sep	Separate the control panel from the bed itself by implementing a wireless control system. The control panel can be detached from the bed, allowing healthcare providers to operate it remotely from a distance. This separation provides convenience and flexibility, enabling caregivers to adjust bed settings or activate features without needing to physically interact with the bed.	Separate the mattress from the frame of a hospital bed to make it easier to clean and maintain. This would also make it easier to transport the bed if necessary.

(Continued)

Table 4.4 (Continued) Natural Design Heuristics with Generative AI

Heuristic	OpenAI ChatGPT	Google Bard
Seg	Divide the bed into modular sections that can be independently adjusted. Each section, such as the head, back, legs, and foot, can have separate adjustment controls. This segmentation allows patients to find the most comfortable position by individually adjusting each section according to their needs, enhancing overall comfort and support.	Segment the bed into different parts, such as the mattress, frame, and headboard. This would make it easier to manufacture and transport the bed. It would also make it easier to replace individual parts if they become damaged.
Rep	Add redundancy to critical bed components such as the power supply and safety systems. By replicating these components, the bed can continue functioning even if one of them fails. Redundancy improves reliability and ensures patient safety, reducing the risk of unexpected system failures.	Replicate the bed in different sizes to accommodate patients of different heights and weights. This would ensure that all patients have a bed that is comfortable and safe for them to use.
Dyn	Implement a dynamic pressure redistribution system based on real-time feedback. By incorporating pressure sensors into the bed surface, the system can dynamically adjust the pressure distribution to alleviate pressure points and prevent bedsores. This dynamic adaptation helps optimize patient comfort and minimize the risk of developing skin ulcers.	Develop a bed that can be adjusted to different heights and angles to accommodate patients of different needs. This would make it easier for patients to get in and out of bed, eat, and use the bathroom.
Max	Optimize energy efficiency by integrating a power-saving mode. The bed can detect periods of inactivity, such as when the patient is not in bed, and automatically enter a low-power state. By minimizing energy consumption during idle times, this maximizes the bed's energy efficiency and reduces overall power usage.	Maximize the comfort of the bed by using soft, supportive materials and by adding features such as a built-in pillow and a reading light. This would help patients to get a good night's sleep and to relax during the day.

Exercises

1. Take a specific business challenge or problem and identify the design heuristics that can be applied to address the challenge and achieve the desired outcomes. For each heuristic, provide a brief explanation of how it can be used and its potential impact on efficiency, resilience, or prominence. Discuss the potential benefits and drawbacks of each heuristic in the given context.

2. Select a product or business service that you admire and examine how design heuristics can be utilized to enhance its prominence. Concentrate on the heuristics of combination, removal, and segmentation. Identify features, attributes, or components that could be combined, removed, or segmented to render the product or service more noticeable, appealing, or memorable to the target audience. Discuss the potential effects on customer perception and market competitiveness.

3. Organize a group innovation workshop where participants apply the natural design heuristics described in this chapter. Divide participants into small teams and assign each team a different heuristic to explore. Encourage teams to brainstorm and present their ideas, highlighting how each heuristic can be effectively employed to address the challenge and improve ERP factors.

4. Conduct a GenAI exercise to generate various product ideas for addressing a specific organizational problem or business opportunity, employing the seven heuristics as indicated above. What are the most intriguing ideas? Can you instruct the GenAI to assess and score the ideas based on factors that hold significance for you or your organization? Begin by instructing the GenAI about the key factors you consider important and then have it evaluate the range of ideas it produces. Subsequently, attempt to guide the GenAI in synthesizing the best ideas into an overarching concept. How robust is the solution or idea generated by the GenAI? What prompt adjustments did you make throughout the exercise, and what are your next steps?

Notes

1. Gigerenzer, G., & Gaissmaier, W. (2011). Heuristic decision making. *Annual Review of Psychology*, 62, 451–482.
2. Pearl, J. (1984). *Heuristics*. Addison-Wesley.

3. Bettis, R. A. (2017). Organizationally intractable decision problems and the intellectual virtues of heuristics. *Journal of Management*, 43(8), 2620–2637.

4. Banks, A. P., Gamblin, D. M., & Hutchinson, H. (2020). Training fast and frugal heuristics in military decision making. *Applied Cognitive Psychology*, 34(3), 699–709.

5. Yilmaz, S., Daly, S. R., Seifert, C. M., & Gonzalez, R. (2016). Evidence-based design heuristics for idea generation. *Design Studies*, 46, 95–124.

6. Gigerenzer, G., & Brighton, H. (2009). Homo heuristicus: Why biased minds make better inferences. *Topics in Cognitive Science*, 1(1), 107–143.

7. Kahneman, D., Slovic, P., & Tversky, A. (Eds.). (1982). *Judgment under Uncertainty: Heuristics and Biases*. Cambridge: Cambridge University Press.

8. Savransky, S. D. (2000). *Engineering of Creativity: Introduction to TRIZ Methodology of Inventive Problem Solving*. CRC Press.

9. Honegger, R. (1985). Fine structure of different types of symbiotic relationships in lichens. In *Lichen Physiology and Cell Biology* (pp. 287–302). Springer US.

10. Dyer, J. H., Kale, P., & Singh, H. (2001). How to make strategic alliances work. *MIT Sloan Management Review*, 42(4), 37.

11. Bergsmann, S. (2001). The concept of military alliance. In *Small States and Alliances* (pp. 25–37). Physica-Verlag HD.

12. Moura, P. S., López, G. L., Moreno, J. I., & De Almeida, A. T. (2013). The role of smart grids to foster energy efficiency. *Energy Efficiency*, 6, 621–639.

13. Oliver, T. H., Heard, M. S., Isaac, N. J., Roy, D. B., Procter, D., Eigenbrod, F., ... Bullock, J. M. (2015). Biodiversity and resilience of ecosystem functions. *Trends in Ecology & Evolution*, 30(11), 673–684.

14. Keel, A., & Nataraajan, R. (2012). Celebrity endorsements and beyond: New avenues for celebrity branding. *Psychology & Marketing*, 29(9), 690–703.

15. Borowsky, R. (2008). Restoring sight in blind cavefish. *Current Biology*, 18(1), R23–R24.

16. Dahlmann, B. (2005). Proteasomes. *Essays in Biochemistry*, 41, 31–48.

17. Puisis, E. (2022, November 4). *What Is Minimalist Architecture?* The Spruce. https://www.thespruce.com/what-is-minimalist-architecture-5224419.

18. Woolfson, D. (2021, January 8). Coca-Cola puts inspirational messages on cans as part of "Open To Better" campaign. *The Grocer*. https://www.thegrocer.co.uk/marketing/coca-cola-puts-inspirational-messages-on-cans-as-part-of-open-to-better-campaign/651915.article.

19. Kan, P. R. (2011, February 24). Making a sandwich in Afghanistan: How to assess a strategic withdrawal from a protracted irregular war. *Small Wars Journal*. http://smallwarsjournal.com/jrnl/art/making-a-sandwich-in-afghanistan.

20. Jang, W. E., Ko, Y. J., Morris, J. D., & Chang, Y. (2015). Scarcity message effects on consumption behavior: Limited edition product considerations. *Psychology & Marketing*, 32(10), 989–1001.

21. Bandholz, E. (2023, June 16). Brandless exec on acquisitions, AI, more. *Practical Ecommerce*. https://www.practicalecommerce.com/brandless-exec-on-acquisitions-ai-more.

22. Guiterman, A. (1936). The march of science. In *Gaily the Troubadour* (p. 38). E. P. Dutton & Company, Incorporated.

23. Fleming, P. A., Muller, D., & Bateman, P. W. (2007). Leave it all behind: A taxonomic perspective of autotomy in invertebrates. *Biological Reviews*, 82(3), 481–510.

24. *IBM Completes the Separation of Kyndryl*. (2021, November 3). IBM Newsroom. https://newsroom.ibm.com/2021-11-03-IBM-Completes-the-Separation-of -Kyndryl.

25. Nicholson, L. B. (2016). The immune system. *Essays in Biochemistry*, 60(3), 275–301.

26. Mosig, Y. (2015, September 21). *New Perspectives on the Battle of Cannae - Hannibal and the Punic Wars*. The History Herald. https://thehistoryherald .com/articles/ancient-history-civilisation/hannibal-and-the-punic-wars/new -perspectives-on-the-battle-of-cannae/amp/.

27. De Win, B., Piessens, F., Joosen, W., & Verhanneman, T. (2002). *On the Importance of the Separation-of-Concerns Principle in Secure Software Engineering*. In Workshop on the Application of Engineering Principles to System Security Design (pp. 1–10).

28. Gouda, M. G., & Liu, A. X. (2007). Structured firewall design. *Computer Networks*, 51(4), 1106–1120.

29. Drucker, P. F. (1984). Beyond the Bell breakup. *The Public Interest*, 77, 3.

30. Edwards, C. A., & Arancon, N. Q. (2022). Earthworm morphology. In *Biology and Ecology of Earthworms* (pp. 1–31). Springer US.

31. Taylor, M. J. (2014). Roman infantry tactics in the mid-Republic: A reassessment. *Historia: Zeitschrift für Alte Geschichte*, 301–322.

32. Kunkel, T. A., & Bebenek, K. (2000). DNA replication fidelity. *Annual Review of Biochemistry*, 69(1), 497–529.

33. Zolghadri, A. (2000). A redundancy-based strategy for safety management in a modern civil aircraft. *Control Engineering Practice*, 8(5), 545–554.

34. Bradach, J. L. (1997). Using the plural form in the management of restaurant chains. *Administrative Science Quarterly*, 276–303.

35. Weinerth, G. (2010). The constructal analysis of warfare. *International Journal of Design & Nature and Ecodynamics*, 5(3), 268–276.

36. Steele, G. C. (1923). Decoy as a weapon in naval warfare. *Royal United Services Institution Journal*, 68(469), 99–108.

37. González-Alonso, J. (2012). Human thermoregulation and the cardiovascular system. *Experimental Physiology*, 97(3), 340–346.

38. *Sensi Smart Wi-Fi Thermostat | Sensi US*. Copeland. Retrieved November 7, 2023, from https://sensi.copeland.com/en-us/products/wifi-thermostat.

39. Kannan, P. K., & Kopalle, P. K. (2001). Dynamic pricing on the Internet: Importance and implications for consumer behavior. *International Journal of Electronic Commerce*, 5(3), 63–83.

40. Salinas, S., Li, M., Li, P., & Fu, Y. (2013). Dynamic energy management for the smart grid with distributed energy resources. *IEEE Transactions on Smart Grid*, 4(4), 2139–2151.

41. DeWitt, T. J., Sih, A., & Sloan Wilson, D. (1998). Costs and limits of phenotypic plasticity. *Trends in Ecology & Evolution*, 13(2), 77–81.
42. Gerwehr, S., & Glenn, R. W. (2000). *The Art of Darkness: Deception and Urban Operations*. Santa Monica, CA: RAND.
43. Red Dot. (2023, March 22). *Red Dot Design Award: Petit Pli – Clothes That Grow*. Red Dot. https://www.red-dot.org/project/petit-pli-clothes-that-grow -37022.
44. Steinberg, D. (2022, November 10). DeepOptics 32°N adaptive focus sunglasses: The 200 best inventions of 2022. *Time*. https://time.com/collection/ best-inventions-2022/6229141/deepoptics-32n-adaptive-focus-sunglasses/.
45. Drinkwater, E., Allen, W. L., Endler, J. A., Hanlon, R. T., Holmes, G., Homziak, N. T., Kang, C., et al. (2022). A synthesis of deimatic behaviour. *Biological Reviews*, 97(6), 2237–2267.
46. Zilincik, S. (2023). Awe for strategic effect: Hardly worth the trouble. *Journal of Strategic Studies*, 1–26.
47. Butler, D. (2013). Fungus threatens top banana: Fears rise for Latin American industry as devastating disease hits leading variety in Africa and Middle East. *Nature*, 504(7479), 195–197.
48. The exercise was conducted on May 18, 2023.

References

Banks, A. P., Gamblin, D. M., & Hutchinson, H. (2020). Training fast and frugal heuristics in military decision making. *Applied Cognitive Psychology*, 34(3), 699–709.

Borowsky, R. (2008). Restoring sight in blind cavefish. *Current Biology*, 18(1), R23–R24.

Bradach, J. L. (1997). Using the plural form in the management of restaurant chains. *Administrative Science Quarterly*, 42(2), 276–303.

Dahlmann, B. (2005). Proteasomes. *Essays in Biochemistry*, 41, 31–48.

De Win, B., Piessens, F., Joosen, W., & Verhanneman, T. (2002). On the importance of the separation-of-concerns principle in secure software engineering. In *Workshop on the Application of Engineering Principles to System Security Design* (pp. 1–10).

DeWitt, T. J., Sih, A., & Sloan Wilson, D. (1998). Costs and limits of phenotypic plasticity. *Trends in Ecology & Evolution*, 13(2), 77–81.

Drinkwater, E., Allen, W. L., Endler, J. A., Hanlon, R. T., Holmes, G., Homziak, N. T., Kang, C., et al. (2022). A synthesis of deimatic behaviour. *Biological Reviews*, 97(6), 2237–2267.

Dyer, J. H., Kale, P., & Singh, H. (2001). How to make strategic alliances work. *MIT Sloan Management Review*, 42(4), 37.

Edwards, C. A., & Arancon, N. Q. (2022). Earthworm morphology. In C. A. Edwards & N. Q. Arancon (Eds.), *Biology and Ecology of Earthworms* (pp. 1–31). Springer US.

Fleming, P. A., Muller, D., & Bateman, P. W. (2007). Leave it all behind: A taxonomic perspective of autotomy in invertebrates. *Biological Reviews*, 82(3), 481–510.

Gerwehr, S., & Glenn, R. W. (2000). *The Art of Darkness: Deception and Urban Operations*. RAND.

Gigerenzer, G., & Brighton, H. (2009). Homo heuristicus: Why biased minds make better inferences. *Topics in Cognitive Science*, 1(1), 107–143.

Gigerenzer, G., & Gaissmaier, W. (2011). Heuristic decision making. *Annual Review of Psychology*, 62, 451–482.

González-Alonso, J. (2012). Human thermoregulation and the cardiovascular system. *Experimental Physiology*, 97(3), 340–346.

Gouda, M. G., & Liu, A. X. (2007). Structured firewall design. *Computer Networks*, 51(4), 1106–1120.

Guiterman, A. (1936). The march of science. In *Gaily the Troubadour* (p. 38). E. P. Dutton & Company, Incorporated.

Honegger, R. (1985). Fine structure of different types of symbiotic relationships in lichens. In Brown, D.H. (eds) *Lichen Physiology and Cell Biology* (pp. 287–302). Springer US.

Jang, W. E., Ko, Y. J., Morris, J. D., & Chang, Y. (2015). Scarcity message effects on consumption behavior: Limited edition product considerations. *Psychology & Marketing*, 32(10), 989–1001.

Kahneman, D., Slovic, P., & Tversky, A. (1982). *Judgment Under Uncertainty*. Cambridge University Press.

Kan, P. R. (2011, February 24). Making a sandwich in Afghanistan: How to assess a strategic withdrawal from a protracted irregular war. *Small Wars Journal*. http://smallwarsjournal.com/jrnl/art/making-a-sandwich-in-afghanistan

Kannan, P. K., & Kopalle, P. K. (2001). Dynamic pricing on the Internet: Importance and implications for consumer behavior. *International Journal of Electronic Commerce*, 5(3), 63–83.

Keel, A., & Nataraajan, R. (2012). Celebrity endorsements and beyond: New avenues for celebrity branding. *Psychology & Marketing*, 29(9), 690–703.

Kunkel, T. A., & Bebenek, K. (2000). DNA replication fidelity. *Annual Review of Biochemistry*, 69(1), 497–529.

Moura, P. S., López, G. L., Moreno, J. I., & De Almeida, A. T. (2013). The role of smart grids to foster energy efficiency. *Energy Efficiency*, 6, 621–639.

Nicholson, L. B. (2016). The immune system. *Essays in Biochemistry*, 60(3), 275–301.

Oliver, T. H., Heard, M. S., Isaac, N. J., Roy, D. B., Procter, D., Eigenbrod, F., ... Bullock, J. M. (2015). Biodiversity and resilience of ecosystem functions. *Trends in Ecology & Evolution*, 30(11), 673–684.

Pearl, J. (1984). *Heuristics: Intelligent Search Strategies for Computer Problem Solving*. Addison-Wesley Longman Publishing Co., Inc.

Salinas, S., Li, M., Li, P., & Fu, Y. (2013). Dynamic energy management for the smart grid with distributed energy resources. *IEEE Transactions on Smart Grid*, 4(4), 2139–2151.

Savransky, S. D. (2000). *Engineering of Creativity: Introduction to TRIZ Methodology of Inventive Problem Solving.* CRC Press.

Steele, G. C. (1923). Decoy as a weapon in naval warfare. *Royal United Services Institution Journal,* 68(469), 99–108.

Taylor, M. J. (2014). Roman infantry tactics in the mid-Republic: A reassessment. *Historia: Zeitschrift für Alte Geschichte,* 63(3), 301–322.

Weinerth, G. (2010). The constructal analysis of warfare. *International Journal of Design & Nature and Ecodynamics,* 5(3), 268–276.

Yilmaz, S., & Seifert, C. M. (2011). Creativity through design heuristics: A case study of expert product design. *Design Studies,* 32(4), 384–415.

Zilincik, S. (2023). Awe for strategic effect: Hardly worth the trouble. *Journal of Strategic Studies,* 46(6–7), 1434–1459.

Zolghadri, A. (2000). A redundancy-based strategy for safety management in a modern civil aircraft. *Control Engineering Practice,* 8(5), 545–554.

Chapter 5

Mixed Design Heuristics

Nature is pleased with simplicity, and affects not the pomp of superfluous causes.

–Isaac Newton

DOI: 10.4324/9781032715315-6

Table 5.1 Mixed Design Heuristics

Dyncom	Dynrem	Dynsep	Dynseg	Dynrep	Dynmax	**Dyn**
Maxcom	Maxrem	Maxsep	Maxseg	Maxrep	**Max**	Maxdyn
Repcom	Reprem	Repsep	Repseg	**Rep**	Repmax	Repdyn
Segcom	Segrem	Segsep	**Seg**	Segrep	Segmax	Segdyn
Sepcom	Seprem	**Sep**	Sepseg	Seprep	Sepmax	Sepdyn
Remcom	**Rem**	Remsep	Remseg	Remrep	Remmax	Remdyn
Com	Comrem	Comsep	Comseg	Comrep	Commax	Comdyn

In this chapter, we undertake an exploration of mixed design heuristics. Mixed heuristics entail the concurrent (simultaneous or sequential) application of two or more of the seven natural heuristics introduced in the previous chapter. These natural heuristics are combination (Com), removal (Rem), separation (Sep), segmentation (Seg), replication (Rep), maximization (Max), and dynamics (Dyn). Our discussion begins with the introduction and examination of 42 (21 x 2) mixed design heuristics, emerging from the amalgamation of two distinct natural heuristics. Similar to their natural counterparts, these mixed heuristics serve as analytical tools, enhancing our comprehension of the design dynamics within diverse systems, encompassing living organisms, commercial entities, products, and constructed environments. Furthermore, they facilitate the generation of innovative design concepts and the identification of strategic courses of action. The nomenclature of these heuristics is derived through the concatenation of the contractions corresponding to the natural heuristics, as highlighted in Table 5.1.

Comrem and Remcom

Comrem and Remcom are mixed heuristic strategies involving the combination and removal heuristics that are used or appear together. Comrem refers to the process of combining two components of a system and subsequently removing another component. A common case of Comrem is when two entities are combined, resulting in the removal of one or more of the combining entities. An example of Comrem in nature is the process of photosynthesis, which involves the combination of carbon dioxide and water to produce glucose and oxygen. At the same time, oxygenic photosynthesis also removes carbon dioxide from the atmosphere. Another form of Comrem is when two components are combined, but the resulting whole is materially smaller than the sum of its constituent entities. An example of this is evident in mergers, where redundant departments are eliminated or employees are laid off.[1] Comrem can also represent a predatory "parasite" strategy, where one entity combines itself with another host (such as a leech), uses the resources of the host, and sometimes destroys the second entity/host before eventually disassociating itself.[2] This strategy can also be observed in companies, where larger companies buy out and eventually destroy smaller competitors.

Remcom, on the other hand, refers to the removal or elimination of a component of a system, followed by the combination or integration of the remaining components. A product might undergo a design simplification, with certain features or components being removed, followed by the integration of the remaining features to create a more streamlined and efficient design. Remcom also represents the "substitution" heuristic, where an entity is removed to be replaced with another. An example of Remcom is seen in embryonic development, where cells undergo a process called apoptosis, in which some cells are selectively removed to form specialized structures. For example, in the development of the human hand, cells between the digits are removed to create individual fingers.[3] Here, removal is often a precondition for combination, as an existing entity in place can prevent the combination from materializing. For instance, one might consider if a material used in manufacturing could be replaced with another material. This involves figuring out how the material can be removed from the existing entity and how the alternate material can be combined with the remaining entity to complete it. Many reductive machining and fabrication processes utilize Remcom. Material may be milled, drilled, or turned away from one form and fastened, pressed, or welded to another material to form higher-level components such as struts, braces, and actuators. Given that both Rem and Com are associated with efficiency, Comrem and Remcom can be considered quintessential efficiency strategies and can be found in organizational design as well. For instance, Joint Base Anacostia Bolling combined Air Force and Naval installations in Maryland on the D.C. border, removing Air Force contracting/buying offices and relying on the Navy to handle it for both services at this location. However, this model has not performed well, and they are switching back and giving this function back to the Air Force.

Seprem and Remsep

Seprem and Remsep involve separating components of the system as well as removing or eliminating a component of the system. Seprem refers to the process of separating components of a system in space or time and then removing or eliminating one or more of those components. Furthermore, "Seprem" encompasses strategic approaches wherein a specific component undergoes physical isolation from the broader system, subsequently culminating in its removal. One well-known example of Seprem is the gecko's tail autotomy strategy, where the reptile separates and removes its appendage to distract potential attackers.[4] In this form of strategic action, a system is separated into non-identical components, and subsequently one of the two parts is removed and eliminated to save the other part. This strategy can also be used as a diversionary tactic where an attractive part of an entity is separated to save the rest. For instance, in the case of a business, an attractive yet small unit of the company might be spun off to be devoured by a predatory firm, ensuring the independent survival of the rest of the company.

Another illustration of the Seprem principle involves sacrificing one member of a group or herd to save the overall group. The sacrificed individual could be a weak member, which is more expendable or difficult to protect, or a strong member to "wear down" the predator so that the rest of the herd is saved. Depending on the context, the leader or the weakest member might be sacrificed to save the group. This may also be characterized as the "sacrificial lamb" or the "scapegoat" strategy. Similarly, in military strategy, the weakest or strongest entity may be sacrificed based on the context for the survival of the rest of the entity. Seprem can also serve as an adversarial/deception strategy where an entity is separated into dissimilar components that depend on each other to eliminate the entity. In military strategy, Seprem can be observed in the tactic of dividing an enemy army into smaller groups, isolating them from each other, and then attacking each group separately.

On the other hand, Remsep is the reverse process of removing a component of the system and then separating components in space or time. An example of Remsep from living organisms is the process of regeneration, where a component of the organism is removed or eliminated, and then the remaining components are separated in space and time to allow for the growth of new tissues and organs. As a predator's strategy, Remsep involves first weakening, immobilizing, or killing a part of a larger entity and then escaping before retaliation. The scorched earth tactics used by Russian soldiers during the Napoleonic Wars involved destroying or removing valuable resources before retreating.[5]

In historical innovation, Remsep can be seen in the development of new technologies or systems that eliminate the limitations of previous generations, and then separate components in space and time to allow for new levels of performance or functionality. Public policy objectives can drive a Remsep strategy. For example, many large federal development contractors in the United States were forced to remove elements of their business that provided advisory and assistance services to the government due to potential organizational and personal employee conflicts of interest. This conflict arose from having a development contractor's employees advise the government on development requirements (perceived as "a fix") while having personal incentives tied to the firm's overall performance. These entities were then separated into their own independent service firms that had no connection to the original development firm, maintaining the advisory talent but removing conflicts of interest.

Comsep and Sepcom

Comsep and Sepcom are heuristics that encompass both combination and separation. Comsep refers to the combination or integration of two components within a system, followed by their subsequent separation in space or time. One common example is when products are combined for storage purposes and then later separated for use. A laptop with a detachable screen that can be used as a tablet is an illustration of Comsep in product design. An exemplar of Comsep from historical military strategy is the Trojan Horse tactic employed by the Greeks during the Trojan War, wherein they combined a wooden horse with soldiers hidden inside and left it outside the gates of Troy. Once the horse was brought inside the city walls, the soldiers emerged and captured the city. An instance from historical innovation is the development of the telephone, involving the integration of electrical signals with sound waves, succeeded by the separation of the transmitter and receiver, enabling greater clarity in communication. In the realm of marketing strategy, Comsep appears as a pragmatic tactic when enterprises introduce novel products or services. This strategy involves the initial integration of the new offering with an existing product line, followed by a deliberate separation to engender a distinct brand identity.

Sepcom, on the other hand, pertains to the separation of components within a system in space or time, followed by their subsequent combination or integration. This approach proves advantageous, as the components, when separated, are more likely to endure in intermediate scenarios. Dynamic Adaptive Streaming over HTTP (MPEG-DASH) serves as an exemplar of the Sepcom strategy. It functions by dividing the content into a series of small segments, each of which is delivered via HTTP to a client.[6] Furthermore, Sepcom is employed as a predatory strategy, wherein an entity is deliberately separated to render it inert and subsequently combined for utilization in a similar or modified manner. Seed banks, such as the Svalbard Global Seed Vault, strategically employ the Sepcom heuristic to isolate and collectively store critical components (seed specimens of plant species).[7] In this context, diverse forms of vital components undergo separation, being maintained independently and then combined when the need arises. Another manifestation of this heuristic is discernible in the division of labor, where two entities undergo separation but later unite to constitute a single entity, subsequently opting to specialize in distinct tasks. For instance, initially, two individual workers may independently perform both Task A and Task B without coordination. Subsequently, they choose to collaborate, coordinating their efforts while each continues to perform both tasks. Ultimately, they separate, with one exclusively handling Task A and the other exclusively managing Task B, thus optimizing efficiency. Within military contexts, the Sepcom heuristic manifests in the establishment of new departments or forces within the Department of Defense, such as the creation of the Space Force. This phased approach involves the separation of the space component from the Navy, Air Force, and Army, subsequently consolidating it under the newly established Space Force.

Sepseg and Segsep

Sepseg and Segsep represent strategies featuring both separation and segmentation. Sepseg refers to a strategy where components of a system are first separated in space or time into distinctive units, and then each of these separated units is segmented into similar subunits. This approach is commonly used to improve the efficiency, reliability, and resilience of a system. Sepseg is observed in organisms and organizations where an entity is first separated into smaller dissimilar entities and then segmented to make it smaller and more flexible. For example, the wings of birds are separated from their bodies and then segmented into feathers, allowing for independent control. Military organizations have historically utilized the Sepseg strategy in their command structures. The overall military organization is separated into distinct branches (army, navy, marines, air force) and then segmented further into multiple similar units and divisions. Sepseg is also observed in the strategy where a car manufacturer first separates the car into its distinct functional components and then segments those components into subassemblies that can be easily manufactured and assembled by specialized suppliers within a supply chain. Early computers were separated into distinct components such as the central processing unit (CPU), memory, and storage, which were then segmented into smaller, similar components like registers and caches, allowing for greater efficiency. In business, a company might first separate its operations into different units, such as marketing, sales, and finance. Then, it might segment each of these units even further into similar teams focused on different products or markets.

Segsep, on the other hand, refers to a process where components of a system are first segmented or modularized into similar units and then separated into distinctive units in space or time. This approach can be used to improve the scalability, flexibility, and adaptability of a system. The division of labor in eusocial insects is also a case of the Segsep principle in nature. Insects such as ants and bees have different castes that perform specialized tasks such as foraging, nest building, and caring for the young.[8] The division of labor is a result of segmenting the colony consisting of similar organisms into different roles (Seg) and then separating the individuals in space and time (Sep) to perform those roles. Staged space rockets may be the best example of a Segsep design strategy. These rockets are built in segmented stages that separate at various transition periods during the launch and deployment of a space asset. Historically, military strategy has also employed Segsep to improve the effectiveness of armies. For example, the Roman army was divided into legions, each with its own command structure and support staff. This segmentation allowed for greater flexibility and adaptability on the battlefield. Sepseg may appear dynamically as part of a Sepdynseg strategy, where the entity appears separated under certain conditions and segmented under other conditions. For example, a military unit or company might decide to organize itself into smaller units that are functionally identical or functionally focused based on the external environment, such as fire teams. Segsep is also seen in the piecemeal strategy. This involves dividing the enemy forces into smaller, more manageable groups (Seg) and then separating them in space and time (Sep) by attacking them at different locations and times to prevent them from regrouping and mounting a counter-attack.

Segrem and Remseg

Segrem and Remseg represent strategies that involve both segmentation and removal. Segrem involves segmenting, dividing, or modularizing a system or its components and then removing or eliminating one or more of those components. In some cases, Segrem is akin to a "chocolate bar" strategy, where the bar is segmented into similar pieces and consumed sequentially. Here, the purpose of segmentation in Segrem is to facilitate balanced or equalized removal or elimination of the entity over time. Segrem is also observed in various designs, such as snap-off blade knives where segmentation facilitates easy removal of sub-units. Philanthropic foundations are devised to completely spend money over a certain period by making segmented payments every year. In several financing schemes, debt is broken into smaller units of similar payments to eventually eliminate the overall debt. Segrem can also be an adversarial or deceptive strategy ("divide and conquer") where a predator divides a large entity into smaller units to destroy it either by making it too small to survive or by attacking it one by one in sequence.[9] This concept is famously captured in Sun Tzu's quote, "the art of using troops is this: When ten to the enemy's one, surround him; When five times his strength, attack him; If double his strength, divide him." The military or a global firm may segment areas of interest/responsibility into manageable, achievable geographic segments to conquer and then work to remove them from their list of targets. A company may also segment a large department into smaller, more specialized teams and then eliminate the teams that are redundant or not performing well.

Remseg involves removing or eliminating a component of the system and then segmenting, dividing, or modularizing the remaining components. This operation is useful when a system is too complex and needs to be simplified or when a component is no longer necessary but can be repurposed. This operation can reduce the impact of the removed component on the overall system while maintaining or improving the system's performance. Another case of Remseg is plant propagation through stem cuttings, where a plant is removed from its parent system, and its stem is segmented into smaller pieces, which can grow into new plants.[10] In historical military strategy, when a defending army retreats from a territory and then sets up smaller, more easily defensible positions, it is using the Remseg operation. By retreating, the army reduces the enemy's ability to attack it with overwhelming force, and by setting up smaller positions, it can better defend itself against enemy attacks by diffusing the enemies' unity of effort. In product design, a manufacturer can remove certain features from a product that are not in demand and then create a modular design that allows customers to choose which features they want. A company may use the Remseg operation to streamline its operations. By identifying non-essential components or departments, the company can remove them and then segment or divide the remaining components to create a more efficient structure. Remseg also represents an operational strategy where a company may eliminate a department that is not performing well and then segment the remaining work among other departments to maintain productivity.

Comseg and Segcom

Comseg and Segcom heuristics represent strategies that involve both combination and segmentation. Comseg refers to the process of combining, integrating, or connecting two components of a system and then segmenting, dividing, or modularizing the system or its components. Fungi are an example of Comseg in biological systems. Fungi form networks of hyphae that integrate different parts of their environment, such as soil and other organisms, but are segmented into different mycelial cords, which can grow and forage in different directions.[11] The Comseg strategy of combining dissimilar entities and then segmenting them equally can introduce efficiency and reliability. For example, two different units in a business organization can be combined and then split into multiple similar units that contain parts of both original units. The development of the modern subway system is also an example of Comseg. Subway lines integrate different parts of a city, but are segmented into different stations and stops, making it easier for people to get to their destination efficiently. Social media platforms such as Facebook or LinkedIn employ Comseg by facilitating global connections among individuals. Users can forge integrated networks with people of diverse backgrounds and from different locations, yet the platform also enables segmentation of the overall network into discrete groups.

Segcom refers to the process of segmenting or modularizing a system or its components, followed by combining or integrating the modularized components to create a more complex and functional system. One example of

Segcom in nature is the formation of a coral reef. Coral reefs are formed by individual coral polyps that are segmented into smaller modular parts.[12] However, these polyps are then integrated to form a larger, more complex structure held together by calcium carbonate. The honeycomb structure of beehives is another example of Segcom in nature. The hexagonal cells are segmented and integrated to create a complex structure that maximizes storage efficiency and functionality. Segcom also appears as an escape strategy where a system is first split into similar units in the face of a threat and then combined later in time after the danger ceases to exist. The smaller, independent segments may be more agile and find it easier to survive in a hostile environment. Once the entities overcome the hostile environment, the segments are combined for efficiency. Segcom is also a repair strategy, similar to Sepcom, where a component is broken into smaller similar components to identify or rectify a defect and then combined again to create the whole. Segcom is also seen in the case where a product segments itself into a partial product and combines with another partial product to form a combined product that possesses an intermediate nature compared to the two constituent entities. For instance, Milan's Radiobus is a segmented combination of a taxi and a bus.[13]

Segrep and Repseg

The Segrep and Repseg heuristics involve strategies that utilize both segmentation and replication. Segrep refers to the process of dividing a system into segments or modules and then replicating those segments or modules. This can be useful for improving efficiency, creating redundancy, increasing reliability, or enhancing performance by distributing the workload across multiple components. In ecology, the process of Segrep can be observed in the way some species disperse their seeds. For example, the burdock plant produces burrs (or burs) with hooked bristles designed to stick to the fur of animals and clothing. The burrs are segmented into small hooks that grab onto the fur, and they are replicated many times on each burr to increase the chances of successful seed dispersal.[14] In the human body, the heart is divided into chambers, and these chambers are replicated on the left and right sides of the body, allowing the heart to pump blood efficiently and reliably throughout the body. This strategy is observed in various human organ redundancies that allow for efficiency and resilience, such as the brain, lungs, kidneys, and eyes.[15] While it is less than ideal for a human to lose one of these organs, they can survive or operate with the loss of a portion of the organ system that incorporates replication. In manufacturing, a production line may be divided into multiple segments, with each segment replicating a particular step in the manufacturing process. This can improve efficiency and reduce the risk of errors. The Segrep strategy breaks an entity into similar components and introduces redundancy through replication. This strategy may be used when the segmented unit is easily replicated. For instance, a portion of a document may be divided and given to several individuals to copy.

Repseg refers to the process of replicating a component or module of a system and then dividing or segmenting those replicated components or modules. Repseg can be seen in the development of the printing press by Johannes Gutenberg, where the individual letters of the alphabet were first replicated and then segmented into different units for printing various texts. Similar to Segrep, manufacturing operations can also follow a Repseg strategy. In these cases, firms may replicate groups of similar manufacturing, such as milling machines, and then segment them for redundancy and agility in producing various customer parts in parallel or overcoming machine downtime, commonly referred to as a "cell" design. Repseg can be observed in the way some organisms such as yeasts reproduce asexually, such as by budding or fission.[16] The organism first replicates its genetic material and then segments itself into multiple parts that develop into new individuals. Repseg can also be observed in the way some animals regenerate lost body parts. For example, salamanders can regenerate their limbs by first replicating the cells needed to form the new limb and then segmenting those cells into the appropriate tissues. This can be useful for creating flexibility, adapting to changing conditions, or improving performance by allowing different segments to work on different tasks. Thus, Repseg is a strategy where components are replicated before being segmented. For example, suppose a company is considering splitting into two units that focus on two different geographical areas. In such cases, some of the previously shared resources should be replicated to ensure that each entity can survive independently. Repseg can be observed in the way some products are marketed. For example, a soda company may replicate its brand in multiple countries and then segment its advertising to cater to local cultures.

Seprep and Repsep

Seprep and Repsep heuristics involve strategies that employ both separation and replication. Seprep refers to the process of separating components of a system and then replicating or adding redundancy to those components. In the Seprep strategy, an entity is first broken down into dissimilar components, and then redundancy is introduced through replication. Examples of Seprep in nature include asexual reproduction in organisms like bacteria and some plants, where a cell separates into two identical daughter cells, thereby replicating the system. Companies may create multiple branches or divisions to separate their operations, allowing for redundancy and risk mitigation in case of failure or market shifts. For example, a tech company may have separate divisions for hardware and software development. Seprep can also represent a "Reverse Engineering" strategy, where a system is broken down to replicate it. This strategy can be useful in situations where it is necessary to replicate a complex system or process, but it is not feasible to do so without first breaking it down into simpler components. The Seprepcom strategy is a related approach where an entity is first segmented into dissimilar units and then replicated for an uncertain journey or season, and then combined when the conditions are favorable. This approach is often used in industries such as manufacturing and transportation, where it may be necessary to temporarily split a larger entity into smaller, more manageable components to optimize efficiency and minimize risk.

Repsep, on the other hand, refers to the process of replicating or adding redundancy to components of a system and then separating those components in space or time. Another related strategy is the Repsep approach, where many progenies of an entity are forced to separate to reduce competition among themselves. This can be seen in living organisms, where a single plant can generate a plethora of offspring, each destined to embark on a unique life trajectory, strategically distanced from each other to improve survivability by mitigating the intensity of competition among siblings for vital resources. Many plant species produce multiple identical copies of their seeds, which can then be dispersed over a wide area, distant from the parent plant, to increase the chances of successful germination and growth.[17] In such cases, the Repsep strategy can help to ensure the survival of the species by allowing each individual to find its own niche and reduce competition for resources. In historical military strategy, Repsep has been used to create multiple lines of defense by replicating and dispersing troops across multiple locations, and then separating them in space or time to create barriers that an enemy must overcome. During World War II, the Allies employed a Repsep strategy of "double envelopment" or "pincer movement" where they would attack an enemy from both sides, surrounding and cutting off their supplies and support. Repsep is also observed in organizations grappling with leadership succession challenges, wherein business units are replicated and strategically separated, often across different geographies, to minimize competition among potential leadership contenders.

Reprem and Remrep

The Reprem and Remrep heuristics involve strategies that utilize both removal and replication. Reprem is a strategy in which the replication of an entity is followed by the removal of one or all of the entities. The rationale behind Reprem is that the entity faces uncertain conditions and creates a replica so that at least one of them will survive. The replica is generated for a temporary purpose and is then eliminated either by endogenous or exogenous forces. Reprem is also observed in the transmission of crucial information. A copy of records is maintained temporarily and then eliminated once the transmission is completed. For example, when transporting a critical document, one might maintain a copy during the journey, but the copy is destroyed once the document arrives safely. The Reprem strategy can be implemented in different ways. The first way is when the replica is kept on the sidelines while the primary entity faces the uncertain situation. The second application of the Reprem strategy is when the replica is created to confront the uncertain situation, either as a distraction mechanism or to be ultimately destroyed or eliminated. The key point is that the replica is removed after the uncertainty is overcome because it might be confusing or perceived as a threat to the main entity.

The Reprem also signifies the "Dictator's doppelganger" or the "political decoy" strategy.[18] For instance, a dictator might dispatch a doppelganger to perilous locations, like the battlefield, to motivate soldiers. However, once the purpose is fulfilled, the replica is terminated – either during the hazardous action, such as combat, or by the dictator later on to eliminate competition or confusion. The Reprem strategy is evident in the Co-CEO concept, previously implemented in companies like SAP, Salesforce, and Oracle.[19] In certain companies, during uncertain times or when two individuals seem suitable candidates, the firm allows for Co-CEOs to coexist. The idea is that one of the Co-CEOs is eventually removed based on the evaluation of relative performance. Similarly, a company entering a new geography might employ Co-executives, one from the home country, with the plan to remove one of them over time. Reprem is also an adversarial/predatorial strategy where the predator creates a replica that attacks the entity with the objective of killing it. For example, a new entrant in a lucrative industry might be eradicated by establishing a very similar company that utilizes the same resources to destroy the new entrant. Reprem can also manifest as a strategy where a large number of replicas are created to destroy an original entity, as seen in diseases. Furthermore, Reprem represents the strategy where the parent entity dies in the process of reproduction or soon afterward, as observed among octopuses.[20]

Remrep is the reverse strategy, wherein the system removes or eliminates a component and then replicates or copies the remaining components. Typically, in this strategy, a non-essential or harmful element is removed, and then the rest is replicated. In business strategy, Remrep can be observed in the process of restructuring, where a company removes or eliminates non-essential functions or departments, and then replicates and maintains its core business functions. In historical military strategy, Remrep has been used to create strategic depth by removing or eliminating weaker or less effectively trained troops, and then replicating the more effectively trained troops while dispersing the stronger, better-trained troops. Remrep can be observed in the military within positions that have specialty codes.[21] They may remove a specialization but not eliminate the military member, unlike some businesses where they simply remove the position and the employee. The military retrains the member to replicate additional manpower in another area. For example, the Air Force removed multiple heavy equipment operator positions and retrained those personnel into other critical jobs such as contracting.

Comrep and Repcom

The Comrep and Repcom heuristics involve strategies that utilize combination and replication. Comrep refers to the process of combining two components of a system and then replicating or adding redundancy to that system or its components. In other words, it involves integrating two components and then duplicating that integrated system or component for improved efficiency and reliability. In the human body, the immune system employs a Comrep strategy to combat infections. The immune system combines various cells and proteins to form a complex defense mechanism, then replicates it to produce many copies of the same mechanism, which helps eliminate the invading pathogen more efficiently. One example of Comrep in nature is the way trees transport water from their roots to their leaves. Trees have evolved a system of interconnected tubes that transport water throughout the tree. The tubes are composed of cells called tracheids, which are connected (Com) end-to-end to form a long, continuous tube. This system of interconnected tubes is replicated (Rep) throughout the tree, providing redundancy in case one section of the tree becomes damaged or diseased. In historical military strategy, an example of Comrep would be the construction of fortifications. Fortifications involve integrating multiple walls and structures to create a complex system that is difficult for attackers to breach. These structures are often replicated multiple times, creating redundancy in case one section of the fortification is breached.

Repcom, on the other hand, involves replicating or adding redundancy to a component of a system and then combining or integrating those replicated components. This process improves the reliability or efficiency of the system by creating multiple redundant components that can work together. This is similar to hybrid vehicles, where an electric engine and a gas-powered engine are combined to create a more efficient system. Another example of Repcom in nature is the way that many animals have multiple eyes. For example, spiders have eight eyes, each with a slightly different function.[22] By having multiple eyes, spiders can detect prey more easily and avoid predators more effectively. The redundant eyes work together to improve the spider's overall visual system. Repcom can be compared to the nesting or the "Matryoshka doll" strategy, where different sizes of dolls are nested within each other. Analogical nesting strategies are seen in biology[23] and political warfare.[24] Companies like the advertising company WPP plc use the Repcom strategy by combining a large number of similar entities under one roof.[25] This strategy can also be seen in companies that have several brands of similar products that compete with each other. Another form of Repcom involves combining two similar elements with opposite properties to create a new benefit. One example of this is the rete mirabile, or "the wonderful net," found in vertebrates that act as a countercurrent exchanger.[26] The proverb in the Biblical book of Ecclesiastes, "And if one prevail against him, two shall withstand him; and a threefold cord is not quickly broken (Ecc. 4:12)," exemplifies Repcom. Samsung's hybrid management system, which incorporates both traditional Japanese and Western principles, is an example of Repcom in business practice.[27]

Repmax and Maxrep

The Repmax and Maxrep heuristics involve strategies that utilize replication and maximization. Repmax is a strategy employing replication to maximize a specific attribute, such as reliability. For instance, bubble wrap with numerous small individual units is employed to prevent damage to goods during transportation. Repmax proves beneficial when a large number of small units are more effective than a single large unit. It may resemble other strategies, like Segmax. Portfolio diversification, as seen in mutual funds, can be considered an extension of the Repmax strategy. Repmax is also utilized in information broadcasting, religious or political propaganda, where a considerable number of replicas (individuals or messages) increase attention in a short period. For instance, the widespread circulation of important informational documents requires maximized replication in terms of both quantity and various forms of information. This strategy is observed in the spawning of a large number of eggs or pollen, aiming to maximize distribution and the chance of reproductive success. Species like guppies employ Repmax by producing numerous offspring to maximize the chances of passing on their genes to the next generation.[28] By replicating genetic material in multiple offspring, they enhance the likelihood of some surviving and reproducing. A company can employ Repmax by replicating a successful product or service and then maximizing profitability through economies of scale, cost-cutting measures, or targeted marketing campaigns. During World War II, the Allied Forces used the tactic of carpet (saturation) bombing, dropping a large number of bombs over a wide area to maximize damage to enemy targets.[29]

The Maxrep operation involves maximizing an attribute of the system and then replicating the resulting system or component. The goal of this operation is to increase the distribution or reach of the system or component by first optimizing its performance and then replicating it. The reproductive strategy of some plants involves maximizing the size or quality of their seeds before dispersing them over a wide area. This is a process of maximizing the reproductive success of the plant before replicating it through the distribution of its seeds. Certain species of bacteria, such as *Bacillus subtilis*, when under stress, can undergo a process called sporulation, wherein they maximize their survival chances by producing a small number of highly resistant spores that can endure extreme conditions.[30] These spores are then replicated to create a large population of resistant bacteria. In business, companies may maximize the performance of a successful product or service in a main market before replicating it through expansion into new markets or geographies. In product design, Maxrep is observed when a product is designed with a focus on maximizing its performance or features before replicating it to create a range of similar products with slight variations to cater to different markets.

Segmax and Maxseg

The Segmax and Maxseg heuristics involve strategies that utilize segmentation and maximization. Segmax is a process that includes segmenting a system or its components and then maximizing an attribute of the segmented components. An example is the vertebrate spine, which is segmented into individual vertebrae that are then maximized for strength and flexibility through the development of specific bones, muscles, and ligaments. Segmax also refers to strategies in which segmentation is employed to maximize a specific attribute. This process may involve splitting a unit to search far and wide, as seen in the example of a company segmenting its salesforce for maximum coverage. Similarly, a herd might split itself into individual units and run in different directions to evade a predator. An organization might also maximize segmentation and distribution as a concealment mechanism. The underlying rationale of Segmax is similar to that of the Repmax heuristic, which also aims to maximize an attribute by creating multiple similar units. A transportation network may segment its routes and schedules to maximize efficiency and minimize travel time for its users. For example, a city's public transportation system might segment its bus routes into different lines that serve specific neighborhoods or destinations. In the field of finance, portfolio optimization involves segmenting a portfolio into different asset classes to maximize returns and minimize risks. This strategy, known as asset allocation, involves selecting a mix of stocks, bonds, and other investments based on an individual's goals, risk tolerance, and time horizon.[31] Another example of Segmax at work is in the field of urban planning. City planners use a technique called zoning, which involves segmenting land into different use categories such as residential, commercial, industrial, or recreational. This segmentation maximizes the efficient use of land and resources and also helps to minimize conflicts between different land uses.

Another strategy is Maxseg, which involves maximizing a component and segmenting it or maximizing the segmentation process itself. For instance, an entity may be pulverized to increase its total available area, as seen in the case of mushroom spores. In computer science, some algorithms use a divide-and-conquer approach to solve complex problems by breaking them down into smaller, more manageable sub-problems. This segmentation maximizes the effectiveness of the algorithm by reducing the computational complexity of the problem. Maxseg is also evident in art, where some artists use a technique called pointillism, creating an image by applying small dots of color to a surface.[32] This technique maximizes the segmentation of the image, producing a diverse and varied texture. In materials science, certain materials are strengthened through shot peening, a process where the surface is bombarded with small metal balls.[33] This process maximizes the segmentation of the material, increasing its surface area and strengthening its structure. In the field of music composition, some composers employ a technique called granular synthesis, maximizing the segmentation of a sound by breaking it down into small overlapping grains that can be independently manipulated and recombined. This technique allows for greater control over the texture and timbre of the sound, enabling the creation of complex and evolving sonic landscapes.

Sepmax and Maxsep

The Sepmax and Maxsep heuristics involve using separation and maximization strategies to achieve a desired outcome. Sepmax is the operation of first separating components of the system in space or time and then maximizing or extremizing an attribute of the system. This operation can be observed in various natural and artificial systems where components need to be separated to optimize their function or performance. Specifically, the process involves breaking down a larger system into smaller, dissimilar entities with the goal of maximizing a particular attribute. The rationale behind this approach is that separating the system into distinct parts can facilitate the maximization of each part's potential. As a Sepmax strategy, a large corporation may choose to spin off a subsidiary company focused on a specific market or product, allowing it to concentrate on maximizing its potential in that area. Sepmax is also a survival strategy, involving the splitting up of a larger entity to maximize its chances of survival. For example, a company may choose to divide its operations into smaller companies to "unlock value," or a smaller number of component entities may be selected for focused attention to ensure their survival.[34] This often leads to the development of hierarchies between the separated entities, with some entities being perceived as more important than others. Sepmax can also be used as an adversarial or attack strategy. In World War II, the Allies used the tactic of "island hopping" in the Pacific theater.[35] This involved separating Japanese-held islands in space and then attacking the weaker ones first, gradually moving closer to the Japanese mainland. This is an example of Sepmax because the Allies were separating the Japanese islands (Sep) and then maximizing their chances of victory by attacking the weaker ones first (Max).

Maxsep, on the other hand, is the operation of first maximizing or extremizing an attribute of the system and then separating its components in space or time. Examples of Maxsep can be found in the viral marketing campaigns of companies like Nike and Apple. By maximizing the appeal and shareability of their messaging, they can separate their products from the competition, creating a highly adaptive and influential brand. The Maxsep strategy was employed by the Wright brothers in the development of the first airplane.[36] They maximized the lift and stability of the wings through a series of experiments and then separated the wing design from the rest of the aircraft, creating a modular component that could be adapted to different types of planes. Maxsep also represents the strategy of maximally separating components of a system from each other. This involves isolating each component with a specific goal in mind, such as locating servers far apart from each other to maximize coverage and minimize the risk of concurrent damage in the event of a natural disaster. Cloud service providers like Amazon Web Services (AWS) use the Maxsep strategy by physically separating data centers in various geographic locations.[37] An example of Maxsep in nature is the migration of animals. Animals such as birds and wildebeest migrate long distances to maximize their access to food, water, and breeding opportunities (Max), often achieving this by separating themselves from their original location (Sep).

Remmax and Maxrem

The Remmax and Maxrem heuristics involve employing removal and maximization strategies. Remmax entails initially eliminating or discarding certain parts of a system or its components, followed by maximizing or optimizing the performance of the remaining parts. An illustrative instance of Remmax in product design is a "streamlining" process, wherein companies eliminate unnecessary features or components from their products to curtail manufacturing costs and enhance user satisfaction. After the removal of superfluous components, the remaining elements can be optimized for superior performance and functionality. Investors could potentially implement the Remmax strategy by strategically restructuring their investment portfolios, systematically removing underperforming assets or those associated with higher risk, and strategically reallocating resources to optimize returns. A similar approach can be taken for product portfolios within large companies.[38] Remmax also encompasses strategies where a section of the system is eliminated to maximize another attribute of the system, for example, reducing a vehicle's weight to enhance its speed. In historical military strategy, Remmax is evident in streamlining the logistical requirements of an army before a battle. Armies may discard non-essential equipment, supplies, or personnel to optimize their mobility and speed. With minimized logistical demands, the army can then optimize its combat performance, augmenting its likelihood of victory. Another manifestation of Remmax involves armies relinquishing or abandoning challenging-to-defend territories to concentrate on maximizing the defense of more valuable territories. For instance, during the Punic Wars, Rome abandoned certain territories in Spain that were difficult to defend and redirected their efforts toward fortifying their more strategic territories in Italy.

Maxrem refers to the process of initially maximizing or optimizing an attribute of a system or its component and subsequently removing or eliminating some of its parts to sustain the optimized performance. An instance of Maxrem in nature is exemplified by the bone remodeling process in vertebrates.[39] Bones undergo continuous remodeling to uphold their strength and flexibility. The body maximizes bone density in response to mechanical loads and then removes excess bone tissue through a process known as osteoclastic bone resorption to maintain optimal bone density. In the realm of business strategy, Maxrem is observable in the company downsizing process following the streamlining and optimization of its operations. A company might first optimize operations by enhancing efficiency, reducing costs, and maximizing profits. After achieving this, the company may then decide to eliminate certain divisions or employees to uphold its optimized performance. In an alternative Maxrem strategy, a segment of the attribute is maximized and subsequently removed once it has exhausted its utility from maximization. For example, airbags inflate momentarily but must be removed once the danger has passed. Another illustration of Maxrem occurs when a system accentuates a single attribute to survive, drawing resources from other components and ultimately leading to their removal. For instance, a company may maximize investment in a particular business, resulting in the elimination of another component.

Commax and Maxcom

The Commax and Maxcom heuristics encompass strategies involving a combination and maximization. Commax involves combining or integrating two components of a system, followed by maximizing or extremizing an attribute of the system. An example of Commax in nature is the establishment of symbiotic relationships between different species, such as the intricate connection between bees and flowers. Bees combine with flowers to create a mutually beneficial system, where bees collect nectar for food while inadvertently pollinating the flowers. This relationship is then maximized through the development of specialized structures, such as the bee's tongue or front legs, enabling access to nectar or fatty oil deep within flowers.[40] Commax also signifies the strategy of combining two dissimilar entities to maximize an attribute of either or both. Typically, the first entity combines with a second entity providing access to a vital resource previously limiting the original system's maximization. For instance, a firm might opt for vertical mergers to consolidate strategic suppliers in an industry. Companies may also acquire potential competitors or strategic resources to maximize their competitive position or maintain leadership or monopolies. In marketing, a firm might integrate numerous services to offer a comprehensive "suite" covering all potential customer needs, eliminating the need for another service provider. Similarly, a company might form a cartel or coalition with various independent entities to maximize a common goal.

Maxcom involves maximizing a specific attribute of the system and then combining two components of the system to create a new, more specialized or efficient component that maintains that attribute. The successful online retailer Amazon is an example of Maxcom in business strategy. Amazon began as an online bookseller, and over time, it has maximized its ability to sell books through its website, using customer data and algorithms to recommend books and create personalized shopping experiences. Integrating its initial prowess in book sales with formidable logistics capabilities, Amazon has fashioned a remarkably efficient and potent online retail system, seamlessly expanding its reach to encompass a vast array of product categories including electronics, clothing, and groceries. Antibiotics have been developed to maximize their ability to kill bacteria, and then combined with other drugs to create potent treatments against bacterial infections.[41] This combination of drugs allows for a targeted attack on specific bacteria while minimizing the risk of resistance and side effects.

Maxcom also refers to strategies that involve maximizing an attribute of an entity until its utility is exhausted, after which it is combined with another entity. Marketing campaigns sometimes focus on maximizing the promotion of a single differentiating attribute of a new product or service, such as its convenience or reliability, until it reaches its saturation point. Once this attribute is exhausted, the campaign can shift focus to another attribute or combine it with other attributes to create a more compelling value proposition that appeals to a broader customer base. Another case of Maxcom occurs when a system maximizes a single attribute to survive, drawing resources from other components, which eventually leads to their combination with the entity. An example of this case of Maxcom can be seen in the development of plants. Some plants, like cacti, are adapted to optimize their water storage capacity for survival in arid environments.[42] This entails extracting resources from various components, such as their leaves, which undergo modifications and transform into spines. These spines serve a dual purpose by shielding the plant, thus acting as a defensive mechanism against predators, while also contributing to efficient water conservation.

Maxdyn and Dynmax

The Maxdyn and Dynmax heuristics involve both maximization and dynamics. Maxdyn refers to maximizing or extremizing a system attribute, followed by dynamically varying or modifying a system or component feature based on external input. Maxdyn also pertains to strategies when a system exhibits an extreme attribute only in specific situations. For example, a cheetah is built for maximum speed to catch prey, but it cannot sustain its top speed for long.[43] To optimize its hunting ability, a cheetah alternates between rest and high-speed pursuit, dynamically varying its activity based on prey availability. In biological systems, an attribute may exaggerate when threatened, resulting in the system becoming larger or smaller. For instance, an animal might exaggerate features when threatened by a predator. This heuristic is also present in marketing strategies, where companies may engage in aggressive price cutting or discounts at specific times (such as Amazon Prime Day) to maximize sales or consumer attention. Maxdyn is also employed by companies facing competitors or predators they wish to eliminate, such as keeping oil prices low to divert investment or eliminate competitors. The key feature of Maxdyn is that attribute maximization is highly inefficient and unsustainable in the long term. Maxdyn is observed in emergency situations, like engaging redundant systems during a crisis. Additionally, Maxdyn is employed by militaries using the "Shock and awe" tactic.[44]

The Dynmax operation entails dynamically varying or modifying a system or component feature based on external input, followed by maximizing or extremizing a system attribute. One instance of Dynmax in biological adaptations is observed in some plants' ability to alter their leaf angle in response to light intensity. In low light, these plants adjust their leaves to maximize light absorption. However, with increasing light intensity, they dynamically change the leaf angle to prevent overheating. Through this combination of dynamic adjustments, focusing on maximizing light absorption, and avoiding damage, these plants thrive in diverse environments. Dynmax is also exemplified in targeted advertising on social media, where advertisers dynamically modify ads based on user behavior and preferences, concurrently maximizing the reach and effectiveness of their campaigns. In product design, a manifestation of Dynmax could be seen in the development of smart thermostats. These devices dynamically adjust temperatures based on user behavior and external factors, such as weather conditions, and subsequently maximize energy efficiency by learning the user's preferences over time.[45]

Repdyn and Dynrep

The Repdyn and Dynrep heuristics consist of strategies that employ both maximization and dynamics. Repdyn involves initially replicating or copying a component of the system or the entire system and then dynamically varying or modifying a feature of that component or the replicated system based on external input. The Repdyn strategy encompasses maintaining a replica or backup system capable of taking over the primary function under specific conditions. This strategy is commonly applied in systems where the failure of the primary component can lead to catastrophic consequences, such as in critical infrastructure systems or life-critical applications. In such systems, ensuring redundancy is crucial to guarantee a backup system that can take over in the event of primary system failure. An example of Repdyn is a dynamic redundancy management system, where a standby or replacement is maintained to be switched over based on contingent conditions, such as when the primary component fails. Dynamic redundancy ensures continuous system availability and operation, even in the face of failure, and is particularly important for safety-critical systems such as aerospace hardware.[46] Another instance of Repdyn is evident in dynamic political replacements, where coalition partners may choose to share power by alternating between the prime minister position. This practice ensures a smooth transition of power and allows different parties to share power and influence. In the Repdyn approach to marketing, companies generate multiple versions of a product and then dynamically vary their marketing strategy to appeal to different target markets, such as age, gender, location, etc. Examples of Repdyn in product design include the development of modular components that can be dynamically varied and combined to create different products with similar functionality. For instance, LEGO building blocks can be dynamically varied and combined to create a wide range of different structures.

The Dynrep operation involves initially dynamically varying or modifying a feature of a component or the system based on some external input and subsequently replicating or copying the modified component or system. It also encompasses strategies of "dynamic replication," where components in a system are replicated based on changing conditions to maintain system reliability.[47] Within the Dynrep heuristic, a primary component is maintained alongside one or more replicas, capable of assuming the primary function in the event of failure or other adverse conditions. In contrast to the Repdyn strategy, these replicas are dynamically generated, meaning they are created only when needed and may not exist at all times. This approach offers several advantages, such as reduced cost, increased efficiency, and enhanced fault tolerance. In the realm of autonomous vehicles, Dynrep is employed to dynamically replicate communication nodes within the vehicle-to-vehicle (V2V) network. As the vehicle traverses diverse environments, the system dynamically generates supplementary communication nodes to uphold dependable connectivity. In emergency response systems, the Dynrep heuristic can be applied to dynamically replicate pivotal communication hubs. In critical scenarios, where the need for communication infrastructure is heightened, supplementary communication hubs are dynamically generated to ensure the resilience of communication channels.

Segdyn and Dynseg

The Segdyn and Dynseg heuristics encompass strategies that integrate segmentation and dynamics to achieve optimal results. Segdyn involves a process where a system or its components undergo segmentation or division into distinct parts. Subsequently, one or more features of these segments are dynamically varied or modified based on external input or changing conditions. Typically, when employing Segdyn, a unitary entity is divided into similar parts under specific conditions while maintaining its integrity as a single entity in normal circumstances. This is evident in products like modular bending systems, where a system is segmented to enable flexible motion. Segdyn systems exhibit the ability to navigate complex environments by swiftly splitting up for agility and uniting for strength. The phenomenon of Segdyn is observable in bird flocks. Birds often adopt V-shaped formations, representing a form of dynamic segmentation.[48] The flock segments into smaller groups, with each bird flying in the slipstream of the one in front. This segmentation aids in reducing air resistance and energy expenditure for the birds in the formation. However, the positioning and coordination within the formation dynamically change based on various factors, such as wind direction and speed.

Military formations also utilize Segdyn to maximize efficiency and coordination. In nature, ants employ Segdyn strategies, swiftly changing formations to adapt to evolving environments. Another instance of Dynseg is evident in the development of modular smartphones, allowing users to dynamically modify their phone's features and functions by swapping out modules (e.g., camera, battery, processor) based on their needs. The modular design also segments the phone into different components, facilitating easier repair and replacement of parts. In the field of aviation, the development of variable-geometry wings (also known as variable-sweep wings) represents a significant example of Segdyn.[49] These segmented wings could be dynamically adjusted during flight to optimize performance at different speeds and altitudes. Segdyn is also observed in marketing through tiered-pricing models, where the price may increase in steps based on quantity. Such models could be used to meet demand and limit the number of units of a product purchased by a single customer.[50]

Dynseg refers to a dynamic process that entails the adaptive variation or modification of a system or its components based on external input. This is followed by the segmentation, division, or modularization of the system or its components. Moreover, Dynseg represents a process wherein a dynamic operation is segmented into smaller steps to facilitate more effective management. For instance, rather than abruptly increasing the temperature in a container, it may be raised incrementally to prevent damage or undesired reactions. In the realm of business strategy, Dynseg manifests in product diversification. A company may dynamically adjust its product offerings in response to market demand and customer preferences (Dyn), and subsequently segment its product line into distinct categories or models (Seg) to effectively cater to different consumer segments. Furthermore, Dynseg embodies a dynamic segmentation approach where a system or organization dynamically divides or segments its operations, resources, or target market based on specific inputs or changing conditions. To illustrate, a software development company could implement a dynamic segmentation strategy for its project teams. Depending on the project requirements, the company forms specialized teams with specific expertise in programming languages, frameworks, or domains. This enables the company to efficiently allocate resources and ensure that each project is handled by a team with the most relevant skills.

Sepdyn and Dynsep

Sepdyn and Dynsep are heuristics that represent strategies combining both dynamics and separation techniques. Sepdyn refers to a process where components of a system are first separated in space or time and then subjected to dynamic variation or modification based on some external input. This combination of operations allows for independent variation and adaptation of the separated components. In the human body, Sepdyn can be observed in the immune system's response to pathogens. When the body encounters a new pathogen, it separates the specific immune cells capable of recognizing and targeting that pathogen. These immune cells then undergo dynamic variation and modification through processes such as clonal expansion and mutation to enhance their effectiveness in combating the specific pathogen. Sepdyn can also be applied in marketing campaigns through the use of A/B testing.[51] In this case, the separation occurs by creating multiple versions of an advertisement or marketing message. These versions are then dynamically varied by exposing different segments of the target audience to each version. By analyzing the response and feedback from each segment, marketers can adapt their messaging to optimize effectiveness. The Sepdyn strategy also represents operations that involve separating a system into dissimilar parts under certain conditions while remaining unitary at other times. For instance, a company may appear unified in some situations but may seem like distinct entities in other locations. For example, a company's consulting division might appear separate from its technology implementation division during the marketing process but might work together to implement a project. However, such arrangements can raise conflict-of-interest flags, particularly when a consultant recommends a technology provider owned by the same holding company.

Dynsep refers to a process where a feature or component of a system is dynamically varied or modified based on external input, followed by a subsequent separation of the components or elements within the system. This sequence allows for adaptation and differentiation of the system based on the dynamic changes. In the human body, Dynsep can be observed in the process of tissue regeneration. When an injury occurs, such as a cut or a broken bone, the body responds by dynamically varying cellular and molecular processes to initiate healing. Cells undergo dynamic changes, such as proliferation and differentiation, to repair the damaged tissue. Following this dynamic adaptation, a separation occurs as new tissue or bone forms, separating it from the damaged or non-functional components. Historical military strategy provides an example of Dynsep in the concept of a feigned retreat, most famously observed in the Battle of Hastings in 1066.[52] During battles, some military commanders strategically employed a feigned retreat, where they would dynamically vary their position and create the perception of weakness or vulnerability. The opposing forces would pursue the retreating troops, leading to a separation between the pursuing force and the remaining troops of the retreating army. This separation allowed the retreating force to regroup, reorganize, and launch a surprise counterattack against the now isolated and vulnerable pursuing forces.

Dynrem and Remdyn

The Dynrem and Remdyn heuristics encompass strategies integrating both dynamic and removal operations. Dynrem involves a process wherein a component undergoes dynamic variation or modification before its removal from the system. This entails adjusting or adapting the component's features based on external inputs or changing conditions before removal. For example, in one manifestation of Dynrem, a product's part disappears at specific time points, reappearing at others, akin to emergency systems activated only under rare conditions. Another instance is the "dynamic hiding" of product features, where certain capabilities remain concealed to mitigate feature fatigue and enhance usability but become visible under specific conditions. A design of this nature can also elicit a sense of surprise from the user.[53] Animals employ a Dynrem strategy as a defense mechanism, withdrawing into their shells when facing danger, akin to playing dead to evade attention. Dynrem also serves as a predatory or attack strategy involving the rapid dynamic removal or elimination of a component or entity through changing conditions, compelling the entity to allocate resources in response to the alterations. Additionally, it represents an adversarial/predator strategy akin to boiling the frog, where an attribute is conditionally modified over time to eliminate another entity. In a business context, Dynrem manifests in practices such as phasing out or discontinuing underperforming product lines. Before the complete removal of products from the market, companies may introduce modifications, pricing adjustments, or marketing campaigns to optimize their potential or salvage their value.

Remdyn describes a process wherein a component is initially removed or eliminated from the system, and then the remaining components or the system as a whole undergo dynamic modification or adaptation based on the changes resulting from the removal. In nature, the removal of a key species, such as a predator or a keystone species, can lead to Remdyn. The absence of that particular species can cause a cascade of effects on the remaining organisms and the overall structure of the reef. The remaining species may dynamically modify their behaviors, population sizes, or interactions to fill the ecological niche left vacant by the removed species, resulting in a new equilibrium and potentially reshaping the entire ecosystem. After a natural disaster, like a forest fire, the ecosystem undergoes Remdyn. The elimination of specific plant species facilitates dynamic modifications, giving rise to regrowth and succession. The remaining plants and organisms adapt to the altered environment, thereby instigating novel ecological dynamics and species interactions. In wound healing, Remdyn can be observed.[54] After a damaged tissue or organ is surgically removed or naturally detached, the body initiates dynamic modifications, such as cell proliferation, extracellular matrix remodeling, and blood vessel formation, to facilitate the healing process and restore functionality. In the business context, Remdyn is observed during the practice of downsizing. Following the elimination of specific departments or the reduction of the organization's size, dynamic modifications, such as restructuring, reorganizing, and streamlining operations, can be instituted to enhance efficiency and profitability.

Comdyn and Dyncom

Comdyn and Dyncom strategies encompass both combination and dynamics. Comdyn refers to a strategy where two or more different entities are initially combined or integrated, and then their combined system undergoes dynamic variations or modifications based on some external input or condition. An example of Comdyn is the human eye, which has two types of photoreceptor cells: rods sensitive to light intensity and cones sensitive to color. The human eye utilizes Comdyn to combine these photoreceptor cells, providing the perception of both color and brightness. In a common form of Comdyn, two different entities are integrated so that one is active at one point in time, and the other is active at another. For instance, an aircraft seat designed with Comdyn would inflate and act as a flotation device upon impact with water. Another example is a combined air-dryer and water spigot system, like the Dyson Airblade Wash+Dry, that switches automatically based on the sensed condition of the hands.[55] In some cases, Dyncom may exhibit characteristics reminiscent of "Jekyll and Hyde," with opposite effects or features (e.g., hot/cold, off/on). In other cases, the combined entities may perform similar functions, resulting in functional replications. In such instances, Comdyn often appears similar to Repdyn, as observed in the case of a hybrid vehicle that automatically switches between modes. Comdyn also represents cases where a single entity can perform two different functions, but only one is activated at a time.

Dyncom is a distinct heuristic from Comdyn, representing a strategy where two entities remain separate or independent under certain conditions but combine or integrate under others. For instance, two automobile manufacturers may form a partnership to develop and share technology in one market while remaining competitors in other territories. Another illustration from nature is the symbiotic relationship between cleaner fish and larger "client" fish.[56] The cleaner fish often remain separate from the clients in open water but combine and interact with them when they seek cleaning services, removing parasites and dead skin from the predators' bodies. In the business world, joint ventures between companies exemplify Dyncom. In a joint venture, two or more companies collaborate on a specific project or venture while remaining separate entities in other aspects. The North Atlantic Treaty Organization (NATO) provides an example of Dyncom in international relations. NATO is an alliance of multiple countries working together to ensure mutual defense and security. While NATO members are partners in terms of collective defense, they may have different geopolitical interests or compete in other aspects, such as trade or diplomacy, demonstrating the combination and separation between allied countries based on specific circumstances.

Complex Strategies

Complex heuristic strategies are invaluable in various fields, particularly in ensuring efficient response times during emergencies or disasters. One such strategy is the Sepsegcom, which combines the Sepcom and Segcom strategies. This strategy offers a general direction for improving resilience and achieving adaptability in challenging circumstances. To illustrate the Sepsegcom strategy, consider an organizational entity with three crucial assets: A, B, and C. By separating, segmenting, and then combining the entity into three smaller units, each encompassing a part of two or three assets, the organization establishes a distributed structure. In uncertain situations like crises, pandemics, wars, or economic depressions, the Sepsegcom strategy may prove more robust than the original structure. Even if one of the three units is destroyed, the surviving units can reconstruct all three different asset types. This versatility strengthens the organization's resilience and ensures continuity even in the face of significant disruptions.

Another similar strategy is the Segrepcom strategy, exemplified by Paul Baran's patent on Packet switching (US Patent No. 4,438,511). Baran's invention aimed to design communication systems that could withstand a first strike from the USSR during the Cold War. To achieve this, he introduced the concept of breaking down information into packets, which could be replicated and finally combined at the destination. By segmenting the data and introducing redundancy, the system could endure noise and losses in transmission while maintaining the integrity of the message. This Segrepcom strategy was instrumental in creating resilient communication networks that could withstand attacks and ensure reliable information exchange. Comseprepdyn is a case of a complex "spatial" strategy seen in military organizations. In such cases, the organization consists of a central command center or "brain" that directs the overall response, followed by intermediate centers or "lungs" that have focused roles and possible redundancies, and appendages or "limbs" that can quickly respond to local changes prominently.

One application of spatial strategies is in responding to Weapons of Mass Destruction (WMD) incidents. The US National Guard Bureau has established 57 Weapons of Mass Destruction Civil Support Teams (WMD-CST) across the states and territories. The WMD-CST's mission is to support civil authorities in identifying CBRNE agents/substances, assessing current or projected consequences, advising on response measures, and assisting with appropriate requests for additional follow-on state and federal military forces. The unit can also provide an immediate response to intentional and unintentional CBRN or hazardous material (HAZMAT) releases and natural or man-made disasters that could result in catastrophic loss of life or property.

Each WMD-CST is composed of 22 full-time, Title 32 Active/Guard/Reserve (AGR) personnel, including Army (ARNG) and Air National Guard (ANG) members, with an average distribution of 18 ARNG and 4 ANG personnel. The unit is divided into six sections: command, operations, communications, administration/logistics, medical/analytical, and survey. The assigned transportation includes a command vehicle, an operations trailer, a communications vehicle called the Unified Command Suite, an analytical laboratory system vehicle, and several general-purpose vehicles. The WMD-CST normally deploys using its assigned vehicles or can be airlifted as required. These CSTs operate independently, reporting to their respective states. They are supposed to respond to national emergencies in a three-tiered fashion: immediate (Gold Team), short-term (Silver Team), and then longer-term (Bronze Team). The responsibilities of the response teams rotate among the 57 CSTs based on a pre-established schedule. The CST capability has been replicated 57 times and separated to ensure efficient response times to unknown locations for as-yet-to-happen emergencies. They create some level of redundancy by having multiple CSTs, but the main goal is to quickly cover the response area within the US and its territories.

Heuristic-Based Product Ideation Using Gen-AI

Generative AI tools such as OpenAI's ChatGPT, Anthropic's Claude, and Google's Gemini can also support heuristic-based ideation, involving the generation of concepts for a given theme or topic using natural and mixed heuristics. To illustrate this concept, the following prompt was given to ChatGPT as an instruction to generate ideas using multiple design heuristics for a children's storybook. ChatGPT was instructed to generate ideas using natural and mixed heuristics. These ideas can serve as a baseline for generating further concepts during an idea generation session and as a benchmark for evaluating the quality of human-generated ideas (Table 5.2). For this purpose, a prompt like the one below can be utilized.

"You will be playing the role of an ideator. For each product that I present to you, you will provide an idea that involves applying each of the following thirteen operations: (1) COM: Combining, integrating, or connecting two components of the system; (2) REM: Removing or eliminating a component of the system; (3) SEP: Separating components of the system in space or time; (4) SEG: Segmenting, dividing, or modularizing the system or its components; (5) REP: Replicating, copying, or adding redundancy to the

Table 5.2   Mixed Heuristics with Generative AI

Heuristic	Product System: Children's Storybook
COM	Combine two different genres of children's books, such as adventure and mystery, to create a unique and engaging story. This could help to keep children interested and engaged in the book.
REM	Remove unnecessary characters or plot points to streamline the story and make it more accessible to young readers. This could make the story easier to follow and understand.
SEP	Separate the story into different chapters or sections, with each section featuring a different character or aspect of the story. This could create a sense of progression and help to build anticipation throughout the book.
SEG	Segment the story into different story arcs or subplots, each with its own climax and resolution. This could add complexity and depth to the story, and help to keep children engaged throughout the book.
REP	Replicate the successful formula of the book in a sequel or spin-off book, with similar characters and themes but with different settings or scenarios. This could help to maintain the book's fanbase and keep them interested in future installments.
MAX	Maximize the book's illustrations by using bright colors and bold designs. This could make the book visually appealing and help to capture children's attention.
DYN	Dynamically vary the book's pacing and tone based on the protagonist's emotional state. For example, the book could start off slow and contemplative, and then become more action-packed and thrilling as the protagonist's adventure unfolds.
REMCOM	Remove the protagonist's usual allies and give them a new partner to work with, with whom they have a complicated relationship. This could create a more interesting dynamic between the two characters and add some dramatic tension to the book.
SEPCOM	Separate the book into two distinct settings – one in the real world and one in a fantastical world. This could create a more diverse range of storylines and make the book feel more epic in scale. Then, combine these two settings by having the protagonist transition from one to the other in a magical set-piece.
SEGCOM	Segment the storybook into different sections, and then combine each section with a related craft activity that children can do at home, allowing them to engage with the story in a more hands-on way.

(Continued)

Table 5.2 (Continued)   Mixed Heuristics with Generative AI

Heuristic	Product System: Children's Storybook
REPCOM	Replicate the storybook and create a choose-your-own-adventure style book, where children can make choices that impact the story's outcome, leading to multiple different endings.
MAXCOM	Maximize the emotional impact of the storybook by incorporating music, sound effects, or other multimedia elements that enhance the story's mood and tone.
DYNCOM	Dynamically modify the storybook's illustrations or text based on a child's real-time reactions or feedback, creating an interactive storytelling experience that adapts to the child's needs and interests.
COMREM	Combine the book with a companion app that allows children to explore the story's world and characters in more depth, removing the limitations of the physical book.
SEPREM	Separate the physical book into different parts and remove certain pages or elements, creating a physical puzzle that children need to solve to access the full story.
SEGREM	Segment the story into different parts and remove certain parts, creating a mystery that children need to solve by piecing together the missing parts of the story.
REPREM	Replicate the story with different characters and settings, but remove certain elements or plot points, creating a different interpretation of the story.
MAXREM	Maximize the emotional impact of the story by removing extraneous details and focusing on the core emotions and relationships that drive the story.
DYNREM	Dynamically remove or add story elements based on the child's responses, creating a unique and personalized reading experience.
COMSEP	Combine two different stories into one book, but separate them by chapter or section to keep them distinct.
REMSEP	Remove a character or subplot from the story, and create a separate book or activity book that focuses on that specific character or topic.
SEGSEP	Segment the story into multiple books or activities, each with a different theme or topic, but separate them by age group or reading level.

(Continued)

Table 5.2 (Continued)   Mixed Heuristics with Generative AI

Heuristic	*Product System: Children's Storybook*
REPSEP	Replicate the story into different formats, but separate them by language, age group, or reading level.
MAXSEP	Maximize the educational value of the book by creating a series of companion materials, such as flashcards or worksheets, that reinforce the lessons learned in the story.
DYNSEP	Dynamically vary the difficulty of the text or activities, based on the child's performance or progress, and separate them by age group or reading level.
COMSEG	Combine the storybook with a set of accompanying toys or figurines that represent the characters in the story. This allows children to play with the toys as they read the story, enhancing their imaginative experience.
REMSEG	Remove certain characters or elements from the story to create a more streamlined and focused narrative. This can help young readers better understand the central message of the story.
SEPSEG	Separate the story into smaller, more digestible sections or chapters, making it easier for children to read and comprehend. This can also help with pacing and keep children engaged.
REPSEG	Replicate the storybook in multiple languages to make it accessible to children of different backgrounds and cultures. This can help promote diversity and inclusivity.
MAXSEG	Maximize the modularity of the storybook by creating different versions with different endings or story paths. This can allow children to explore different possibilities and enhance their problem-solving skills.
DYNSEG	Dynamically change the size or shape of the character based on their emotions or actions. For example, when the character is happy or excited, they might grow larger, and when they are sad or scared, they might shrink in size.
COMREP	Combine two existing stories into one cohesive narrative, while also replicating the book with slight variations in characters, settings, or plot.
REMREP	Remove any elements of the story that may be inappropriate for children, while also replicating the book with slight variations in characters, settings, or plot.

(Continued)

Table 5.2 (Continued)   Mixed Heuristics with Generative AI

Heuristic	Product System: Children's Storybook
SEPREP	Separate the book into multiple volumes, each with its own set of characters and storylines, while also replicating the book with slight variations in characters, settings, or plot.
SEGREP	Segment the book into chapters, each focusing on a different character or aspect of the story, while also replicating the book with slight variations in characters, settings, or plot.
MAXREP	Maximize the book's interactivity by including augmented reality features that bring the story to life, while also replicating the book with slight variations in characters, settings, or plot.
DYNREP	Dynamically vary the story based on reader input, such as choosing the path of the story or selecting the ending, while also replicating the book with slight variations in characters, settings, or plot.
COMMAX	Combine two existing stories into one cohesive narrative, while also maximizing the book's interactivity by including augmented reality features that bring the story to life.
REMMAX	Remove any elements of the story that may be inappropriate for children, while also maximizing the book's interactivity by including augmented reality features that bring the story to life.
SEPMAX	Separate the book into multiple volumes, each with its own set of characters and storylines, while also maximizing the book's interactivity by including augmented reality features that bring the story to life.
REPMAX	Create a series of children's storybooks that follow the adventures of the same set of characters, but with each book emphasizing and maximizing a different attribute of the story.
SEGMAX	Segment the book into chapters, each focusing on a different character or aspect of the story, while also maximizing the book's interactivity by including augmented reality features that bring the story to life.
DYNMAX	Dynamically vary the story based on reader input, such as choosing the path of the story or selecting the ending, while also maximizing the book's interactivity by including augmented reality features that bring the story to life.
COMDYN	Combine the children's storybook with a digital platform that allows children to interact with the story in different ways, such as by changing the storyline or characters.

(Continued)

Table 5.2 (Continued)   Mixed Heuristics with Generative AI

Heuristic	*Product System: Children's Storybook*
REMDYN	Remove certain parts of the children's storybook and replace them with dynamic elements that allow children to create their own versions of the story.
SEPDYN	Separate the children's storybook into different physical components that children can manipulate to create their own story.
SEGDYN	Segment the children's storybook into different sections that can be dynamically modified based on the child's interactions with the story.
MAXDYN	Maximize the emotional impact of the children's storybook by incorporating dynamic elements that adjust based on the child's emotional response.
REPDYN	Replicate certain parts of the children's storybook to create a redundant storyline that reinforces key messages and lessons.

system or its components; (6) MAX: Maximizing or extremizing an attribute of the system; (7) DYN: Dynamically varying or modifying a feature of the system or its component based on some external input; (8) REMCOM: Both REM and COM; (9) SEPCOM: Both SEP and COM; (10) SEGCOM: Both SEG and COM; (11) REPCOM: Both REP and COM; (12) MAXCOM: Both MAX and COM; (13) DYNCOM: Both DYN and COM…"

Exercises

1. Identify a business process or system that could benefit from an efficiency strategy. Choose one of the mixed design heuristics discussed in this chapter and apply it to the process/system. For example, you might choose Comrem and apply it to a manufacturing process where you combine two components and remove a redundant third component to increase efficiency. Analyze the potential benefits and challenges of implementing this strategy in your chosen context.

2. Pick a product that has undergone a redesign or update in the past few years. Research the details of the redesign or update and analyze how some of the mixed heuristic strategies were used in the process. Evaluate the effectiveness of the strategies and the impact on the product's performance and user experiences.

3. Find a process in your workplace or personal life that could benefit from improvement. Use different mixed heuristics to brainstorm possible solutions. Apply the strategies to the process and evaluate the effectiveness of the solutions. Implement the most effective solution and evaluate the impact on the process.
4. Teach these heuristics to ChatGPT or another LLM application, similar to the example of the children's storybook in this chapter. Use the trained model to ideate on new concepts based on the procedure outlined in this chapter. See if you can create prompts that lead to ideas that are both highly novel, feasible, and likely to attract new customers. How do these compare to ideas you have generated or observed using traditional methods, such as group brainstorming?

Notes

1. O'Shaughnessy, K. C., & Flanagan, D. J. (1998). Determinants of lay-off announcements following M&As: An empirical investigation. *Strategic Management Journal*, 19(10), 989–999.
2. Thomas, F., Frédéric, S. P., Brown, S. P., Sukhdeo, M., & Renaud, F. (2002). Understanding parasite strategies: A state-dependent approach? *Trends in Parasitology*, 18(9), 387–390.
3. National Human Genome Research Institute. (2022, May 10). *Apoptosis*. Genome.gov. https://www.genome.gov/genetics-glossary/apoptosis.
4. Jagnandan, K., & Higham, T. E. (2017). Lateral movements of a massive tail influence gecko locomotion: An integrative study comparing tail restriction and autotomy. *Scientific Reports*, 7(1), 1–8.
5. Fitzgerald, C. (2022, April 19). *The Devastating History of Scorched Earth Tactics in War*. Warhistoryonline. https://www.warhistoryonline.com/war-articles/scorched-earth-tactics.html.
6. Stockhammer, T. (2011). Dynamic adaptive streaming over HTTP – standards and design principles. In *Proceedings of the Second Annual ACM Conference on Multimedia Systems* (pp. 133–144).
7. Qvenild, M. (2008). Svalbard global seed vault: A "Noah's Ark" for the world's seeds. *Development in Practice*, 18(1), 110–116.
8. Robinson, G. E. (1992). Regulation of division of labor in insect societies. *Annual Review of Entomology*, 37(1), 637–665.
9. Peck, M. (2020, December 8). Russia's best strategy for controlling The Black Sea: Divide and conquer. *Forbes*. https://www.forbes.com/sites/michaelpeck/2020/12/08/russias-best-strategy-for-controlling-the-black-sea-divide-and-conquer/.
10. Evans, E., & Blazich, F. (2019). *Plant Propagation by Stem Cuttings | NC State Extension Publications*. NCSU. https://content.ces.ncsu.edu/plant-propagation-by-stem-cuttings-instructions-for-the-home-gardener.

11. Boswell, G. P., & Davidson, F. A. (2012). Modelling hyphal networks. *Fungal Biology Reviews*, 26(1), 30–38.
12. Goreau, T. F., Goreau, N. I., & Goreau, T. J. (1979). Corals and coral reefs. *Scientific American*, 241(2), 124–137.
13. *Radiobus di Quartiere ATM, Azienda Trasporti Milanesi.* ATM. Retrieved November 10, 2023, from https://www.atm.it/en/ViaggiaConNoi/Radiobus/Pages/Radiobus.aspx.
14. Damalas, C. A., Alexoudis, C., & Koutroubas, S. D. (2015). Common burdock: A common weed of nonarable land in Orestiada, Greece. *Hellenic Plant Protection Journal*, 8(1), 15–20.
15. Glassman, R. B. (1987). An hypothesis about redundancy and reliability in the brains of higher species: Analogies with genes, internal organs, and engineering systems. *Neuroscience & Biobehavioral Reviews*, 11(3), 275–285.
16. Kurtzman, C. P., Fell, J. W., & Boekhout, T. (2011). Definition, classification and nomenclature of the yeasts. In *The Yeasts* (pp. 3–5). Elsevier.
17. McConkey, K. R., Prasad, S., Corlett, R. T., Campos-Arceiz, A., Brodie, J. F., Rogers, H., and Santamaria, L. (2012). Seed dispersal in changing landscapes. *Biological Conservation* 146(1), 1–13.
18. Kingsley, P. (2012, January 15). Fallen dictators and their doppelgangers. *The Guardian.* https://www.theguardian.com/world/2012/jan/15/dictators-looka-likes-kim-jong-il.
19. Evans, B. (2020, April 22). SAP, Oracle and salesforce agree on one thing: co-CEO model is dead. *Acceleration Economy.* https://accelerationeconomy.com/cloud/sap-oracle-and-salesforce-agree-on-one-thing-co-ceo-model-is-dead/.
20. Wang, Z. Y., Pergande, M. R., Ragsdale, C. W., & Cologna, S. M. (2022). Steroid hormones of the octopus self-destruct system. *Current Biology*, 32(11), 2572–2579.
21. Dahl, L. K. (2010). *Stability Operations: Creating a New Air Force Specialty Code.* Air Command and Staff College.
22. Morehouse, N. (2020). Spider vision. *Current Biology*, 30(17), R975–R980.
23. Woyke, T., & Schulz, F. (2019). Entities inside one another – a matryoshka doll in biology? *Environmental Microbiology Reports*, 11(1), 26.
24. Quinn, T. C. (2018). *The Matryoshka Doll: A Model for Russian Deception, Disinformation, and Chaos.* Marine Corps University, Quantico, VA.
25. Graham, M. (2023, October 17). WSJ News Exclusive | WPP Merging VMLY&R With Wunderman Thompson. *Wall Street Journal.* https://www.wsj.com/articles/wpp-merging-vmly-r-with-wunderman-thompson-37ec147b.
26. Scholander, P. F. (1957). The wonderful net. *Scientific American*, 196(4), 96–110.
27. Khanna, T., Song, J., & Lee, K. (2011). The paradox of Samsung's rise. *Harvard Business Review*, 89(7–8), 142–147.
28. Magurran, A. E. (2005). *Evolutionary ecology: The Trinidadian guppy.* Oxford University Press.
29. Bonura, M. A. (2012). Saturation (carpet) bombing. In G. Martel (Ed.), *The Encyclopedia of War* (Vol. 4, pp. 1918–1925). Blackwell Publishing.

30. Piggot, P. J., & Hilbert, D. W. (2004). Sporulation of *Bacillus subtilis. Current Opinion in Microbiology,* 7(6), 579–586.

31. Brennan, M. J., Schwartz, E. S., & Lagnado, R. (1997). Strategic asset allocation. *Journal of Economic Dynamics and Control,* 21(8–9), 1377–1403.

32. Yang, C.-K., & Yang, H.-L. (2008). Realization of Seurat's pointillism via non-photorealistic rendering. *The Visual Computer,* 24, 303–322.

33. Diepart, C. P. (1992). Controlled shot peening today. In *Materials Science Forum,* 102, 517–532. Trans Tech Publications Ltd.

34. Krishnaswami, S., & Subramaniam, V. (2015). Unlocking value by improving transparency: The case of spinoffs. *Corporate Ownership & Control,* 13(1), 701–711.

35. The National WWII Museum. (2017, July 10). *The Pacific Strategy, 1941–1944.* The National WWII Museum | New Orleans. https://www.nationalww2museum.org/war/articles/pacific-strategy-1941–1944.

36. Padfield, G. D., & Lawrence, B. (2003). The birth of flight control: An engineering analysis of the Wright brothers' 1902 glider. *The Aeronautical Journal,* 107(1078), 697–718.

37. AWS. (2022). *Global Cloud Infrastructure | Regions & Availability Zones | AWS.* Amazon Web Services, Inc. https://aws.amazon.com/about-aws/global-infrastructure/

38. Shunko, M., Masha, T., Yunes, T., Fenu, G., Scheller-Wolf, A., Tardif, V., & Tayur, S. (2018). Product portfolio restructuring: Methodology and application at Caterpillar. *Production and Operations Management,* 27(1), 100–120.

39. Hadjidakis, D. J., & Androulakis, I. I. (2006). Bone remodeling. *Annals of the New York Academy of Sciences,* 1092(1), 385–396.

40. Vogel, S. (1984). The Diascia flower and its bee – an oil-based symbiosis in southern Africa. *Acta Botanica Neerlandica,* 33(4), 509–518.

41. Jawetz, E., & Gunnison, J. B. (1952). An experimental basis of combined antibiotic action. *Journal of the American Medical Association,* 150(7), 693–695.

42. Kim, K., Kim, H., Park, S. H., & Lee, S. J. (2017). Hydraulic strategy of cactus trichome for absorption and storage of water under arid environment. *Frontiers in Plant Science,* 8, 1777.

43. Wilson, J. W., Mills, M. G. L., Wilson, R. P., Peters, G., Mills, M. E. J., Speakman, J. R., Durant, S. M., Bennett, N. C., Marks, N. J., & Scantlebury, M. (2013). Cheetahs, *Acinonyx jubatus* balance turn capacity with pace when chasing prey. *Biology Letters,* 9(5), 20130620.

44. Ullman, H., Wade, J. Jr, Edney, L. A., Franks, F. Jr, Horner, C., & Brendley, K. (1996). *Shock and Awe: Achieving Rapid Dominance.* National Defense University.

45. Stopps, H., & Touchie, M. F. (2020). Managing thermal comfort in contemporary high-rise residential buildings: Using smart thermostats and surveys to identify energy efficiency and comfort opportunities. *Building and Environment,* 173, 106748.

46. Patton, R. J. (1990). Fault detection and diagnosis in aerospace systems using analytical redundancy. In *IEE Colloquium on Condition Monitoring and Fault Tolerance* (pp. 1–1). IET.

47. Tang, M., Lee, B.-S., Yeo, C.-K., & Tang, X. (2005). Dynamic replication algorithms for the multi-tier data grid. *Future Generation Computer Systems*, 21(5), 775–790.

48. Lissaman, P. B., & Shollenberger, C. A. (1970). Formation flight of birds. *Science*, 168(3934), 1003–1005.

49. Harvey, J. W. (1968). Structural considerations for variable sweep wings. *SAE Transactions*, 2765–2772.

50. Finkenstadt, D. J., Handfield, R., & Eapen, T. T. (2022). Certainty satiation marketing for disrupted supply chains. *California Management Review Insights*. https://cmr.berkeley.edu/2022/01/certainty-satiation-marketing-for-disrupted -supply-chains/.

51. Siroker, D., & Koomen, P. (2015). *A/B Testing: The Most Powerful Way to Turn Clicks into Customers*. John Wiley & Sons.

52. Bachrach, B. S. (1971). The feigned retreat at Hastings. *Mediaeval Studies*, 33, 344–347.

53. Ludden, G. D. S., Schifferstein, H. N. J., & Hekkert, P. (2008). Surprise as a design strategy. *Design Issues*, 24(2), 28–38.

54. Kirsner, R. S., & Eaglstein, W. H. (1993). The wound healing process. *Dermatologic Clinics*, 11(4), 629–640.

55. *Dyson Airblade Wash+Dry Short Hand Dryer*. (2019). Dyson. https://www .dyson.com/commercial/hand-dryers/airblade-wash-dry-short.

56. Grutter, A. S. (2010). Cleaner fish. *Current Biology*, 20(13), R547–R549.

References

Bachrach, B. S. (1971). The feigned retreat at Hastings. *Mediaeval Studies*, 33, 344–347.

Boswell, G. P., & Davidson, F. A. (2012). Modelling hyphal networks. *Fungal Biology Reviews*, 26(1), 30–38.

Brennan, M. J., Schwartz, E. S., & Lagnado, R. (1997). Strategic asset allocation. *Journal of Economic Dynamics and Control*, 21(8–9), 1377–1403.

Dahl, L. K. (2010). *Stability Operations: Creating a New Air Force Specialty Code*. Air Command and Staff College.

Damalas, C. A., Alexoudis, C., & Koutroubas, S. D. (2015). Common burdock: A common weed of nonarable land in Orestiada, Greece. *Hellenic Plant Protection Journal*, 8(1), 15–20.

Diepart, C. P. (1992). Controlled shot peening today. In *ASM Heat Treatment and Surface Engineering Conference I*, 517–532. Materials Science Forum, 102. Trans Tech Publications Ltd. https://doi.org/10.4028/www.scientific.net/MSF.102-104.517.

Finkenstadt, D. J., Handfield, R., & Eapen, T. T. (2022). Certainty satiation marketing for disrupted supply chains. *California Management Review Insights*. https://cmr.berkeley.edu/2022/01/certainty-satiation-marketing-for-disrupted-supply-chains/.

Glassman, R. B. (1987). An hypothesis about redundancy and reliability in the brains of higher species: Analogies with genes, internal organs, and engineering systems. *Neuroscience & Biobehavioral Reviews*, 11(3), 275–285.

Goreau, T. F., Goreau, N. I., & Goreau, T. J. (1979). Corals and coral reefs. *Scientific American*, 241(2), 124–137.

Grutter, A. S. (2010). Cleaner fish. *Current Biology*, 20(13), R547–R549.

Hadjidakis, D. J., & Androulakis, I. I. (2006). Bone remodeling. *Annals of the New York Academy of Sciences*, 1092(1), 385–396.

Harvey, J. W. (1968). Structural considerations for variable sweep wings. *SAE Transactions*, 2765–2772.

Jagnandan, K., & Higham, T. E. (2017). Lateral movements of a massive tail influence gecko locomotion: An integrative study comparing tail restriction and autotomy. *Scientific Reports*, 7(1), 1–8.

Jawetz, E., & Gunnison, J. B. (1952). An experimental basis of combined antibiotic action. *Journal of the American Medical Association*, 150(7), 693–695.

Khanna, T., Song, J., & Lee, K. (2011). The paradox of Samsung's rise. *Harvard Business Review*, 89(7–8), 142–147.

Kim, K., Kim, H., Park, S. H., & Lee, S. J. (2017). Hydraulic strategy of cactus trichome for absorption and storage of water under arid environment. *Frontiers in Plant Science*, 8, 1777.

Kirsner, R. S., & Eaglstein, W. H. (1993). The wound healing process. *Dermatologic Clinics*, 11(4), 629–640.

Krishnaswami, S., & Subramaniam, V. (2015). Unlocking value by improving transparency: The case of spinoffs. *Corporate Ownership & Control*, 13(1), 701–711.

Kurtzman, C. P., Fell, J. W., & Boekhout, T. (2011). Definition, classification and nomenclature of the yeasts. In C. P. Kurtzman, J. W. Fell, & T. Boekhout (Eds.), *The Yeasts* (Fifth Edition) (pp. 3–5). Elsevier. https://doi.org/10.1016/B978-0-444-52149-1.00001-X

Lissaman, P. B., & Shollenberger, C. A. (1970). Formation flight of birds. *Science*, 168(3934), 1003–1005.

Ludden, G. D. S., Schifferstein, H. N. J., & Hekkert, P. (2008). Surprise as a design strategy. *Design Issues*, 24(2), 28–38.

Magurran, A. E. (2005). *Evolutionary Ecology: The Trinidadian Guppy*. Oxford University Press.

McConkey, K. R., Prasad, S., Corlett, R. T., Campos-Arceiz, A., Brodie, J. F., Rogers, H., & Santamaria, L. (2012). Seed dispersal in changing landscapes. *Biological Conservation*, 146(1), 1–13.

Morehouse, N. (2020). Spider vision. *Current Biology*, 30(17), R975–R980.

O'Shaughnessy, K. C., & Flanagan, D. J. (1998). Determinants of layoff announcements following M&As: An empirical investigation. *Strategic Management Journal*, 19(10), 989–999.

Padfield, G. D., & Lawrence, B. (2003). The birth of flight control: An engineering analysis of the Wright brothers' 1902 glider. *The Aeronautical Journal*, 107(1078), 697–718.

Patton, R. J. (1990). Fault detection and diagnosis in aerospace systems using analytical redundancy. In *IEE Colloquium on Condition Monitoring and Fault Tolerance* (pp. 1–1). IET.

Quinn, T. C. (2018). *The Matryoshka Doll: A Model for Russian Deception, Disinformation, and Chaos.* Marine Corps University.

Qvenild, M. (2008). Svalbard global seed vault: A 'Noah's Ark' for the world's seeds. *Development in Practice*, 18(1), 110–116.

Robinson, G. E. (1992). Regulation of division of labor in insect societies. *Annual Review of Entomology*, 37(1), 637–665.

Scholander, P. F. (1957). The wonderful net. *Scientific American*, 196(4), 96–110.

Shunko, M., Masha, T., Yunes, T., Fenu, G., Scheller-Wolf, A., Tardif, V., & Tayur, S. (2018). Product portfolio restructuring: Methodology and application at Caterpillar. *Production and Operations Management*, 27(1), 100–120.

Siroker, D., & Koomen, P. (2015). *A/B Testing: The Most Powerful Way to Turn Clicks into Customers.* John Wiley & Sons.

Stockhammer, T. (2011). Dynamic adaptive streaming over HTTP—Standards and design principles. In *Proceedings of the Second Annual ACM Conference on Multimedia Systems* (pp. 133–144).

Stopps, H., & Touchie, M. F. (2020). Managing thermal comfort in contemporary high-rise residential buildings: Using smart thermostats and surveys to identify energy efficiency and comfort opportunities. *Building and Environment*, 173, 106748.

Tang, M., Lee, B.-S., Yeo, C.-K., & Tang, X. (2005). Dynamic replication algorithms for the multi-tier data grid. *Future Generation Computer Systems*, 21(5), 775–790.

Thomas, F., Frédéric, S. P., Brown, S. P., Sukhdeo, M., & Renaud, F. (2002). Understanding parasite strategies: A state-dependent approach? *Trends in Parasitology*, 18(9), 387–390.

Ullman, H., Wade, J. Jr., Edney, L. A., Franks, F. Jr., Horner, C., & Brendley, K. (1996). *Shock and Awe: Achieving Rapid Dominance.* National Defense University.

Vogel, S. (1984). The Diascia flower and its bee – An oil-based symbiosis in southern Africa. *Acta Botanica Neerlandica*, 33(4), 509–518.

Wang, Z. Y., Pergande, M. R., Ragsdale, C. W., & Cologna, S. M. (2022). Steroid hormones of the octopus self-destruct system. *Current Biology*, 32(11), 2572–2579.

Wilson, J. W., Mills, M. G. L., Wilson, R. P., Peters, G., Mills, M. E. J., Speakman, J. R., Durant, S. M., Bennett, N. C., Marks, N. J., & Scantlebury, M. (2013). Cheetahs, *Acinonyx jubatus*, balance turn capacity with pace when chasing prey. *Biology Letters*, 9(5), 20130620.

Woyke, T., & Schulz, F. (2019). Entities inside one another—A Matryoshka doll in biology? *Environmental Microbiology Reports*, 11(1), 26.

Yang, C.-K., & Yang, H.-L. (2008). Realization of Seurat's pointillism via non-photo-realistic rendering. *The Visual Computer*, 24, 303–322.

Chapter 6

ERP-Focused Strategic Planning

In nature, strategy is less about long-term planning and more about responding to quickly changing conditions.

–Elizabeth Kolbert

DOI: 10.4324/9781032715315-7

In this chapter, we will delve into the applications of the ERP (efficiency–resilience–prominence) framework within the realm of strategic thinking in organizations. We will commence by examining the role of the ERP factors in scenario planning, a widely utilized strategic planning method that involves exploring potential future scenarios to pinpoint risks, challenges, and opportunities for the organization. These scenarios serve as the foundation for identifying strategic actions that constitute appropriate responses to each scenario. The conventional approach to scenario planning can be enhanced by integrating the ERP framework, which posits that the survivability of an organization hinges on three capabilities – efficiency (resource management), resilience (management of external forces), and prominence (management of observers).

In the realm of scenario planning, the ERP framework proves invaluable for swiftly generating multiple scenarios based on available data and aiding organizations in readiness to respond to a myriad of potential situations by pinpointing strategic actions. Effective strategic actions necessitate organizations to prepare for all three ERP factors. In the scenario context, planning for efficiency (E) mandates that the organization optimize its resources to attain goals across diverse potential scenarios. Likewise, gearing up for resilience (R) compels the company to rebound from unforeseen disruptions and sustain operations in the face of external forces across various scenarios. Ultimately, cultivating prominence (P) capabilities for the future requires the organization to enhance its ability to manage attention from both friendly and antagonistic observers across all potential scenarios.

Scenario Planning

Scenario planning has become a widely used tool for businesses to anticipate and prepare for potential changes in the business environment.[1] Recently, there has been an increasing call for its adoption, particularly in the aftermath of the extensive disruptions to the supply chain caused by the COVID-19 pandemic.[2] In his 1996 book *The Art of the Long View*, Peter Schwartz, a pioneer in the field of future-oriented thinking, suggests that small businesses may derive particular benefit from this approach, given the heightened levels of uncertainty they typically encounter.[3] The scenario planning approach involves envisioning multiple alternate scenarios that represent different possible future realities. The organization then identifies the best ways to prepare for one or more of these scenarios. Fictional scenarios that help to create a sense of urgency, engage stakeholders, and encourage creative thinking may also be utilized. These scenarios may not be perfect, accurate representations of the future, but they aid organizations in anticipating and preparing for potential changes in the business environment.[4] Traditionally, scenario planning found application in time horizons spanning hree to five years or even longer. However, amid the COVID-19 pandemic, we witnessed the emergence of contingency scenario planning (CSP) to aid in near-term decision-making, exemplified by its use in planning for the 2020 Tokyo Olympics.[5]

Scenario planning is a crucial tool for strategic foresight, or anticipatory thinking, involving the preparation for low-probability, high-impact events across multiple alternative futures. It is becoming increasingly important for both firms and governments. The global energy company Shell has been using scenario planning since the late 1960s to navigate the unpredictable nature of the oil and gas industry. Shell's scenario planning approach involved creating "what-if" scenarios that explored multiple potential future realities. By considering a range of scenarios, Shell could identify strategies potentially adaptable to various futures. When the Yom Kippur War broke out in 1973, causing oil prices to increase sixfold, Shell was well-prepared.[6] The company's utilization of scenario planning resulted in its ability to act quickly during the crisis, which has been credited as the primary reason behind its subsequent success in the oil and gas industry. The National Intelligence University (NIU) in the United States has an entire center developed specifically for futures intelligence, and notable defense and business strategists are writing about concepts like "Fictional Intelligence" that involve melding non-fictional information with futures forecasting and creative narratives to imagine alternate future challenges and opportunities.[7]

Scenario-planning methods have generally been established and led by practitioners, starting with Shell's planners such as Pierre Wack.[8] Over time, several methodologies have been created, sharing many common characteristics. Peter Schwartz's and Paul J.H. Schoemaker's methodologies are particularly popular, and their works are among the most frequently cited in the field of scenario planning.

The Scenario Planning Process

The scenario planning process described below has been adapted from the approach outlined by Schoemaker in his influential article published in *Sloan Management Review* in 1994.[9]

1. Scope Definition: The initial step in scenario planning involves defining the scope by establishing the time frame and analyzing products, markets, geographic areas, and technologies. Additionally, past uncertainties and changes should be considered to anticipate future ones.

2. Identify Key Stakeholders: The subsequent step is to recognize the major stakeholders, and understand their interests, power positions, and how these factors have evolved. This includes customers, suppliers, competitors, employees, shareholders, government, etc.

3. Identify Trends and Uncertainties in the Environment: In the third step of scenario planning, the planner must identify political, economic, societal, technological, legal, and industry trends and uncertainties that will impact the organization. It is crucial to determine whether their impact is positive, negative, or uncertain.

4. Develop Learning Scenarios: Next, the company must identify strategically relevant themes by organizing possible outcomes and trends around them, creating learning scenarios for research and study.

5. Scenario Research: The company may need to conduct additional research and develop quantitative models to analyze and compare different scenarios and better understand their potential impacts.

6. Develop Decision Scenarios: To converge toward decision scenarios, a company must repeat the previous steps iteratively until its scenarios are relevant, internally consistent, archetypal, and describe a system that may exist for some time, and they should cover a wide range of possibilities and highlight competing perspectives.

7. Strategic Ideation: The company can use decision scenarios as the basis for identifying strategic actions that can help the company succeed in each of the different scenarios. By considering the potential impacts of various scenarios and assessing the company's strengths and weaknesses in each, companies can develop strategies that are robust and adaptable to a range of possible futures.

We aim to highlight the framework outlined above to emphasize the shortcomings of conventional methods of scenario planning and to suggest an ERP-centric approach that can overcome some of these limitations.

Limitations in Traditional Scenario Planning

Despite the popularity of the tool, there have been several criticisms of the scenario planning approach.[10] For example, management guru Henry

Mintzberg and his co-authors of the book *Strategy Safari* criticized the traditional scenario planning approach as time-consuming and ineffective.[11]

The process of creating scenarios is complex and fraught with challenges. It is unclear how to select the optimal scenarios, and there is little formal guidance on how organizations can best prepare for multiple scenarios, especially extreme ones. Moreover, the risks of preparing too much for the wrong scenarios may be as damaging as not preparing for any at all. Limitations can be clustered around the three relevant stages of scenario planning: (1) generating scenarios, (2) selecting scenarios, and (3) preparing for scenarios.

Generating Scenarios: One limitation of the traditional scenario planning outlined above is its lack of formal guidance on where to locate trends and uncertainties. Without a structured process for identifying and analyzing potential trends and uncertainties, organizations may succumb to tunnel vision and overconfidence – two biases that scenario planning aims to help managers avoid.[12]

Selecting Scenarios: The next set of challenges in scenario planning relates to how the best set of scenarios may be selected. There are clear trade-offs to consider in this process. Scenario planning experts, such as Peter Schwartz, have recommended a small number of scenarios, typically three to five, to allow planners to focus. However, this often means that the scenarios planned for are likely to be extreme cases, which may be unrealistic.

Preparing for Scenarios: The third set of challenges in scenario planning relates to preparing for the decision scenarios. A key limitation of traditional scenario planning is that it doesn't offer guidance on how organizations can prepare for multiple potential realities simultaneously. This limitation is concerning because actions that are consistent with success in one scenario may be inadequate or even detrimental to the company's success under another scenario. For example, a company may need to prepare for two scenarios: one in which global oil prices continually rise and another in which they remain stable. To satisfactorily prepare for each scenario, the company may need to apply different strategies that may be at odds with each other. Organizations have several options to prepare for multiple, potentially contradictory scenarios.

■ One approach is to focus on actions consistent with the most likely scenario based on available data and insights. However, this approach may not always be sufficient as the future is inherently uncertain.

- Another option is to take action for an intermediate scenario, which involves finding a balance between the different scenarios. This approach can be useful in situations where the company is unsure which scenario is more likely or when the cost of preparing for one scenario is too high.
- Finally, the company can develop competencies to adapt actions based on emerging information about scenarios. This involves building a culture of agility and flexibility, where the company can quickly pivot and adjust its strategies based on new information and changing circumstances.

The first approach prepares an organization for only the most likely scenario, leaving it unprepared for less likely but still possible scenarios. The second approach may be suitable in some situations, but it may not optimize for any one scenario. The third approach, which involves developing adaptability, is the most promising. However, it is difficult to examine adaptability at the level of every action, given that actions across scenarios may be different. For example, investing in new product development in a new category might be the appropriate action in one scenario, while investing in the technical efficiency of existing products might be the right course of action in another scenario. The advantage of taking an ERP-focused look at scenario planning is that it provides a model of competing strategic objectives that are generalizable to any organization or context. All scenarios will require some trade among ERP factors to optimize survivability. In this way, organizations can develop agility and adaptability by viewing all possible futures as optimal ERP trades given possible conditions.

ERP-Focused Scenario Planning

Next, we will describe how the use of the ERP framework, in conjunction with the traditional scenario planning model, can address some of the limitations identified above. Firstly, in generating scenarios, it allows us to systematically and comprehensively identify trends and uncertainties, forcing us to consider resources, forces, and observers, as well as their interactions. Many companies struggle with identifying the appropriate trends in their industry, but the ERP framework can alleviate this challenge by directing planners to precisely where to look for trends and opportunities. Secondly, in selecting scenarios, the ERP framework helps us quickly identify the advantages and limitations of each scenario, thereby enabling us to choose and combine the appropriate scenarios. Finally, the ERP framework helps organizations systematically prepare for multiple scenarios by assisting us in identifying trade-offs among different possible actions across various scenarios and how these actions relate to the underlying capabilities of the organization.

By integrating the ERP framework into scenario planning, organizations can assess their efficiency, resilience, and prominence across different potential scenarios. Organizations can identify inconsistencies across different scenarios and understand the level of adaptability required by examining the impact of each action on the ERP factors. This helps identify gaps in existing capabilities and develop more robust strategies that can adapt to different futures. For example, if one scenario requires high prominence towards customers and another also dictates the same, then there is no need to worry about prominence adaptability. However, if the analysis reveals that one scenario requires high prominence towards a major competitor while another requires low prominence, then high prominence adaptability is required for actions targeted at this competitor. To incorporate ERP analysis within traditional scenario planning, we can follow these steps:

- Generating Scenarios: Perform a comprehensive analysis of the organization using the Ro/Fo/Ob (Resource–Forces–Observers) analysis. Identify the nature of survivability concerns and their interlinkages. Identify trends and uncertainties for each relevant Ro/Fo/Ob variable and investigate their relationships. Create learning scenarios focused on resources, forces, and observers based on combinations of resources (high/low), forces (strong/weak), and observers (attract/avoid).
- Selecting Scenarios: Combine learning scenarios to create decision scenarios that reflect multiple trends for a single survivability concern or all concerns for a single trend. This process helps identify the key scenarios that the organization needs to prepare for.
- Preparing for Scenarios: Create a set of potential actions for each scenario that can assist the organization in achieving its goals. Evaluate each action based on its impact on the ERP factors.
- Organizations can develop a comprehensive approach to scenario planning that considers all ERP-relevant factors by following these steps. This approach can assist in preparing for a variety of scenarios and minimizing the risks associated with contradictory options. Generative AI tools, such as large language models (LLMs), can support

ERP-focused scenario planning by identifying baseline scenarios, formulating scenarios based on trends, generating ideas, combining scenarios, and evaluating ideas.

ERP-Focused Scenario Planning for a Business School Using Generative AI

Next, let's delve into a hypothetical scenario planning exercise at a business school in 2023, elucidating the utilization of the ERP framework alongside the traditional scenario planning process. We'll initiate the process by generating scenarios. The initial step encompasses the consideration of all pertinent survivability concerns – resources, forces, and observers – that hold significance for the business school. Additionally, we can leverage the support of Large Language Models (LLMs) such as OpenAI's ChatGPT, Anthropic's Claude, or Google Bard to generate a foundational list. In our simulation, the following prompt was employed to compile a list of pertinent resources, forces, and observers.

Let's consider a hypothetical scenario planning exercise for a standalone international business school. In the first step, we need to identify and evaluate all the relevant resources, external forces, and observers of significance. Can you please list some of the critical resources, external forces, and observers in order of their significance?

The following set of survivability concerns was obtained:

- Resources – faculty members and staff, facilities, financial resources, curriculum and educational resources, alumni network
- External forces – economic conditions, technological changes, regulatory environment, competition, demographic changes
- Observers – students, industry partners, accrediting bodies, government agencies, media, and ranking organizations

The next step is to identify trends related to the above concerns. To illustrate, we prompted ChatGPT to generate hypothetical trends that could affect a standalone business school, specifically relating to faculty members and staff, economic conditions, and students. The following prompt was used in this step:

Please identify three hypothetical trends for each of the following categories: (1) faculty members and staff, (2) economic conditions, and (3) students, which could impact a standalone business school.

The following trends were identified by the LLM:

Faculty members and staff:

1. Increased demand for remote work options and flexible scheduling due to the COVID-19 pandemic, resulting in a need for updated policies and procedures.
2. Growing importance of diversity, equity, and inclusion initiatives to attract and retain top talent.
3. Increased competition for faculty and staff due to the proliferation of online education platforms and other alternative career paths.

Economic conditions:

1. Increased demand for specialized, niche programs and certifications to meet the needs of the changing job market.
2. Economic downturn resulting in decreased enrollment and reduced funding for the school, leading to a need for cost-cutting measures.
3. Increased government regulation and oversight of for-profit educational institutions, leading to increased compliance costs.

Students:

1. Increased focus on practical, hands-on learning experiences and opportunities for real-world application.
2. Greater emphasis on online and hybrid learning formats due to changing demographics and preferences.
3. Increased demand for sustainability and social responsibility in educational programs and institutional practices.

From the trends generated above, we have selected three trends – one from each of the three concerns – to form the basis for developing initial learning scenarios. The three trends (Tn) we have chosen are as follows:

1. T1: Increased competition for faculty and staff due to the proliferation of online education platforms and other alternative career paths.
2. T2: Economic downturn resulting in decreased enrollment and reduced funding for the school, leading to a need for cost-cutting measures.
3. T3: Increased focus by students on practical, hands-on learning experiences and opportunities for real-world application.

Table 6.1 Learning Scenarios

Trends	Resources (faculty members and staff, facilities, financial resources, curriculum and educational resources, alumni network)	Forces (economic conditions, technological changes, regulatory environment, competition, demographic changes)	Observers (students, industry partners, accrediting bodies, government agencies, media, and rankings organizations)
T1	LS11	LS12	LS13
T2	LS21	LS22	LS23
T3	LS31	LS32	LS33

The next step is to use the trends T1 to T3 to create a set of learning scenarios LS11 to LS33 (Table 6.1) by assessing the relationships between the trends and the resources, observers, and forces of the business school.

To generate the first learning scenario LS11, we asked ChatGPT to identify the impact of the first trend T1 on the various resources of the business school, using the following prompt:

Examine how the increased competition for faculty and staff, resulting from the proliferation of online education platforms and alternative career paths, impacts the following resources of a standalone international business school: faculty members and staff, facilities, financial resources, curriculum, educational resources, and alumni network.

The following impacts of trend T1 on different resources of the business school were identified by the LLM:

1. Faculty Members and Staff: Increased competition could lead to higher salaries and benefits packages to attract and retain top talent, which may strain the school's financial resources.
2. Facilities: The school may need to upgrade and improve its facilities to remain competitive and attract top talent, which could be costly.
3. Financial Resources: Increased competition could lead to higher salaries and benefits packages for faculty and staff, which may strain the school's financial resources.
4. Curriculum: The school may need to update and improve its curriculum to remain competitive and relevant, which could be time-consuming and costly.

5. Educational Resources: The school may need to invest in technology and other resources to offer more flexible learning options to remain competitive.
6. Alumni Network: If alumni leave for alternative career paths or online education platforms, they may become less involved with the school, which could impact the school's fundraising and networking efforts.

Now, we can generate the resource-focused learning scenario LS11 by combining the trend and its impact on the resources identified above, using the following prompt:

Create a scenario for a standalone business school that considers the impact of [trend T1] and its relationship to the following resources: [list of resources].

A detailed description of the scenario was generated, which is summarized below:

Learning Scenario LS11: ABC International Business School has been experiencing increased competition for faculty and staff due to the proliferation of online education platforms and alternative career paths. To attract and retain top talent, the school decides to offer higher salaries and benefits packages, which puts a strain on its financial resources. The school also invests in upgrading and improving its facilities to remain competitive and attract top talent, which incurs significant costs. To remain relevant, the school updates and improves its curriculum, which is time-consuming and costly. Additionally, the school invests in technology and other resources to offer more flexible learning options to remain competitive. Despite these efforts, the school's alumni network is impacted as some alumni leave for alternative career paths or online education platforms, which leads to a decrease in fundraising and networking efforts.

Similarly, a second scenario LS12, which focused on external forces, can be created by looking at the relationship between the trend T2 and external forces using the following prompt.

Examine how the increased competition for faculty and staff, resulting from the proliferation of online education platforms and alternative career paths, relates to the following external forces of a standalone international business school: economic conditions, technological changes, regulatory environment, competition, demographic changes.

The following response was provided by ChatGPT about how trend T2 relates to the different external forces:

1. Economic Conditions: Economic conditions can influence the availability of funding for salaries, benefits, and other incentives that may attract and retain top faculty and staff. Increased competition for faculty and staff may drive up salaries and benefits, making it more difficult for a standalone international business school to remain competitive.

2. Technological Changes: Technological changes, such as the proliferation of online education platforms, have led to increased competition for faculty and staff. Online platforms offer flexible schedules, competitive compensation, and other incentives that may be attractive to faculty and staff. A standalone international business school may need to adopt new technologies to remain competitive and attract top talent.

3. Regulatory Environment: The regulatory environment may impact the ability of a standalone international business school to attract and retain top faculty and staff. For example, visa restrictions may limit the ability of international faculty to work at the school. Changes in regulatory requirements may also impact the compensation and benefit packages offered to faculty and staff.

4. Competition: Increased competition from other schools, online platforms, and alternative career paths may make it more challenging for a standalone international business school to attract and retain top talent. The school may need to differentiate itself by offering unique programs, competitive compensation packages, and other incentives.

5. Demographic Changes: Demographic changes, such as the aging workforce and the influx of millennials, may impact the recruitment and retention strategies of a standalone international business school. Younger faculty and staff may prioritize work–life balance, flexible schedules, and a sense of purpose in their career. The school may need to adapt its recruitment and retention strategies to align with the needs of this demographic group.

The following external forces–focused learning scenario LS12 can be generated by combining the trend and its relationship to different external forces using a prompt of the following type:

Create a scenario for a standalone business school that considers the impact of trend: [trend T2] and its relationship to the following economic forces: [list of forces].

Learning Scenario LS12: ABC International Business School has been providing high-quality business education for over a decade, but the school is now facing increased competition for faculty and staff from online education platforms and alternative career paths. Economic conditions have driven up salaries and benefits, making it challenging for the school to attract and retain top talent. Technological changes have made online platforms attractive to faculty and staff, and the school may need to adopt new technologies and develop online programs to remain competitive. Regulatory changes, including visa restrictions, could impact the compensation and benefits packages for faculty and staff, and the school must adapt its strategies accordingly. With increased competition from other institutions and demographic changes, ABC International Business School must differentiate itself by offering unique programs and competitive compensation packages and aligning its recruitment and retention strategies with the needs of the younger demographic group.

Similarly, the third learning scenario LS13, which focuses on external forces, can be created by examining the relationship between trend T3 and the observers of the business school, with the help of the following prompt.

For a standalone international business school, examine how the increased competition for faculty and staff, resulting from the proliferation of online education platforms and alternative career paths, relates to the following external observers: students, industry partners, accrediting bodies, government agencies, and media and rankings organizations.

The following points were generated using the input above as input to ChatGPT:

1. Students: Students are likely to be impacted by the quality of faculty and staff members in international business schools. If the school is not able to attract and retain highly qualified and experienced faculty members, students may receive a lower quality of education. As competition for faculty and staff members increases, it may become more difficult for schools to maintain high standards of education, which can negatively impact student satisfaction and future job prospects.

2. Industry Partners: Industry partners are often interested in collaborating with business schools to help train their future workforce or to develop research partnerships. The quality of faculty and staff members in a business school can be an important factor in determining whether or not industry partners are interested in collaborating with a particular institution. If the school is unable to attract highly qualified faculty and staff, it may struggle to build partnerships with industry leaders.

3. Accrediting Bodies: Accrediting bodies play a critical role in determining the quality of education offered by business schools. They assess the curriculum, faculty, and staff members to ensure that the school meets certain standards. The increased competition for faculty and staff members may make it more challenging for schools to maintain the required standards, which can negatively impact their accreditation status.

4. Government Agencies: Government agencies may be interested in promoting the quality of education in their country. They may provide funding or other support to business schools that meet certain criteria. The quality of faculty and staff members can be an important factor in determining whether or not a school receives this type of support. If the school is unable to attract highly qualified faculty and staff, it may miss out on government funding or support.

5. Media and Rankings Organizations: Media and rankings organizations are often interested in promoting the best business schools. They may create rankings or publish articles about the top schools in the world. The quality of faculty and staff members can be a critical factor in determining a school's ranking. If the school is unable to attract highly qualified faculty and staff, it may receive lower rankings or less media attention.

The following observer-focused learning scenario LS13 can be generated by combining the trend and its relationship to different observers, using a prompt of the following type:

Create a scenario for a standalone business school that describes the trend: [increased competition for faculty and staff, resulting from the proliferation of online education platforms and alternative career paths] and its relationship to the following observers related factors: [list of observer related outcomes].

Learning Scenario LS13: As online education platforms and alternative career paths proliferate, ABC International Business School is facing intense competition for faculty and staff members, which is causing significant challenges for the school. The quality of faculty and staff members in a school is critical for maintaining high standards of education, and this impacts various stakeholders. Students may receive lower quality education and have negative impacts on their satisfaction and future job prospects if the school cannot attract and retain highly qualified faculty members. Industry partners may be unwilling to collaborate with a school that cannot attract highly qualified personnel, resulting in missed opportunities for collaboration. Accrediting bodies play a critical role in determining the quality of education offered by business schools, and the increased competition for faculty and staff members may make it challenging for schools to maintain required standards. Government agencies may provide funding or other support to business schools that meet certain criteria, and the quality of faculty and staff members can be an important factor in determining whether or not a school receives this type of support. Finally, media and rankings organizations often promote the best business schools, and the quality of faculty and staff members can be a critical factor in determining a school's ranking or media attention.

The same approach was used to create the learning scenario LS21 for trend T2, using the following prompt:

For a standalone international business school, examine how economic downturn resulting in decreased enrollment and reduced funding for the school, leading to a need for cost-cutting measures, relates to the following resources: faculty members and staff, facilities, financial resources, curriculum, educational resources, and alumni network.

Here are some of the resource-related factors identified as relevant to trend T2:

1. Faculty Members and Staff: One of the primary costs of running an international business school is the salary and benefits of faculty members and staff. If the school is facing financial difficulties, it may need to reduce the number of faculty members and staff or reduce their salaries and benefits. This could lead to a reduction in the quality of education provided by the school and could also negatively impact the morale of the remaining faculty and staff.

2. Facilities: Another major expense for an international business school is its facilities. The school may need to reduce the size or quality of its facilities in order to save money. This could make it more difficult for the school to attract students and faculty members, and could also negatively impact the quality of education provided by the school.

3. Financial Resources: A decrease in enrollment and funding will likely result in a reduction in the school's financial resources. The school may need to cut back on expenses, such as marketing and advertising, in order to save money. This could make it more difficult for the school to attract new students and could lead to a further decrease in enrollment.

4. Curriculum: An economic downturn may force the school to re-evaluate its curriculum in order to make it more relevant to the current job market and attract more students. This could involve cutting back on certain courses or programs that are not in high demand, or adding new courses or programs that are more relevant to the current job market.

5. Educational Resources: An international business school relies on various educational resources to provide its students with a quality education. These resources include textbooks, online resources, and other learning materials. The school may need to cut back on these resources in order to save money, which could negatively impact the quality of education provided by the school.

6. Alumni Network: The alumni network is an important resource for an international business school, as it can provide support and funding to the school. However, if the school is facing financial difficulties, it may be more difficult to maintain a strong alumni network. This could lead to a decrease in donations and support from alumni, which could further exacerbate the school's financial problems.

Create a scenario for a standalone business school that describes the trend: [economic downturn resulting in decreased enrollment and reduced funding for the school, leading to a need for cost-cutting measures] and its relationship to the following resource-related factors: [list of resource-related factors].

Learning Scenario LS21: ABC International Business School, a reputable institution in a major city, has been hit by an economic downturn causing decreased enrollment and funding. In order to remain financially viable, the school has had to consider cost-cutting measures. These measures include reducing the number of faculty members and staff, reducing the size and quality of its facilities, cutting back on expenses and scholarships, re-evaluating its curriculum, and considering cutting back on various educational resources. The school is also trying to maintain its strong alumni network to provide support and funding to the institution. However, the school's financial difficulties may make it difficult to maintain the network, further exacerbating the school's problems.

Next, the above approach was used to create learning scenario LS31 for trend T3.

Learning Scenario LS31: ABC International Business School has observed an increasing trend among its students for practical, hands-on learning experiences and opportunities for real-world application. The trend is driven by students' desire to gain skills and experience that will prepare them for the job market and help them stand out to potential employers. The school needs to focus on several resource-related factors to meet this demand. These include ensuring that faculty members have relevant industry experience and can incorporate hands-on activities into the curriculum, investing in specialized facilities, allocating more financial resources to support practical learning experiences, revising the curriculum to include more real-world applications, investing in new educational resources, and engaging with its alumni network to provide mentorship, internships, and networking opportunities for students. By addressing these factors, the school can provide students with practical, real-world knowledge and skills that are aligned with industry needs and help them prepare for their careers.

ERP-Focused Ideation for Learning Scenarios

The learning scenarios described in the previous section can serve as the foundation for generating preliminary ideas for strategic actions. These initial ideas can be generated using generative AI tools as a starting point, and then further refined by human ideators. As an example, one could ask ChatGPT to generate three ideas that could assist the business school in achieving success in learning scenario LS11.

Generate three ideas that can help a standalone business school succeed in the following scenario: [learning scenario LS11].

The three ideas presented below were generated by ChatGPT in response to the aforementioned prompt.

1. Diversify Revenue Streams: The school can explore different ways to generate revenue beyond tuition fees and alumni donations. For example, the school can offer executive education programs or consulting services to businesses or government agencies. These programs can provide an additional source of income for the school while also enhancing its reputation and expanding its network.

2. Develop a Strong Online Presence: To compete with online education platforms, the school can develop a strong online presence by offering high-quality online courses and programs. This will enable the school to reach a wider audience, increase its visibility, and attract more students. Additionally, the school can leverage social media and other digital marketing channels to engage with prospective students and showcase its expertise.

3. Foster a Strong Community: The school can invest in fostering a strong sense of community among its students, faculty, staff, and alumni. This can be achieved through networking events, mentorship programs, and alumni reunions. By building a strong community, the school can enhance its reputation and improve its fundraising efforts. Additionally, alumni who feel connected to the school are more likely to recommend it to others, which can help attract new students and faculty.

These baseline ideas can be used for comparison with human-generated ideas or as a starting point to inspire more focused ideation by human ideators. The next step involves evaluating the potential impact of each idea (potential strategic action) on the ERP factors.

Examine the impact of the following idea on the efficiency (management of resources), resilience (management of external forces), and prominence (management of observers) of a standalone business school: [idea].

The above prompt was employed to assess the impact of the first idea – diversifying revenue streams. The following impacts of this idea on ERP factors were identified:

1. Efficiency (Management of Resources): By diversifying revenue streams, the business school can reduce its reliance on tuition fees and alumni donations, which can be unpredictable and subject to market

fluctuations. By generating additional income from executive education programs or consulting services, the school can create a more stable financial base, allowing it to better manage its resources and invest in its infrastructure and faculty. Moreover, these additional revenue streams can create new job opportunities for faculty members, thereby enhancing the overall efficiency of the school.

2. Resilience (Management of External Forces): Diversifying revenue streams can also make the business school more resilient to external forces such as economic downturns, changes in government policies, or shifts in the education landscape. For example, if there is a decline in the number of students applying to business schools, a diversified revenue stream can help the school weather the storm by providing a steady source of income. Similarly, if the government cuts funding for higher education, the school can still rely on its diversified revenue streams to support its operations.

3. Prominence (Management of Observers): Finally, diversifying revenue streams can enhance the prominence of the business school by expanding its network and enhancing its reputation. By offering executive education programs or consulting services to businesses or government agencies, the school can build stronger relationships with these organizations and position itself as a thought leader in its field. This can lead to increased visibility, more opportunities for collaboration, and a greater sense of prestige and influence.

Nevertheless, it should be noted that the above evaluations may not be entirely accurate and may require further evaluation and discussion by human planners. For instance, diversification could result in a decrease in efficiency in existing operations – a point that was not identified by ChatGPT. Moving forward, we can ask ChatGPT to generate three ideas that could aid the business school in achieving success in learning scenario LS12.

Generate three ideas that can help a standalone business school succeed in the following scenario: [learning scenario LS12].

The following ideas were garnered for the above prompt.

■ Develop a Flexible Online Program: To stay competitive with online education platforms, ABC International Business School should consider developing a flexible online program that allows students to balance their education with other commitments. The program could be designed to accommodate students who work full-time or have other obligations, such as family or travel. This would require investment in technology and infrastructure, but could attract a wider pool of students, while also appealing to faculty members who value the flexibility of online teaching.

■ Foster a Strong Alumni Network: One way to differentiate the school from competitors is to build a strong alumni network. This could involve providing opportunities for alumni to connect with each other, hosting events, and offering mentorship programs. A strong alumni network can help to increase the school's reputation, attract new students and faculty, and provide valuable resources and opportunities for graduates.

■ Emphasize Social Responsibility: Another way for the school to differentiate itself is to emphasize its commitment to social responsibility. This could involve integrating sustainability and ethics into the curriculum and promoting initiatives that give back to the community. Faculty members who are passionate about social responsibility may be more likely to stay with the school if they feel that their values are aligned with those of the institution. This could also appeal to younger students, who are increasingly interested in social and environmental issues.

Lastly, we can request that ChatGPT generate three ideas to assist the business school in achieving success in learning scenario LS13. The following three ideas were generated:

1. Industry Partnerships and Collaborations: The school can partner with various industries and businesses to provide practical learning experiences for its students. Through collaborations with companies, students can participate in internships, work on real-life projects, and gain industry insights that can prepare them for the job market. The school can also offer industry-sponsored scholarships or grants to students, providing financial support while building relationships with businesses. Additionally, the school can invite industry experts as guest speakers or instructors to provide students with practical knowledge and insights.

2. Virtual and Augmented Reality (VR/AR) Technology Integration: The school can invest in specialized facilities and educational resources that incorporate VR/AR technology to create simulated learning environments. This technology can help students gain practical experience in a safe, controlled environment, providing them with hands-on training

that can prepare them for real-world scenarios. The school can also develop virtual internship programs, enabling students to work with companies remotely and gain practical experience from anywhere in the world.

3. Alumni Engagement and Mentorship: The school can leverage its alumni network to provide mentorship, networking opportunities, and internships for its students. Alumni can provide guidance and support, share their industry experience, and connect students with potential employers. The school can also organize alumni networking events, where students can connect with alumni and learn from their experiences. This can help students build their professional networks and gain valuable insights into the job market.

From Learning Scenarios to Decision Scenarios

The individual learning scenarios are crafted to be standalone, each focusing on a single trend and one of the three organizational survivability concerns: resources, forces, and observers. Nonetheless, real-world decision scenarios frequently encompass multiple trends and necessitate the scrutiny of all three concerns. To accomplish this, we need to amalgamate pertinent learning scenarios to construct decision scenarios. For example, combining LS11, LS22, and LS33 produces the subsequent decision scenario, centering on a single trend and assessing its influence on all three survivability concerns – resources, forces, and observers – pertaining to the business school.

Decision Scenario: ABC International Business School is facing fierce competition for faculty and staff members, causing significant challenges for the school and impacting various stakeholders. To remain competitive, the school has responded by offering higher salaries and benefits packages, which has strained its financial resources. Additionally, the school has invested in upgrading and improving its facilities, curriculum, and technology to offer more flexible learning options. Economic conditions have driven up salaries and benefits, making it challenging for the school to attract and retain top talent. Technological changes have made online platforms attractive to faculty and staff, and the school may need to adopt new technologies and develop online programs to remain competitive. The quality of faculty and staff members is crucial for maintaining high standards of education, which affects students, industry partners, accrediting bodies, government agencies, and media and rankings organizations. If the school cannot attract and retain highly qualified faculty members, students may receive lower quality education, industry partners may be unwilling to collaborate, and the school's rankings and media attention may suffer.

Alternatively, we can combine LS11, LS21, and LS31 to create the following decision scenario, which concentrates on resource-related challenges arising from multiple trends. It is crucial to ensure that the selected trends can coexist and are consistent and likely to occur simultaneously.

Decision Scenario: ABC International Business School is facing multiple challenges and opportunities that require a multi-faceted approach. Firstly, to attract and retain top talent, the school plans to offer higher salaries and benefits packages and invest in upgrading its facilities. However, this is putting a strain on its financial resources, so the school needs to identify alternative funding sources. Secondly, due to a decrease in enrollment and funding, the school is considering cost-cutting measures. It must ensure that the quality of education and student experience is not compromised and explore alternative revenue streams such as online courses. Lastly, the school needs to address the increasing demand for practical, hands-on learning experiences. This requires ensuring that faculty members have relevant industry experience, investing in specialized facilities, allocating more financial resources, revising the curriculum, investing in new educational resources, and engaging with alumni networks. These efforts will enable the school to provide practical, real-world knowledge and skills that align with industry needs and prepare students for their careers. The school must prioritize the quality of education while effectively managing financial resources, ensuring that it remains competitive and attractive to top talent while providing students with the best possible educational experience.

This process should result in three to five decision scenarios, which will once again serve as the foundation for strategic ideation. For instance, three decision scenarios may be derived by combining all pertinent trend-related learning scenarios and analyzing their impact on resources, forces, and observers.

Adapting to Multiple Decision Scenarios

To adequately prepare for multiple scenarios, it is essential to consider the ERP-related trade-offs, involving different ideas for both a given scenario and across multiple scenarios. In addition to identifying the appropriate state of ERP factors for different scenarios, the organization must also consider how quickly it can take actions that modify ERP factors if there is a change in parameters relating to scenarios. The following steps are recommended:

- Identify inconsistencies in the required level and direction of ERP factors across different ideas within a single scenario, as well as across different scenarios.
- Determine the degree of ERP adaptability required to address these inconsistencies. Adaptability is crucial because taking actions that prepare for one potential scenario may make the organization less prepared for other scenarios.
- Adjust the set of actions for each scenario based on the ERP analysis and revise the scenarios and ideas if necessary.

This way, ERP analysis can highlight the inconsistencies that may arise when attempting to prepare for multiple potential scenarios.

Exercises

1. Select a product or service from a company of interest that has been significantly affected by a severe adverse event, such as a pandemic or extreme weather occurrence. Utilizing the ERP framework, identify the key trends and uncertainties that have influenced the product or service and examine their impact on the organization's ERP factors.
2. Choose an industry of your preference. Identify recent business news articles and analyze the trends and uncertainties in the described industry using the ERP framework. Identify the key resources, forces, and observers and clarify their interactions. Based on your analysis, devise three distinct learning scenarios that a company in the industry might

confront in the future and discuss the advantages and limitations of each scenario.

3. Envision yourself as the CEO of a company operating in a highly regulated industry, such as healthcare or finance. Employ the ERP framework to formulate two distinct learning scenarios that the company might encounter concerning regulatory changes and market dynamics. For each learning scenario, propose ideas that the organization can embrace to maintain competitiveness. Subsequently, amalgamate the two learning scenarios into a unified decision scenario and generate supplementary ideas for this scenario. Compare and contrast the ideas generated for the learning scenarios with those generated for the decision scenario.

4. Take the learning scenarios developed in the above exercise and, with a team of three to five individuals, generate a set of strategic decisive actions. Utilize OpenAI's ChatGPT or a similar Large Language Model (LLM) to assess the pros and cons of each action based on the ERP framework. Is the pro/con analysis valid? If so, how well did your decisions perform? How should you refine your strategic decision-making to address the cons and enhance the pros?

Note: Readers with ChatGPT Plus may try the custom WhatIf-WhatNow GPT for scenario planning developed by the authors and found at: https://chat .openai.com/g/g-md4aQ7R6M-whatif-whatnow-gpt

Notes

1. Finkenstadt, D. J., Eapen, T. T., Sotiriadis, J., & Guinto, P. (2023, November 30). Use GenAI to improve scenario planning. *Harvard Business Review.* https:// hbr.org/2023/11/use-genai-to-improve-scenario-planning.

2. Handfield, R., Finkenstadt, D. J., & Guinto, P. (2021, February 15). How business leaders can prepare for the next health crisis. *Harvard Business Review.* https://hbr.org/2021/02/how-business-leaders-can-prepare-for-the-next-health -crisis.

3. Schwartz, P. (1996). *The Art of the Long View: Planning for the Future in an Uncertain World.* New York: Currency Doubleday.

4. Fiction Intelligence (FICINT) with Peter W Singer. (2021, February 24). Janes .com. https://www.janes.com/intelligence-resources/open-source-intelligence -podcasts/podcast-details/fiction-intelligence-ficint-with-peter-w-singer.

5. *IOC Executive Board Steps Up "Scenario-Planning" for Tokyo 2020.* (2020, March 23). Olympics; International Olympic Committee. https://olympics.com/ en/news/ioc-executive-board-steps-up-scenario-planning-for-tokyo-2020.

6. Chermack, T. J. (2011). *Scenario Planning in Organizations: How to Create, Use, and Assess Scenarios*. San Francisco: Berrett-Koehler Publishers.
7. *332. Realer than Real: Useful Fiction with P.W. Singer and August Cole*. (2021, June 10). Mad Scientist Laboratory. https://madsciblog.tradoc.army.mil/332 -realer-than-real-useful-fiction-with-p-w-singer-and-august-cole/.
8. Wack, P. (1985). Scenarios: Uncharted waters ahead. *Harvard Business Review*, 63(5), 72–89.
9. Schoemaker, P. J. H. (1995). Scenario planning: A tool for strategic thinking. *Sloan Management Review*, 36(2), 25–50.
10. Cairns, G., & Wright, G. (2017). *Scenario Thinking: Preparing Your Organization for the Future in an Unpredictable World*. Springer.
11. Mintzberg, H., Ahlstrand, B., & Lampel, J. B. (2020). *Strategy Safari*. Pearson UK.
12. Cordova-Pozo, K., & Rouwette, E. A. J. A. (2023). Types of scenario planning and their effectiveness: A review of reviews. *Futures*, 103153.

References

Amer, M., Daim, T. U., & Jetter, A. (2013). A review of scenario planning. *Futures*, 46, 23–40.

Cairns, G., & Wright, G. (2017). *Scenario Thinking: Preparing Your Organization for the Future in an Unpredictable World*. Springer.

Chermack, T. J. (2011). *Scenario Planning in Organizations: How to Create, Use, and Assess Scenarios*. Berrett-Koehler Publishers.

Cordova-Pozo, K., & Rouwette, E. A. J. A. (2023). Types of scenario planning and their effectiveness: A review of reviews. *Futures*, 149, 103153.

Finkenstadt, D. J., Eapen, T. T., Sotiriadis, J., & Guinto, P. (2023, November 30). Use GenAI to improve scenario planning. *Harvard Business Review*. https://hbr.org /2023/11/use-genai-to-improve-scenario-planning

Handfield, R., Finkenstadt, D. J., & Guinto, P. (2021, February 15). How business leaders can prepare for the next health crisis. *Harvard Business Review*.

Mintzberg, H., Ahlstrand, B., & Lampel, J. B. (2020). *Strategy Safari*. Pearson UK.

Schoemaker, P. J. H. (1995). Scenario planning: A tool for strategic thinking. *Sloan Management Review*, 36(2), 25–50.

Schwartz, P. (1996). *The Art of the Long View: Planning for the Future in an Uncertain World*. Currency Doubleday.

Wack, P. (1985). Scenarios: Uncharted waters ahead. *Harvard Business Review*, 63(5), 72–89.

Chapter 7

Bioinspired Product Design

If you truly love nature, you will find beauty everywhere.

–Vincent Van Gogh

DOI: 10.4324/9781032715315-8

In this chapter, we will delve into how bioinspiration principles can guide the generation of new product design concepts. Initially, we will explore the utilization of the ERP framework to identify opportunities for technologically innovative products that incorporate principles observed in living organisms. Following this, we will consider the application of generative AI tools, including large language models and text-to-image tools, to generate and refine novel ideas for products inspired by living organisms.

Bioinspired Technological Product Innovation Using ERP Principles

Numerous technologically innovative products have drawn inspiration from biological systems. The process of designing such products, which model the functions and characteristics of living organisms, is also referred to as biomimicry.[1] Our goal is to explore how the principles of survivability and the ERP (efficiency, resilience, prominence) framework can be applied to technological product innovation. To begin, let's examine some examples of bioinspired innovations and explore how these solutions are linked to one or more of the ERP factors.

- One example of biomimicry in the field of sports is the Cheetah Flex-Foot, a prosthetic foot designed for athletes and individuals with lower limb amputations who require a high degree of flexibility and energy return. This innovative prosthetic, invented by Van Phillips, is named after the cheetah, one of the fastest animals on earth, and is designed to mimic the cheetah's natural running mechanics, allowing the animal to achieve incredible speed and agility.[2] The Cheetah Flex-Foot is an example of bioinspiration that focuses on improving efficiency.
- Another example of biomimicry in product design is the use of the kingfisher's beak to improve the design of the Shinkansen, Japan's high-speed bullet train.[3] In the 1990s, Eiji Nakatsu, an engineer with the Japan Railways Group, was tasked with finding a solution to the train's noise problem. Nakatsu was known for his passion for bird watching and had observed that the kingfisher, a bird renowned for its fast and quiet diving ability, had a unique beak shape that reduced noise and drag in the water. Drawing inspiration from the kingfisher's beak, Nakatsu and his team redesigned the front of the Shinkansen train to decrease the noise produced as the train exited tunnels. The new

design, featuring a beak-like nose cone, not only proved to be more aerodynamic and quieter but also enhanced the train's energy efficiency by reducing air resistance, allowing it to travel faster. The use of bio-inspiration in the redesign of the Shinkansen train is an example of an efficiency-focused design, resulting in a more efficient and sustainable transportation system. Additionally, it impacts prominence, as the unique bird-inspired appearance of the train has helped distinguish it from other high-speed trains.

■ Hippos secrete a reddish, oily fluid known as "red sweat" from specialized glands in their skin. This fluid serves as a moisturizer, water repellent, and antibiotic.[4] Additionally, the unique properties of hippopotamus red sweat could inspire the development of future sunscreens. Similarly, some fish, birds, amphibians, and reptiles possess the genes necessary to produce gadusols, ultraviolet-protective compounds. It has been demonstrated that engineered yeast containing fish genes can also produce and secrete gadusol.[5] This technology exemplifies resilience-focused design through bioinspiration.

■ ORNILUX® bird-protection glass is a product crafted by the German glass manufacturer Arnold Glas.[6] Birds possess the ability to perceive ultraviolet light, enabling them to steer clear of orb webs constructed from UV-reflective silks embedded in the glass.[7] This product feature is an example of a prominence-focused design. However, this feature can also potentially enhance the resilience of the glass by making it stronger.

■ Cephalopod-inspired dynamic materials are an exceptional example of bioinspired design that is prominence-focused. These systems are developed by drawing inspiration from the remarkable appearance-changing abilities of cephalopods, such as squids and octopuses.[8] These creatures can quickly change their skin color, texture, and shape to blend into their surroundings, communicate with others, and deter predators. Such dynamic materials can have numerous applications, such as camouflage and shapeshifter-like technologies. For example, they can be used to create smart clothing, vehicles, or buildings that can adapt to changing environments, enhance their aesthetics, or provide sensory feedback to their users.

■ In other cases, the efficiency and resilience of a product are not only inspired by nature but intricately constructed from materials sourced from living organisms. The Mercedes Biome concept car is crafted entirely from fibers of various genetically modified seeds, producing an ultra-lightweight material that surpasses steel in strength when fully matured. This includes not only the interior and exterior materials but also the wheels. The car is also powered by plant juices, dubbed "BioNectar4534". This juice is taken from trees that Mercedes engineers have modified with receptors that collect excess solar energy.[9] Furthermore, additional solar energy can be stored in the car's biofibers themselves, and the vehicle releases only oxygen into the atmosphere. Interestingly, these concepts help elevate the model's prominence and attract attention.

■ One successful example of nature-inspired product design comes from the United States military. Biologically-Informed Unmanned Underwater Vehicles, or BIUUVs, are a line of small unmanned submarines that specifically seek to mimic the motion efficiency and quietness of fish. This is a traditional practice in military design. For example, after WWII, submarine hull designs emerged through the bioinspiration of sperm whales.[10]

We note from the above examples that the application of biomimicry in product innovation commonly arises from the desire to enhance one or more ERP factors but may also eventually impact other ERP factors. Interestingly, we also observe that the inspiration for such innovative solutions is more likely to emerge from organisms that appear to possess a highly developed capability in the ERP factor of primary interest. For instance, when seeking ideas to improve the efficiency of a system, organisms with biological adaptations that strongly exemplify efficiency should be the first to be considered. To assist in the exploration of identifying solutions to technological challenges where nature-inspired solutions are sought, a list of animals and their key adaptations, along with the ERP factor that the adaptation affects, can be useful. A limited table is provided (Table 7.1) to illustrate this application.

To systematically identify bioinspired product ideas and technological solutions, a structured approach can be followed, guided by a series of questions. These questions can help identify the core challenges of a given product system, the relevant living organisms that face similar challenges, and how the adaptations of these organisms can be leveraged for product development. Here is a list of eight questions that can guide the process:

1. What is the product system of interest? Defining the product system of interest is the starting point of the process. The product system can be any type of product or system that has a specific function and purpose.

Table 7.1 ERP Capabilities and Exemplary Organisms

Capability	Exemplary Organisms
Efficiency (E)	Algae, Arctic Fox, Arctic Tern, African Wild Dog, Bighorn Sheep, Capybara, Cactus, Cheetah, Chimpanzee, Dolphin, Echidna, Fungi, Giant Anteater, Gray Wolf, Honeybee, Humpback Whale, Hummingbird, Kangaroo, Kangaroo Rat, Koala, Lichen, Mule Deer, Ostrich, Peregrine Falcon, Sea turtle, Sloth, Snow Leopard, Spider, Termite
Resilience (R)	Acacia Tree, African Elephant, Axolotl, Baobab Tree, Bison, Camels, Camphor Tree, Coral, Crocodile, Eucalyptus Tree, Gila Monster, Giant Clam, Honey Badger, Humpback Whale, Komodo Dragon, Mangrove Tree, Narwhal, Octopus, Pine Tree, Polar Bear, Saguaro Cactus, Sagebrush, Sea Anemone, Sea Cucumbers, Seahorse, Tardigrades
Prominence (P)	Anglerfish, Blue Jay, Butterflies, Cephalopods, Chameleons, Cuttlefish, Electric Eel, Fireflies, Flamingos, Giraffe, Golden Pheasant, Gorilla, Jellyfish, Lion, Mandarin Duck, Mandarin Fish, Monarch Butterfly, Peacocks, Poison Dart Frogs, Rainbow Lorikeet, Regal Tang, Sea Dragon, Snow Leopard, Toucan, Venus Flytrap, Zebra

2. What is the core challenge? Once the product system is identified, the core challenge should be identified. The core challenge can be a problem or limitation of the product system that needs to be addressed or improved.

3. How is the core challenge related to the ERP factors? The core challenge should be analyzed in terms of how it relates to the Efficiency, Resilience, and Prominence (ERP) factors. This analysis can aid in identifying the relevant living organisms that face similar challenges.

4. What are the other variables of interest? In addition to the ERP factors, there may be other variables of interest that need to be considered. These variables can include economic, social, or environmental factors such as cost, user insights, and standards.

5. What living organism(s) face a similar core challenge? After identifying the core challenge and relevant variables, living organisms that face similar challenges can be identified. This can be achieved by researching living organisms that have evolved to solve similar problems.

6. Are there analogical resemblances between the organism and the product system? Analogical resemblances between the living organism and the product system should be explored. These resemblances can

provide insights into how the organism's adaptations can be leveraged for product development.

7. What are specific adaptations in the organism that help it to solve the core challenge? The specific adaptations of the organism that help it to solve the core challenge should be identified. This can be achieved by researching the organism's anatomy, physiology, and behavior.

8. Can the identified adaptations be applied directly or analogically to solve the core challenge? Finally, the identified adaptations should be analyzed to determine if they can be applied directly or analogically to the product system. This analysis can provide insights into how the organism's adaptations can be leveraged for product development.

The following tables illustrate how the questions previously discussed were applied to specific example cases involving a drone (Table 7.2), a power grid (Table 7.3), and a social media platform (Table 7.4).

Role of Analogy in Bioinspired Product Ideation

We also observe that the use of analogy is a powerful tool for identifying new bioinspired ideas. By drawing comparisons between seemingly unrelated concepts, we can spark innovative solutions that may not have been previously considered. For instance, consider the connections between spiders and glass. Firstly, broken safety glass displays a spiderweb pattern. This observation could potentially inspire the idea that the natural pattern of spiderwebs could be used as a template for designing stronger and safer glass structures. Additionally, the glass transition in spider silk, where the silk becomes solid when exposed to air, could inspire the development of new glass-like materials with interesting properties. Moreover, the concept of spider glazing in architecture, where a network of cables and rods is used to support a glass façade, can be analogically associated with the strength and flexibility of spider webs for innovative ideas. Analogous similarities also enable consumers to better understand novel ideas, thereby increasing their acceptability.

Using Generative AI for Bioinspired Ideation

The year 2022 marked the beginning of an exciting era for generative AI technologies.[11] Large language models and text-to-image models became

Table 7.2 Identification of Bioinspired Solutions – Drone

Q1	What is the product system of interest?	The product system of interest is a drone, which is an unmanned aerial vehicle (UAV) used for various applications such as delivery, surveillance, and photography.
Q2	What is the core challenge?	The core challenge of a drone is its limited battery life, which restricts the amount of time it can stay in the air.
Q3	How is the core challenge related to the ERP factors?	The core challenge is related to the Efficiency factor of the ERP framework, as a longer battery life would increase the drone's efficiency by allowing it to stay in the air for longer periods.
Q4	What are the other variables of interest?	Other variables of interest could include the drone's weight, size, and cost, as well as the regulatory environment surrounding drone usage.
Q5	What living organism(s) face a similar core challenge?	Hummingbirds face a similar challenge of needing to stay in the air for long periods of time while expending minimal energy due to their small size and high metabolic rate.
Q6	Are there analogical resemblances between the organism and the product system?	There are analogical resemblances between hummingbirds and drones, such as their ability to hover in the air for extended periods and their reliance on efficient flight mechanics.
Q7	What are specific adaptations in the organism that help it to solve the core challenge?	Hummingbirds have several adaptations that help them stay in the air for extended periods, including high metabolic rates, specialized wing structures, and the ability to regulate body temperature.
Q8	Can the identified adaptations be applied directly or analogically to solve the core challenge?	The adaptations of hummingbirds could be leveraged for drone development by incorporating features such as flexible wings, energy-efficient flight patterns, and body temperature regulation to optimize battery usage and increase flight time.

the talk of the town, creating an immense buzz in the business world. Some people were enthusiastic about the new opportunities these technologies could bring, while others expressed apprehension about their impact on human creativity. There were also those who were distrustful of the

Table 7.3   Identification of Bioinspired Solutions – Power Grid

Q1	What is the product system of interest?	The product system of interest is a power grid that is responsible for delivering electricity to customers in a given region.
Q2	What is the core challenge?	The core challenge of a power grid is to maintain reliability and resilience in the face of disruptions, such as natural disasters, cyber-attacks, and equipment failures.
Q3	How is the core challenge related to the ERP factors?	The core challenge is related to the Resilience factor of the ERP framework, as maintaining the resilience and reliability of the power grid is crucial to ensuring its continued operation in the face of disruptive events.
Q4	What are the other variables of interest?	Other variables of interest could include the type and age of equipment, capacity and demand, geographical location, and frequency and severity of disruptions.
Q5	What living organism(s) face a similar core challenge?	Some species of trees, such as the Sitka spruce and balsam fir, have adaptations that help them withstand harsh weather conditions, such as high winds and heavy snow.
Q6	Are there analogical resemblances between the organism and the product system?	There are analogical resemblances between trees and power grids in terms of their ability to withstand and recover from disruptive events.
Q7	What are specific adaptations in the organism that help it to solve the core challenge?	Trees have several adaptations that help them withstand harsh weather conditions, such as flexible trunks and branches that allow them to bend without breaking, deep root systems that anchor them to the ground, and thick bark that protects them from damage.
Q8	Can the identified adaptations be applied directly or analogically to solve the core challenge?	The adaptations of trees could be leveraged for power grid development by incorporating features such as flexible transmission lines that can bend without breaking, redundant power sources and pathways that can keep the grid operational in case of disruptions, and smart sensors and software that can detect and respond to disruptions in real time.

Table 7.4   Identification of Bioinspired Solutions – Social Media Platform

Q1	What is the product system of interest?	The product system of interest is a social media platform that allows users to share and view content, connect with others, and engage in online communities.
Q2	What is the core challenge?	The core challenge of a social media platform is to maintain its prominence in a highly competitive market by attracting and retaining users, generating revenue, and adapting to changing trends and user preferences.
Q3	How is the core challenge related to the ERP factors?	The core challenge is related to the Prominence factor of the ERP framework, as maintaining prominence and market leadership in a highly competitive environment is crucial to the platform's continued success.
Q4	What are the other variables of interest?	Other variables of interest could include user demographics and behavior, content trends and preferences, platform features and functionality, and revenue streams and advertising models.
Q5	What living organism(s) face a similar core challenge?	Some bird species, such as the peacock, have adaptations that help them attract mates and establish dominance within their social group.
Q6	Are there analogical resemblances between the organism and the product system?	There are analogical resemblances between peacocks and social media platforms in terms of their ability to attract and retain attention, establish dominance, and stand out in a crowded environment.
Q7	What are specific adaptations in the organism that help it to solve the core challenge?	Peacocks have several adaptations that help them attract mates and establish dominance, such as elaborate and colorful feathers, impressive displays of vocalization and movement, and territorial behavior.
Q8	Can the identified adaptations be applied directly or analogically to solve the core challenge?	The adaptations of peacocks could be leveraged for social media platform development by incorporating features such as personalized and visually appealing user interfaces, engaging and interactive content formats, and gamification and reward systems that encourage user participation and loyalty.

potential of these technologies to replace humans in creative roles, such as marketing communication, product design, advertising, and software development.

One of the most significant sources of economic opportunities for business organizations and technological advancements for governments lies in utilizing generative AI to augment human creativity.[12] This can be achieved by leveraging the power of generative AI to work in tandem with human ideators. In this chapter, we will explore various ways in which generative AI tools can support bioinspired design.

- The first application we will discuss is the use of large language models (LLMs) like GPT 4, via ChatGPT, to generate remote associations between products and living organisms. LLMs have the unique ability to connect seemingly unrelated concepts and ideas, which can be leveraged to trigger divergent thinking. Divergent thinking is a crucial part of the creative process, and generating remote associations can help designers break out of their usual ways of thinking and generate new, innovative ideas. By drawing on the appropriate capabilities and adaptations of living organisms, LLMs can quickly help us in searching for innovative bioinspired product ideas. For instance, by analyzing the various features and functions of living organisms, LLMs can suggest design solutions that improve the efficiency, resilience, or prominence-related features of a product.
- The second application we will discuss in this chapter is the use of text-to-image models to generate visual concepts of products that draw inspiration from the appearance of living organisms. This approach can be particularly useful in fields such as product design or advertising, where the aim is to create something new by drawing inspiration from existing designs or concepts.
- Generative AI tools can help designers generate a large number of different forms for a product, which can then be used to inspire new ideas for its function. This approach also allows us to apply a 'form leads function' principle, where the function of an object is determined only after its form is available. This represents a new paradigm in design thinking and a powerful approach for divergent thinking to overcome well-known biases such as design fixation.
- Collaborative design detailing is another way to use generative AI to support bioinspired design. This involves using AI tools to facilitate collaboration between different designers or teams, and even customers,

enabling them to work together more effectively and efficiently. By leveraging the power of generative AI, designers can quickly generate a range of design possibilities that can then be refined through collaboration and feedback.

■ Finally, we will discuss how generative AI tools can promote new collaborative models, including collaborative business models and collaboration in new product development. One exciting possibility is the emergence of Generative AI Businesses (GAIBs), which can use AI tools to generate a large number of product concepts in partnership with customers. This approach can create a more collaborative relationship between businesses and customers, leading to increased customer satisfaction and loyalty.

Using Large Language Models for Associative Creativity

Large Language Model (LLM) tools, such as ChatGPT, have the potential to generate innovative and diverse idea descriptions by combining seemingly unrelated concepts. This process of idea generation is guided by the theory of associative creativity. An example of a simple application of LLMs is to ask OpenAI's ChatGPT, a popular early instance of an LLM released in late 2022, to generate ideas for improving a product by drawing inspiration from a living organism. Another approach is to ask ChatGPT to come up with product concepts based on the efficiency, resilience, and prominence strategies of living organisms (Table 7.5). For instance, we can ask ChatGPT to generate product ideas for an electric car inspired by a lion (for efficiency), camel (for resilience), and chameleon (for prominence).

To expand on this approach, we can assign the role of an ideator to ChatGPT, whereby it takes inputs from a human to generate ideas through a process known as "trisociation," connecting three distinct entities – an extension of the bisociation creativity technique. Initially, we task ChatGPT with generating a list of concepts (nouns). We then select two nouns and a living organism. ChatGPT subsequently employs these three concepts to generate a trisociated business idea. Text-to-image models, such as DALL-E, Stable Diffusion, or Midjourney, can then be used to visualize the ideas generated.

To achieve this, we employed the following prompt:

You will play the role of an ideator. You will randomly generate 10 common nouns. You will ask me to select any two of the 10 nouns you have

Table 7.5   ERP-Focused Product Concept Generation Using Gen-AI

Prompt	Summary of Product Concept Generated by ChatGPT
Generate an idea for an electric car inspired the efficiency strategies of the lion	A concept for an electric car inspired by the efficiency of lions would involve regenerative braking and a hybrid powertrain to optimize energy usage. Regenerative braking would recover energy during deceleration, stored in the battery pack, improving the car's overall efficiency and driving range. The hybrid powertrain would switch between electric and gas power based on driving conditions, similar to how lions alternate between running and walking during a hunt. Additionally, the car's design would incorporate aerodynamic features inspired by a lion's sleek body, such as a streamlined body, retractable mirrors, and a low-profile roofline.
Generate an idea for an electric car inspired by the resilience strategies of the camel	A concept for an electric car inspired by the resilience of camels would feature a durable exterior design that can resist damage from harsh environments. The car's suspension and tires would be optimized for rough terrain, and the powertrain would incorporate advanced cooling and temperature control systems to ensure optimal performance in extreme temperatures. The car's interior would be designed for comfort and functionality in harsh environments, featuring durable materials and advanced navigation and communication systems. Additionally, the car's energy usage and range would be optimized through features such as thermal insulation, active cooling systems, and energy-efficient climate control.
Generate an idea for an electric car inspired by the prominence strategies of the chameleon	A concept for an electric car inspired by the prominence strategies of chameleons would feature advanced active camouflage technology and a modular design for customizable options. The car's active camouflage technology would allow drivers to change the car's color, pattern, and texture to their preferences and needs, from paint colors to advanced adaptive camouflage that can mimic the surrounding environment. The modular design would allow for easy customization and upgrades, with interchangeable parts and components to modify the car's performance, appearance, and functionality. The car's interior would also feature adaptable seating arrangements and advanced technology systems that can adjust to the driver's preferences and driving conditions.

identified. You will also ask me for the name of a living organism. You will generate a business idea by combining or associating the two nouns you have identified, drawing inspiration from the living organism I have specified. Table 7.6 displays three ideas generated using this approach.

We can also teach LLMs, like ChatGPT, the ERP model and how to relate ERP factors to various natural analogies using the exemplar species in Table 7.6. Once the model understands these linkages, we can use it to generate a host of novel and feasible concepts that blend ERP factors to enhance

Table 7.6 Ideas Generated by ChatGPT Using Trisociation

Nouns	Organism	Business Idea (ChatGPT)
Shoe, coffee	Elephant	"Elephant Steps Coffee" – A coffee brand that sources its beans from sustainable elephant habitats in Africa. The company could create a line of specialty coffee blends that are named after the different types of elephants found in Africa. Additionally, for every bag of coffee sold, a portion of the profits could be donated to support elephant conservation efforts in Africa. As a unique and socially responsible brand, "Elephant Steps Coffee" would not only appeal to coffee lovers, but also to those who are passionate about animal welfare and conservation. Finally, to tie in with the "Shoe" aspect of the business, they could also offer a limited edition of shoes made from elephant-friendly materials that are inspired by the brand's logo and branding.
Chair, phone	Caterpillar	"ChairCrawler" – A furniture company that creates innovative chairs inspired by the movement and flexibility of a caterpillar. The chairs are designed with modular segments that can be rearranged and connected in various configurations, allowing the user to adjust the shape and size of the chair to fit their specific needs. The chair segments are equipped with built-in charging ports and speakers, turning each segment into a mini-phone station. The ChairCrawler brand promotes adaptability, versatility, and technology for the modern workspace.
Watch, fruit	Panda	"Panda Time" – a line of eco-friendly watches made from sustainable materials, inspired by the black and white colors of pandas. Each watch features a unique design inspired by a different type of fruit, such as a strawberry or watermelon, and is paired with a matching strap made from organic cotton or recycled materials. The brand's mission is to promote sustainable and healthy living, and each watch comes with a free guide on the health benefits of the fruit that inspired its design. A portion of the proceeds from each watch sale is donated to organizations that support panda conservation efforts.

survival. Take this example generated in a matter of minutes after GPT learned the ERP model:

Product Idea: Smart and Sustainable Urban Gardening System.

Imagine a smart and sustainable urban gardening system that incorporates lessons from efficiency, resilience, and prominence in nature.

Efficiency: Taking inspiration from honeybees, the system could optimize resource allocation and maximize efficiency in urban gardening. It could utilize smart sensors and AI algorithms to monitor environmental conditions such as sunlight, temperature, and soil moisture. Based on this data, the system could efficiently allocate water, nutrients, and sunlight to the plants, ensuring their optimal growth and productivity. The system could also provide real-time insights and recommendations to users, enabling them to make informed decisions for efficient gardening practices.

Resilience: Drawing inspiration from tardigrades, the system could be designed to withstand various challenges and promote resilience in urban gardening. It could incorporate modular and durable gardening components that are resistant to extreme weather conditions, pests, and diseases. Additionally, the system could integrate backup mechanisms such as alternative water sources, renewable energy options, and backup seed banks to ensure the continuity of gardening even in unpredictable situations. By incorporating resilience into its design, the system would help urban gardeners adapt and thrive despite potential setbacks.

Prominence: Inspired by peacocks, the system could have a visually striking design that captures attention and promotes urban gardening as a prominent and attractive activity. The gardening system could feature aesthetically pleasing structures, vibrant displays of plants, and visually appealing vertical gardening arrangements. It could also incorporate interactive elements such as educational touchscreens, augmented reality features, and community engagement platforms to create a sense of prominence and draw people's attention to the benefits and beauty of urban gardening.

By blending efficiency, resilience, and prominence in this smart and sustainable urban gardening system, it would provide an all-in-one solution for urban dwellers to efficiently grow their own food, contribute to sustainability, and create visually appealing green spaces in their surroundings.

Using Text-to-Image Models for Visualization of Bioinspired Product Ideas

Generative AI can promote divergent thinking by facilitating the association and visualization of diverse concepts, thus supporting idea generation by connecting product concepts with living organisms. In addition to verbal descriptions, text-to-image models can visually render the generated ideas. To illustrate this approach, we utilized generative AI models to devise product designs inspired by various biological sources (see Figure 7.1). Our concepts span several categories, including sofas (koala), trains (eagle), cars (camel), beds (panda), knives (shark), chairs (sloth), and yachts (dolphin). The appeal of an idea depends on the degree of analogical resemblance between the form or function of the product and the living organism. The greater the resemblance, the more attractive the idea is likely to be. Furthermore, it is advantageous if the key benefit of the product, in terms of the ERP factor, corresponds to the most salient adaptation of the organism being considered. For instance, a tub inspired by a hippopotamus is intriguing because the shape of a hippopotamus resembles that of a bathtub, and hippos spend most of their time in water (Figure 7.1).

Text-to-image models can blend ideas and generate compelling product concepts that draw inspiration from multiple living organisms. For example, we employed text-to-image models to create an image that fuses an elephant and a butterfly, resulting in a griffin-like creature we named Phantafly. We leveraged the Phantafly concept to "bioinspire" and generate ideas for various product categories, including chocolate (Figure 7.2), brooches, bags, and cakes. Similarly, we merged the images of a tortoise and a scorpion to produce a "torscion," which served as a source of inspiration for concept car designs.

When combining imagery from multiple living organisms, it can be beneficial to consider their analogous or complementary ERP properties. For instance, we can combine features that embody efficiency, resilience, and prominence from various living organisms. To illustrate this approach, we conceived a residential concept named "Cameleot," which incorporates

Figure 7.1 HippoTub concepts.

elements from the camel, chameleon, and lion and embodies the ERP principles of efficiency, resilience, and prominence associated with these animals. The name Cameleot combines chameleon, camel, leo (lion), and lot, reflecting our selection of animals with distinct characteristics that represent the three core survival-related capabilities of any living system: efficiency, resilience, and prominence, also known as the ERP factors. The lion, renowned for its potent and efficient hunting tactics, exemplifies efficiency in resource management. The camel, celebrated for its ability to survive in harsh desert environments, epitomizes resilience in the face of extreme conditions. Finally, the chameleon, famed for its color-changing and camouflage

Figure 7.2 Phantafly chocolate concepts.

abilities, represents prominence in the capacity to attract or evade attention. The Cameleot is designed to embody these capabilities, minimizing resource waste, withstanding extreme weather conditions, and altering its appearance to both attract and blend in with its surroundings as needed (Figure 7.3).

Form Leads Function Approach to Product Ideation

In the fast-paced world of product development, generative AI models have emerged as a valuable tool for designers who want to push the boundaries of what's possible. Adopting an innovative approach to product design, known as "form leads function," can help designers overcome common biases that may limit creativity and innovation. Biases, such as design fixation, can impede the ideation process of domain experts.[13] However, by embracing a "form leads function" approach, designers can break free from these biases and unlock new levels of creativity. This is achieved by

Figure 7.3   Cameleot home concept.

exploring a broader search space, thereby avoiding the problem of design fixation.[14]

In contrast to the traditional "form follows function" approach, where functions are determined first and the form is designed to accommodate them, the "form leads function" approach allows for intentional vagueness in the early stages of the ideation process.[15] This approach uses generated images with vague functional features as a catalyst for further ideation. By specifying only that a desired image be a "product" or "toy," without additional functional specifications, designers can generate a plethora of design concepts. Some of these concepts may lack clarity in terms of function. To illustrate the potential of this approach, we generated several generic designs of butterfly-inspired toys (Figure 7.4) using Stable Diffusion, without specifying any functional features.

The ideation process of "form leads function" can lead to innovative bioinspired concepts that may not have been discovered by starting with

Figure 7.4 Fluttertoy concepts.

function first and then deciding on form. By freeing themselves from pre-conceived notions of how form relates to function, designers can expand their thinking and unlock new opportunities for innovation. This approach is not new and can be observed in the design of theme park rides and the development of technologies used by intelligence agencies. For instance, the lipstick pistol, also known as the "kiss of death," carried by KGB agents in the 1960s, is an example of how form drove the limited functionality of the pistol, allowing for a subtle but serious impact.[16]

We can also use what we have taught ChatGPT about our ERP model to both generate a novel concept with a description and generate initial images of the product. For example, ChatGPT was asked to complete a previous design challenge taken on by MBA students. We asked ChatGPT to design a product that considered ERP analogies from nature to support small groups hiking across Pacific island chains, enabling them to have fresh drinking water as they traveled in areas where there are not a lot of sources of standing or running freshwater access points. It generated the following product concept.

"The HydraGen Portable Water Generator draws inspiration from nature to provide a lightweight and versatile solution for small hiking groups in the Pacific islands, enabling them to generate fresh drinking water in locations where standing or running fresh water is scarce.

Efficiency: Similar to how certain desert-dwelling organisms, like cacti and camels, efficiently utilize available resources, the HydraGen employs advanced condensation technology to extract moisture from the air and convert it into clean, drinkable water. This process optimizes efficiency by minimizing water wastage and maximizing the water generation capacity, ensuring a reliable supply of freshwater for the hikers.

Resilience: Taking cues from the resilience of organisms such as mangrove trees and their ability to thrive in challenging coastal environments, the HydraGen Portable Water Generator is designed to withstand the demands of outdoor exploration. Its lightweight yet durable construction ensures it can endure various environmental conditions, making it resilient during the hikers' journey across the Pacific islands. The inclusion of backup power options, inspired by the adaptability of organisms that can utilize different energy sources, ensures a continuous supply of freshwater even when alternative power sources are needed.

Low Prominence: Inspired by nature's creatures that utilize camouflage to blend into their surroundings, the HydraGen Portable Water Generator features a discreet and unobtrusive design. It incorporates muted colors and camouflage patterns, allowing it to maintain a low profile and minimize the chances of attracting unwanted attention during the hiking expedition. The quiet operation of the generator further enhances its low prominence, ensuring the hikers can generate fresh water without drawing unnecessary notice.

By incorporating efficiency, resilience, and low prominence inspired by nature, the HydraGen Portable Water Generator offers a lightweight and self-sufficient solution for small hiking groups in the Pacific islands. It emulates the resourcefulness and adaptability found in nature, enabling hikers to generate fresh drinking water where standing or running water is scarce, ensuring their survival while keeping a low profile throughout their journey."

To help us visualize this product, we then asked ChatGPT to develop a Midjourney prompt for this product using a standard prompt engineering design we taught it earlier. It generated this prompt:

(Content) Hyper-realistic image showcasing the technical details of the HydraGen Portable Water Generator

(Medium) Digital illustration or highly detailed product render

(Style) Photo-realistic with intricate details and textures

(Lighting) Studio lighting to accentuate the product's features and components

(Color) Accurate representation of the product's color and materials

(Composition) Close-up view of the HydraGen Portable Water Generator, highlighting its key technical aspects and functionality. Show the intricate condensation technology, water extraction process, and internal components with exceptional attention to detail. Utilize a combination of sharp focus and shallow depth of field to draw attention to specific features and showcase the generator's inner workings. Incorporate elements that communicate its lightweight and versatile nature, such as showing it in use by hikers in a Pacific island setting, reinforcing its purpose and practicality. By employing a hyper-realistic approach, this image will provide viewers with a vivid and detailed understanding of the technical aspects of the HydraGen Portable Water Generator. The accurate depiction of its components, condensation technology, and functionality will instill confidence in its efficiency and reliability. The careful composition and lighting will create a visually appealing and informative image that showcases the product's technical prowess, inviting viewers to explore and appreciate its design and capabilities.

Different text-to-image models can be employed to explore designs and stimulate fresh thinking. It must be noted that these designs are not actual design specifications; instead, they serve as triggers to initiate creative thinking and as a foundation for interactive refinement. Some concepts generated by DALL-E are shown below (Figure 7.5). These are not necessarily the final designs but serve as a launchpad for further ideation and iterative design.

Collaborative Design Detailing for Bioinspired Ideation

Generative AI tools have the potential to revolutionize the way designers collaborate and innovate. By enabling multiple individuals to collaborate on design projects and build on each other's contributions, this approach, referred to as "collaborative design detailing," can efficiently synthesize requirements across a broader base of users and consumers to generate

Figure 7.5   HydraGen concepts generated using Midjourney.

novel solutions. One key advantage of using generative AI tools in collabora-tive design is the ability to explore a wide range of design possibilities and evaluate them based on specific user requirements and feedback.

To illustrate the potential of collaborative design detailing, let's consider the example of a bioinspired flying car design (Figure 7.6). An ideator gen-erated an initial design using a prompt, yielding several design options. From these choices, a promising design was selected and is displayed below. Subsequently, a second ideator edited the design using prompts to incorporate bioinspired elements, refining and expanding upon the initial design concept (Table 7.7).[17] The collaborative design detailing approach

Figure 7.6 Flying Car concept inspired by dragonflies.

facilitates an iterative and inclusive design process, allowing multiple designers to conveniently contribute conveniently to a single project and build
upon each other's ideas, irrespective of their level of expertise in design or
visualization.

Bioinspired Designs and Generative AI Business Models

The generative approach to AI has the potential to revolutionize product
design by enabling the rapid creation of new and unique products with
minimal need for support from expert designers. This approach can be particularly beneficial for businesses, allowing the quick generation of a wide
range of products that can be rapidly brought to market. We refer to these
business models as Generative AI Businesses (GAIBs). For example, a sports
apparel company could use generative AI to create a large number of new
designs for T-shirts, shoes, and socks. These designs could then be swiftly
prototyped and brought to market, enabling the company to stay ahead of

Table 7.7   Prompts for Collaborative Design Detailing

Initial Concept	*Reimagined Concept*
Prompt: Design me a product that can fly but also drive on the road, a flying automobile.	Prompt: Resembles a robotic dragonfly.

Figure 7.7   Snail-inspired vase concepts.

trends and offer a constantly evolving selection of products to customers. By structuring themselves as GAIBs, companies can rapidly respond to market demands and quickly bring innovative products to market.

To demonstrate the potential of this approach, we utilized text-to-image models to generate design concepts for beds inspired by pandas, as well as design concepts for vases inspired by the appearance of snails (Figure 7.7). This same approach could be employed by GAIBs to generate a vast array of new and unique products or designs that cater to changing market trends and customer demands. By leveraging generative AI tools, GAIBs can stay ahead of the curve, delight their customers with innovative products, and transform the way products are designed, created, and brought to market.

Generative AI tools have the potential to empower consumers to create visually appealing designs that can be submitted to companies or crowdsourcing platforms. Additionally, businesses can leverage Generative AI Business (GAIB) tools to collaborate with customers in generating design concepts for products. This approach enables customers and users to identify unique designs independently of the company, potentially leading to the creation of new product lines or features. Text-to-image models can be used to generate these concepts, allowing users to create visual representations of their ideas even without expertise in computer-aided design (CAD) tools or visualization.

For example, a company could provide a tool that assists customers in generating their designs and submitting them for manufacturing. The company can then partner with consumers to develop and market toy products that are generated using AI. To demonstrate this, we created a concept brand called Platoplays using text-to-image models (Figure 7.8).

Figure 7.8　Generated concepts for Platoplays toys.

Incorporating AI into the design process can aid in generating visually distinct and appealing platypus-inspired toys. Following the creation of these concepts, businesses can create customized versions of the product based on customer designs. Alternatively, customers can submit their designs to crowdsourcing platforms for evaluation by the community, with the top designs being chosen for further development.

Exercises

1. Explain, using examples not cited in this chapter, how the ERP factors can guide the selection of organisms to draw inspiration from when designing products.
2. What are the potential benefits of using generative AI technologies for bioinspired design? How can it solve some of the challenges faced in the past by ideators and organizations?
3. Define the "form leads function" principle and discuss how generative AI tools can be applied to support it. What are some product categories where this approach might be suitable for new product development? What are some products where "form leads function" would be the wrong approach for new product ideation?
4. Can you teach ChatGPT the ERP model? Once taught, can you get it to develop novel concepts using natural analogies? How much better are its ideas once you give it specific natural analogies yourself?
5. Can you generate prompts for text-to-image platforms like Midjourney or Stable Diffusion using the ideas you generated in ChatGPT? How does that help you or your team increase the speed and range of ideation for new product designs?

Note: Readers with ChatGPT Plus may try the custom built BioBuilder GPT tool developed by the authors for aiding them in ideating bio inspired product designs found at: biobuilder.net.

Notes

1. Benyus, J. M. (2002). *Biomimicry: Innovation Inspired by Nature*. Harper Perennial.
2. Davidson, M. (2005, March 9). *Innovative Lives: Artificial Parts: Van Phillips*. Lemelson Center for the Study of Invention and Innovation; Smithsonian

Institution. https://invention.si.edu/innovative-lives-artificial-parts-van -phillips.

3. Snell-Rood, E. (2016). Interdisciplinarity: Bring biologists into biomimetics. *Nature*, 529(7586), 277–278.

4. Saikawa, Y., Hashimoto, K., Nakata, M., Yoshihara, M., Nagai, K., Ida, M., & Komiya, T. (2004). The red sweat of the hippopotamus. *Nature*, 429(6990), 363–363.

5. Osborn, A. R., et al. (2015). De Novo synthesis of a sunscreen compound in vertebrates. *eLife*, four, e05919.

6. *ORNILUX® Bird Protection Glass*. Arnold Glas. Retrieved November 22, 2023, from https://www.arnold-glas.de/en/products/pi-ornilux-bird-protection-glass -704924742.

7. Kennedy, E. B. (2017). Biomimicry: Design by analogy to biology. *Research-Technology Management*, 60(6), 51–56.

8. Phan, L., Kautz, R., Leung, E. M., Naughton, K. L., Van Dyke, Y., & Gorodetsky, A. A. (2016). Dynamic materials inspired by cephalopods. *Chemistry of Materials*, 28(19), 6804–6816.

9. Reid, R. (2010, November 22). *Mercedes-Benz Biome Concept Car is "Grown from DNA-Modified Seeds."* CNET. https://www.cnet.com/roadshow/pictures/ mercedes-benz-biome-concept-car-is-grown-from-dna-modified-seeds/.

10. Peck, M. (2022, October 20). Why the pentagon wants robot subs that swim like fish. *Forbes*. https://www.forbes.com/sites/michaelpeck/2021/10/20/why -the-pentagon-wants-robot-subs-that-swim-like-fish/.

11. Stokel-Walker, C., & Van Noorden, R. (2023). What ChatGPT and generative AI mean for science. *Nature*, 614(7947), 214–216.

12. Eapen, T. T., Finkenstadt, D. J., Folk, J., & Venkataswamy, L. (2023). How generative AI can augment human creativity. *Harvard Business Review*, 101(4), 76–85.

13. Jansson, D. G., & Smith, S. M. (1991). Design fixation. *Design Studies*, 12(1), 3–11.

14. Wiley, J. (1998). Expertise as mental set: The effects of domain knowledge in creative problem solving. *Memory & Cognition*, 26, 716–730.

15. Sullivan, L. H. (1896). The tall office building artistically considered. *Lippincott's Monthly Magazine*, 57, 403–409.

16. Davis-Marks, I. (2020, November 6). You could own a lipstick gun, a poison-tipped umbrella and other KGB spy tools. *Smithsonian Magazine*. https://www .smithsonianmag.com/smart-news/spy-museum-selling-most-its-stealthy-tools -180976223/.

17. Prompt originally appeared in Eapen, Finkenstadt, Folk and Venkataswamy (2023).

References

Benyus, J. M. (2002). *Biomimicry: Innovation Inspired by Nature*. Harper Perennial.

Eapen, T. T., Finkenstadt, D. J., Folk, J., & Venkataswamy, L. (2023). How generative AI can augment human creativity. *Harvard Business Review*, 101(4), 76–85.

Jansson, D. G., & Smith, S. M. (1991). Design fixation. *Design Studies*, 12(1), 3–11.

Kennedy, E. B. (2017). Biomimicry: Design by analogy to biology. *Research-Technology Management*, 60(6), 51–56.

Osborn, A. R., et al. (2015). De novo synthesis of a sunscreen compound in vertebrates. *eLife*, 4, e05919.

Phan, L., Kautz, R., Leung, E. M., Naughton, K. L., Van Dyke, Y., & Gorodetsky, A. A. (2016). Dynamic materials inspired by cephalopods. *Chemistry of Materials*, 28(19), 6804–6816.

Saikawa, Y., Hashimoto, K., Nakata, M., Yoshihara, M., Nagai, K., Ida, M., & Komiya, T. (2004). The red sweat of the hippopotamus. *Nature*, 429(6990), 363–363.

Snell-Rood, E. (2016). Interdisciplinarity: Bring biologists into biomimetics. *Nature*, 529(7586), 277–278.

Stokel-Walker, C., & Van Noorden, R. (2023). What ChatGPT and generative AI mean for science. *Nature*, 614(7947), 214–216.

Sullivan, L. H. (1896). The tall office building artistically considered. *Lippincott's Monthly Magazine*, 57, 403–409.

Wiley, J. (1998). Expertise as mental set: The effects of domain knowledge in creative problem solving. *Memory & Cognition*, 26, 716–730.

Index